NO MORALITY, NO SELF

James Doyle

NO MORALITY, NO SELF

Anscombe's Radical Skepticism

Harvard University Press

Cambridge, Massachusetts, and London, England   2018

Second printing

Library of Congress Cataloging-in-Publication Data

Names: Doyle, James, 1963 November 18– author.
Title: No morality, no self : Anscombe's radical skepticism / James Doyle.
Description: Cambridge, Massachusetts : Harvard University Press, 2018. |
   Includes bibliographical references and index.
Identifiers: LCCN 2017006226 | ISBN 9780674976504 (hardcover : alk. paper)
Subjects: LCSH: Anscombe, G. E. M. (Gertrude Elizabeth Margaret) |
   Ethics—Philosophy. | Self (Philosophy) | Skepticism.
Classification: LCC B1618.A574 D69 2018 | DDC 126— dc23
LC record available at https://lccn.loc.gov/2017006226

For Danielle
ὦ καλή, ὦ χαρίεσσα

Contents

Preface

This book is an exposition and qualified defense of the two papers by G. E. M. Anscombe in which she advances perhaps her most amazing theses: "Modern Moral Philosophy" (1958) and "The First Person" (1975).

Both papers are highly influential, in that they are frequently cited. But the main theses and arguments of "Modern Moral Philosophy" have been widely and deeply misunderstood by critics and advocates alike; and many responses to "The First Person" have not really taken the measure of the problems Anscombe raises for our ordinary understanding of the first-person pronoun.

The main claim of "Modern Moral Philosophy" is that the term "moral," where this is supposed to identify a distinct, sui generis species of obligations, reasons, evaluations, traits of character, and so on, is literally senseless and should therefore be abandoned. The main claim of "The First Person" is that the word "I" (as well as "me," "myself," and so on) is not a referring expression; that is, its role in the language is not to pick something out. In particular, its role is not to pick out the person who utters it, or some special entity called a "self."

Unsurprisingly, philosophers have generally responded to both claims with deep skepticism and even incredulity. Yet Anscombe was the exact opposite of the sort of philosopher, by no means uncommon, who seeks notoriety by arguing ingeniously for outrageous views they do not really believe. The idea that we should do away with the notion of the *moral* does initially sound bizarre and even grotesque. Yet Anscombe advances it with complete seriousness; and I argue that the almost unanimous rejection of it is in every case based on serious misunderstandings of the thesis, or of Anscombe's arguments for it, or of both.

Now, when a philosopher puts forward a weird-sounding view, and then responds to objections to it by protesting that he has been misinterpreted, this response very often turns out to be a more or less thinly disguised way of conceding that the weird-sounding view was no more than weird-*sounding*. The real reason the objections are seen to miss the mark, once the author has clarified his meaning, is that that meaning was much more mundane than the critics had quite reasonably been led to believe by the startling or apocalyptic terms in which it was originally expressed. The novelty, the weirdness, were in the end just a con.

Part of the great interest of "Modern Moral Philosophy," in my view, is that although, as I have said, the objections to its main thesis have been based on misunderstandings, the correct understanding of it does *not* turn out to be banal. The correct interpretation, I argue in Part 1, does make the thesis much more plausible than its opponents have supposed, but it does not make it any less interesting. If Anscombe's main thesis here is correct in the way she intended it to be understood, then, in coming to appreciate its truth, we learn something about ethics that is very much worth knowing.

The main point I want to establish in Part 1 is that, contrary to virtually all subsequent comment on the paper, Anscombe does not maintain in "Modern Moral Philosophy" that the concept of morality was in good order when it was underpinned by a divine command conception of ethics but ceased to be intelligible when this conception was abandoned by philosophers. Her view is rather that the concept of morality was *never* intelligible, and is in fact not a concept at all, but only a word. "Modern Moral Philosophy" does not issue a challenge, in the manner of J. L. Mackie's "error theory," to legitimate morality in the face of skeptical arguments that it could not be instantiated. On Anscombe's view there is nothing there to legitimate.

The case of "The First Person" is in important respects somewhat different. Here the main thesis is generally well understood, so that the numerous arguments against it in the literature are not simply aimed at the wrong target.[1] My defensive action on behalf of this later paper's thesis, which constitutes the second part of this work, is more limited. Anscombe's paper begins with an argument designed to show that any attempt to give an account of "I" as an expression each person uses to refer to herself will be either vulnerable to clear counterexamples or viciously circular. I examine various attempts, by Lucy O'Brien, Gareth Evans, and Ian Rumfitt, among others, to refute the argument by presenting an adequate noncircular account of the very kind she supposes impossible. I show that nearly all these attempts are still vulnerable to Anscombe-style objections. Rumfitt's account avoids the objections, but at the cost of relying on a view of reflexive pronouns that, according to a line of thought suggested by A. N. Prior, seems to lend support to Anscombe's overarching thesis that "I" is not a referring expression. So the overall verdict here is that one of Anscombe's main objections to viewing "I" as a referring expression has not been met. I then make some tentative remarks, drawing on some other ideas of Prior, about how a positive view of "I" as a nonreferring expression might go—an issue about which Anscombe herself was exasperatingly reticent. Finally, I consider and reject attempts to hold on to an understanding of "I" as a singular term: by disallowing Anscombe's conception of a referring expression as inappropriately epistemic, by appealing to the "deflationary" conception of a referring expression Crispin Wright finds in Gottlob Frege's *Grundlagen,* and by constructing a referent for "I" on the basis of an abstraction principle.

NO MORALITY, NO SELF

PART ONE

No Morality: "Modern Moral Philosophy" (1958)

Don't fool yourselves! For in general no creature has any affinity like the one it has for its own personal benefit. So whatever seems to a man to be in the way of this—whether it's a brother, a father, a child, a beloved or a lover—he hates it, repudiates it and curses it. It's in a man's nature, you see, to love nothing so much as his own benefit; *this* is his father and his brother, his kin, his homeland and his god. So if the gods themselves seem to us to be in the way of this, we abuse even *them,* and destroy their shrines and burn down their temples, just like Alexander, who ordered the temple of Asklepios to be burned down when his beloved died. Therefore anyone who lumps all together his benefit and piety and what's noble, and homeland and fathers and friends—he preserves them all. But if he puts his benefit on the one side, and his friends and his homeland and his kin and even what's just on the other, all these things are outweighed and annihilated by his benefit. Because wherever its *I* and *mine* are, that's where a creature is necessarily inclined. If they are in the flesh, that's where a man's ruling passion will be. If they are in reflective decision, it will be there. If they're in external goods, there. But look: if *I* am where reflective decision is, only *there* will I be the sort of friend I should be, and the sort of son, and father. Because then it will benefit *me* to honour my commitments, and my good name, and a spirit of toleration, of temperance, and of co-operation, and to protect and maintain my relationships with others. But if I position myself in one place, and put what's noble somewhere else, then the argument of Epicurus has force, and proves that what is noble is either nothing or, if it is anything at all, mere opinion.

EPICTETUS

It is often felt, even if obscurely, that there is an element of deception in the official line about morality. And while some have been persuaded by talk about the authority of the moral law, others have turned away with a sense of distrust.

PHILIPPA FOOT

1

Virtue Ethics, Eudaimonism, and the Greeks

Introduction: Anscombe's Theses

"Modern Moral Philosophy" (Anscombe 1958; hereafter MMP) is often cited, and is considered enormously influential. But it still has not been properly understood, *at all*.

Anscombe argued for three main claims, which she usefully summarized at the outset:

> [1] The first is that it is not profitable for us at present to do moral philosophy; that should be laid aside at any rate until we have an adequate philosophy of psychology, in which we are conspicuously lacking. [2] The second is that the concepts of obligation, and duty—*moral* obligation and *moral* duty, that is to say—and of what is *morally* right and wrong, and of the *moral* sense of "ought," ought to be jettisoned if this is psychologically possible; because they are survivals, or derivatives from survivals, from an earlier conception of ethics which no longer generally survives, and are only harmful without it. [3] My third thesis is that the differences between the well-known English writers on moral philosophy from [Henry] Sidgwick to the present day are of little importance. (MMP, 1)

The theses turn out to be related, in the following way: The concepts of distinctively *moral* obligation and so on are to be jettisoned (as in [2]) in favor of the concept of a *virtue,* for the purposes of doing philosophical ethics. But it is because we don't yet have the resources in philosophical psychology for understanding what kind of thing a virtue is that we should forget about ethics until we do have such resources (as in [1]). As for the third thesis, when Anscombe says that the differences between Sidgwick and his successors in ethics are of little importance, she mainly means that they are all consequentialists (and few ethicists before Sidgwick were consequentialists). Consequentialism, she thinks, is confused and otherwise bad. It is confused because it depends on taking seriously the special category of the *moral*, which, according to thesis (2), has, with the rise of secular culture in the West, degenerated into a pseudo-concept. Furthermore, the special badness that attaches to consequentialism has been made possible by our not having noticed that the category of the moral *has* degenerated into a pseudo-concept.

Thus thesis (2), that the special category of the *moral* should be jettisoned as a pseudo-concept, is fundamental; it is presupposed by the arguments for theses (1) and (3). Furthermore, it is this claim that makes the paper potentially very profound. If a paper is plausible (and for now I will assume that MMP, or at least thesis [2], is plausible; I will examine the assumption later), one measure of its profundity is how much other philosophy it would put out of business were it true. MMP is profound by this measure in virtue of thesis (2). There is still a huge amount of moral philosophy that takes the category of the moral as *given,* and typically as sui generis. The category is presupposed in investigations into how moral norms are related, for example, to those of prudence, or of rationality more broadly construed. Equally it is presupposed in debates between so-called internalists and externalists about whether it is part of the meaning of a *moral* proposition that it give suitably situated agents a reason for acting in accordance with it. When consequentialists maintain that an action or policy derives its *moral* worth from its likely consequences, or deontologists maintain, to the contrary, that there can be *moral* evaluation of an action or policy that pays no heed to consequences, or expressivists deny that *moral* judgments can be true or false, or experimental philosophers try to discern the content of ordinary people's *moral* intuitions— these philosophers take themselves to be making contentful claims, and so they rely on being able to help themselves to a category of the *moral* already constituted to provide a subject matter—even if they purport to be looking into what that category really amounts to. Certainly, they don't usually rule out the possibility that we might be radically mistaken over some of the details as to which propositions get included in the category, or as to which moral propositions are to count as true or right—but then, again, this would count as news only because we already have, we think, a core concept of the *moral* relative to which such results might turn out to be surprising, or not.

If thesis (2) of MMP is right, then, it is profound, because in that case none of these philosophers will really know what they are talking about. A crucial presupposition of all the debates in moral philosophy I have mentioned, and very many more, will turn out to have been false: this is the presupposition that there is a preexistent category or concept of the *moral*, which we can be said to understand in the minimal way necessary for it to be an intelligible question for us whether an action derives its *moral* worth exclusively from its consequences, or whether *moral* precepts are consistent with prudential ones, and so on. Anscombe's main claim in MMP is that we don't really understand such a sui generis concept of the *moral*, because there is nothing there to understand—there is nothing for the concept of the *moral* to be a concept *of.*

Thesis (2), then, is both fundamental to the structure of MMP and what makes the paper especially profound (if it is). Yet although MMP is frequently mentioned in the literature and rightly considered very influential, thesis (2), its basis, and its implications have not been much examined; and when the thesis has been examined it has usually been badly misconstrued.[1]

My first aim in Part 1 of this book is to rectify the situation by getting clear on what thesis (2) really amounts to, on the reasons there may be for holding it, and on its implications for ethics, including its purported support for (1) and (3).

If thesis (2) has been so ignored, what is it about MMP that has made it so well known and influential? The answer is that it is thought to be a founding document, or even *the* founding document, of the revival of "virtue ethics"—the attempt to place the concept of virtue, rather than that of rule, or of the best state of affairs, at the center of ethics—as it was, supposedly, in the ancient world. That revival has therefore proceeded largely independently of thesis (2), as an explication of the moral realm rather than an alternative to it. Anscombe urged a return to the Greek conception of virtue partly because the Greeks lacked the concept of morality rejected in thesis (2). The many modern virtue ethicists who leave the concept of morality largely undisturbed, but claim inspiration from the Greeks and Anscombe, misunderstand both the Greek notion and the main point of Anscombe's paper. As a result they put forward ethical theories that are not very interestingly different from those they purport to reject. Anscombe had in mind something much more radical, novel, interesting, and, for those sympathetic to thesis (2), promising.

The second aim of Part 1 is to explain these claims in more detail, in the hope of making them plausible.

1.2 My Undergraduate Bewilderment

We first have to get clear on the theses themselves. When I first read, some thirty-five years ago (as an undergraduate and, as it happens, attending Anscombe's lectures on the *Nicomachean Ethics* at the time), "the concepts of [*moral*] obligation, and [*moral*] duty . . . and of what is *morally* right and wrong, and of the *moral* sense of 'ought,' ought to be jettisoned if this is psychologically possible," I was completely bewildered. What *on earth* could this mean? How could we possibly get rid of the concept of moral obligation? The concept seemed too fundamental to be thought of as optional. Wouldn't that mean surrender to moral skepticism? Wouldn't abandonment of these concepts leave self-interest in sole possession of the field, as the only legitimate source of reasons for action?

I can now see that these reactions really expressed how deeply I was immersed in the ideology of morality. For it is part of that ideology that the only alternative to the moral is the immoral or the amoral: naked egotism or dangerous sociopathy. For morality, in this context, as Kantians have insisted, is a matter of "pure" altruism: taking others' interests into account *as such* and not merely when it happens to square with my own interests. So the only alternative seems to be some version of being out for oneself.

I am not embarrassed to confess my youthful misunderstanding, because it is shared to this day by established philosophers. Simon Blackburn, for example, recently wrote in a review of Anscombe (2005a) that "Anscombe's thought [in MMP] was a version of the Dostoievskian claim that if God is dead everything is permitted" (Blackburn 2005, 11). But there is no hint of this in MMP and Anscombe clearly has no doubt that the viciousness of certain actions is or should be apparent to anyone, including the many who disbelieve in divine command. When she wrote, about the person who would wonder whether it might not be OK in a given case to procure judicial murder, "I do not want to argue with him: he shows a corrupt mind" (MMP, 17), she pretty clearly was decrying not a corruption that stems from disbelieving in divine command, but the corruption manifested in *being unjust*—a charge Aristotle, who certainly did not think of ethics in terms of divine command, would have readily understood and agreed with. Yet Blackburn takes Anscombe's unconditional condemnation of acts like judicial murder to indicate that she "had no intention of jettisoning the concepts of moral obligation and duty" after all (2005, 11). Like my youthful self, he does not consider the possibility that a fundamental ethical precept could fail to be a *moral* precept, because he has missed her point, expounded in much more detail by Bernard Williams, that morality is best viewed as a particular form that ethical thought might take, but need not.

Blackburn also wrote, "I suppose it is a permanent feature of the human condition that persons who entangle their notion of morality with some notion of divine authority cannot imagine that there might be people who have the morality, but who have no need of the supernatural prop. This may be a natural enough frailty, but philosophers should be better able to overcome it, both because there is nothing serious to be said for it and because it was refuted by Plato[2]" (2005, 12).

He seems to be making Anscombe say what he expects a theist to say. In MMP Anscombe wrote,

> It would be most reasonable to drop [the notion *morally ought*]. It has no reasonable sense outside a law conception of ethics; [our present-day ethicists] are not going to maintain such a conception; and *you can do ethics without it, as is shown by the example of Aristotle*. It would be a great improvement if, instead of "morally wrong," one always named a genus such as "untruthful," "unchaste," "unjust." We should no longer ask whether doing something was "wrong," passing directly from some description of an action to this notion; we should ask whether, e.g., it was unjust; and the answer would sometimes be clear at once. (8–9; my emphasis)

It is obvious that Anscombe is thinking of terms like "unchaste" and "unjust" as claiming action-guiding force. It is equally obvious that she does not take herself to be addressing only Jews, Christians, and Muslims.

1.3 Unobjectionable Uses of "Moral"

Anscombe's chief objection, as I understand it, is to *moral* purportedly understood as a fully sui generis category. This sense is typified when it is contrasted with other sorts of reason, motive, criticism, consideration, and so on: think of all those qualifications or objections: "I mean a specifically *moral* . . . ," "Yes, but that's not really a *moral* . . . ," and so on. Relatedly, philosophers often suppose that *moral* in this sense is essentially irreducible to other categories of reason, consideration, and so on. This is clear from the routine objection alluded to by Blackburn and supposedly inspired by Plato's *Euthyphro*, to "divine command theories of morality": one might concede that God has, say, forbidden a certain kind of action, but there always remains a further question as to whether that kind of action is *morally* forbidden. Even if God's commands and the moral precepts always coincide, it is often thought, something's being commanded by God can't be *what it is* for it to be a moral precept, nor even (it would usually also be insisted) *that in virtue of which* it is a moral precept.

There are, of course, other senses or uses of "moral." Most of these are clearly unobjectionable, in the sense that Anscombe's criticisms do not apply to them. Some of the harmless locutions sound slightly archaic, precisely because they hark back to an older sense of the word: "moral (as opposed to natural) sciences," for example, and "moral psychology." Some of these occur in contexts that encourage a false assimilation to the objectionable sense, as in the traditional translation of Aristotle's distinction between ἀρεταὶ διανοητικαί and ἀρεταὶ ἠθικαί as being between intellectual virtues and *moral* virtues.

"Virtues of character" is now gaining ground as the preferred (and very much preferable) rendering of the latter phrase. Thomas Aquinas, however, unwittingly muddies the waters for us by translating the Aristotelian distinction, naturally, as between *virtutes intellectuales* and *virtutes morales* (for example, Aquinas 1888–1906 [hereafter *ST*], IaIIae Q100 A2, although there is no consistently reliable translation of the *ST*; the best available is Aquinas [1964–1980]). That the translation is virtually unavoidable only makes it the more intractably misleading to the eye of a culture pervaded by a purportedly sui generis idea of morality. As their Aristotelian provenance should lead us to expect, these expressions in Aquinas do not advert to a sui generis concept at all. I say more about this in Appendix A.

This common translation of Aristotle's ἠθικός, and the ubiquitous translation of Aquinas's *moralis*, which really amount to something very like our "ethical," in turn encourage a tendency to use "moral" and "ethical" interchangeably. This tendency is innocuous if it expresses an assimilation of "moral" to "ethical," so that both words designate merely that the question of how to live is being posed in an especially abstract and general spirit, and understood in such a way that the special, sui generis sense of "moral" gives at best one set of answers among many. More often, however, the identity is intended to be read in the other direction, and so encodes a deplorable assumption that morality, in the sense here deemed objectionable, is identical with ethics, in the sense of what pertains to the most general and authoritative norms governing human character and behavior.

It has been said, correctly, that Anscombe subsequently disregarded her own recommendation in MMP about "*banishing ethics totally* from our minds" until the vast deficiencies she alleged in the philosophy of psychology had been made good (MMP, 15)—unless she thought this had already been accomplished by the time she published on ethics, which seems very unlikely (Pigden 1988, 20). But her own subsequent use of the term "moral" indicates no similar inconsistency with MMP, since it is the innocuous use that matches Aquinas's *moralis*—designating the ethical as such, not any particular conception of it:

> To say [as Anscombe does] that "human action" and "moral action (*sc* of a human being)" are equivalent is to say that all human action *in concreto* is either good or bad simpliciter. There is no need to insert "morally" and say "morally good or bad." The term "moral" adds no sense to the phrase, because we are talking about human actions, and the "moral" goodness of an action is nothing but its goodness as a human action. I mean: the goodness with which it is a good action. "Moral" goodness is: goodness of actions, passions, and habits of action and feeling. (Anscombe 1982, 17)

As she often does, Anscombe here closely follows Aquinas without mentioning him.[3] In this case she echoes *ST* IaIIae Q1 A3 Resp: "Moral acts are the same as human acts" (*idem sunt actus morales et actus humani*), a saying that makes it clear enough that Aquinas's *moralis* does not mean "moral" in its purportedly sui generis sense. She accordingly here takes a softer line on the matter of terminology than that implied in much of MMP; for example, "the notions of 'moral obligation,' 'the moral ought,' and 'duty' are best put on the Index, if [one] can manage it" (MMP, 15).

My main purpose in going into all this is to make it clear, and so obviate any further repetition of the point, that nothing in what I say should be taken as impugning what I here characterize as unobjectionable uses of "moral." Nevertheless, I would still like to record a preference for Anscombe's scorched-earth policy in MMP. We should make a clean break: as I hope to show, the word is hopelessly compromised.

1.4 The Real Point of Virtue Ethics

We can see the mistake, in supposing that we can't abandon the concept of the *moral* without becoming ethical skeptics, if we go back to the Greeks.[4] Anscombe points out that Aristotle, for example, seems to get by rather well without any recourse to the concept of the *moral* in our special sense. The concept is alien because the Greeks were (nearly)[5] all *eudaimonists*— that is, they took it for granted that a reason for action was simply a way in which the action served the interests or contributed to the well-being of the agent. (Socrates, for example, frequently appeals to something like this as an axiom, and the people he is addressing go along with it unquestioningly—including the jury at his trial, who were a random cross section of Athenian citizens.) Now, the pagan world was by our standards in many ways a very cruel place, but it certainly wasn't a world of egotists and sociopaths. Again, looking at the *Nicomachean Ethics* in particular, there are features of Aristotle's portrait of the virtuous man that make us uneasy or indignant, but no one would claim that it doesn't leave room for our ties to other people.

So eudaimonistic virtue ethics can perfectly well make room for other-regarding actions and attitudes. But we have to take care that this point not lead us into an opposite misconception of the Greeks' conception of virtue, as amounting to *moral* virtue.

Robert Louden wrote,

> On the Anscombe model, strong, irreducible duty and obligation notions drop out of the picture, and are to be replaced by vices such as

unchasteness and untruthfulness. But are we to take the assertion literally, and actually attempt to do moral theory without any concept of duty whatsoever? On my reading, Anscombe is not really proposing that we entirely dispose of moral oughts. Suppose one follows her advice, and replaces "morally wrong" with "untruthful," "unchaste," etc. Isn't this merely shorthand for saying that agents *ought* to be truthful and chaste, and that untruthful and unchaste acts are *morally wrong* because good agents don't perform such acts? (1984, 228)

Louden is doubly confused. First, there is nothing in the Greek *or* modern idea of virtue inconsistent with the idea of duty or unconditional requirement. Socrates in the *Apology* plausibly claimed that the virtue of piety required him to obey the commands of the god. Most people think the virtue of justice requires them not to swindle people. Aristotle certainly thought there were sorts of action that a good man would not consider under any circumstances. Anscombe objects not to the idea of an ethical principle—many virtues cannot be understood independently of the disposition to follow such principles—but to a special category of such principles marked off as *moral*. But why can't we call a principle that enters into the definition of a virtue a *moral* principle? In fact—don't we *have* to?

Some modern "virtue ethicists" (for example, McDowell 1979) who claim to be inspired by the Greek conception of virtue (and in many cases by Anscombe's paper!) do seem to think of virtue as what we would call "*moral* virtue"—which is to say, a disposition to act in accordance with just what we would call *moral* precepts and to further *moral* ideals; this accords with what springs to mind nowadays when one hears the word "virtue": highly Christianized and altruistic qualities like kindness (John McDowell's main example) and humility (which in many of its manifestations the Greeks would consider a vice). The point of virtue ethics, on this "Victorian" view (as we might call it), lies in its opposition to a "law conception" (Anscombe's phrase), and so its giving us a "third way" alternative to the two dominant, warring families of law conception: deontology or absolutism, and consequentialism (on which more later). But this gives us an account of ethics that is not very interestingly different from a law conception; and insofar as it claims to appropriate the ancient concept of virtue, it misunderstands that. These faults are related: appropriation of the genuine ancient concept, as on Anscombe's view, gives us a much more novel and interesting account of ethics.

The Victorian view does not give us a very interestingly distinctive account of ethics because it is too close to being a "notational variant" of a law conception (whether deontological or consequentialist). Can't the "moral virtues" and the moral precepts be defined in terms of each other? The virtues are the dispositions to abide by the precepts,[6] and the precepts are those observed by the virtuous. As Louden implies, we can talk about virtue or we can talk about moral duty, but it's the same underlying moral reality we're getting at.

As an account of the Victorian view, this is oversimple. As I understand him, McDowell wants to argue for the *primacy* of the virtue conception, on the Aristotelian ground that ethics cannot be codified without remainder into a system of rules, but involves an ineliminable component of quasi-perceptual sensitivity to the ethically relevant features of concrete situations. This looks plausible as far as it goes (although less plausible if it is taken as far as denying the existence of any ethical precepts at all, as in Dancy [2004]). But it is still a much more superficial departure from standard (deontological and consequentialist) accounts than Anscombe proposes, precisely because it retains their commitment to the sui generis category of the *moral,* with all the problems that brings—in particular, what is the content of the concept? And especially, what is supposed to motivate us to act morally? That is, what makes a *"moral* reason" a reason at all?

The Victorian view fails to pick up on what is distinctive about the Greeks' conception of virtue, which is exactly what makes that conception philosophically promising. That conception is *egoistic-eudaimonistic,* which is to say it is a conceptual truth that a virtue benefits its possessor.[7] "Virtue" as a translation of the Greek term *aretē* is actually quite seriously misleading, and I only use it because it is now too well entrenched to oppose. The English word sounds rather quaint (and Victorian), *precisely because* of connotations of moral earnestness the Greek word lacks. The root meaning of the Greek word is "excellence," in the sense of a quality that makes a thing good of its kind. What counts as such a quality therefore radically depends on what kind of thing is in question: a good knife will standardly be sharp, a good musical instrument in tune—but what makes for a good human being? Here we must be careful, for the category of the *moral* so pervades our thinking about ethics that it can be quite difficult not to hear the phrase "good human being" as "*morally* good human being." But an *aretē* is a quality that makes one good *at being* a human being, and while one may argue that "other-regarding" qualities like benevolence and generosity fit this description, there is nothing in the concept of an *aretē* to prevent one from arguing, as Plato's Callicles did (*Gorgias* 483a–484c), that the true or "natural" virtue of justice comprises the intelligence and courage of the strong natures that enable them to dominate the weaker and appropriate their possessions, and the freedom from inhibition that enables them to magnify and indulge their appetites to the utmost. While Socrates spends the remainder of the *Gorgias* arguing against Callicles's conceptions of *aretē* and *eudaimonia,* the important point for our purposes is that he never once suggests that there is anything immediately contradictory in Callicles's claim that these rapacious and self-indulgent qualities are *aretai* at all—but this would be the obvious retort, if it were part of the *idea* of an *aretē,* as it is part of our idea of many of the virtues, and certainly of justice, that they require one to take others' interests into account. The example of Callicles alone is enough to discredit much that is simply taken for granted (that is, asserted without argument) about ancient ethics.[8]

Thrasymachus in the *Republic,* by contrast, in denying that justice is good for its possessor (he calls it "another's good") is simply denying it is a virtue at all. Roughly speaking, if I have a virtue in the modern "Victorian" sense, this is, by definition, good news for other people, but it is an open question whether it is good news for me; whereas if I have an *aretē,* this is, by definition, good news for me, but it is an open question whether it is good news for other people.[9]

Someone might object at this point that we, and even the Greeks, are after all entitled to restrict our attention to, roughly, what Callicles calls a "conventional," that is, other-regarding, understanding of justice, and the same sort of understanding of the other virtues. (This would of course in the end be a terminological point; the further we move back to such a modern understanding of virtue, the more vulnerable we become, all over again, to the objection that it's really not clear what reason we have to cultivate *those* qualities.) The conclusion that real justice is the "natural" quality that Callicles praises, it might be said, is not a possible outcome for *ethics,* but the collapse of the whole inquiry, as well as of any prospect of social cooperation on decent terms, insofar as such a conclusion gains credence. And doesn't Anscombe herself, notoriously, refuse to argue with one whose principles leave it open that procuring the judicial execution of the innocent might sometimes be the thing to do, for the reason that he "shows a corrupt mind" (MMP, 17)?

But, first, Anscombe is here following Plato, whose Socrates in the *Republic* addresses his most important arguments not to the corrupt Thrasymachus but to the ethically sound Glaucon and Adeimantus, and Aristotle, who addresses his *Nicomachean Ethics* to mature people who already know how to behave. An understandable disdain for real-life ethical (as opposed to moral) skeptics does not absolve us, as philosophers, from seeking refutations of their positions, and there is much in the *Ethics* and the *Republic* to help equip us for that job. I may rightly refuse to entertain even the possibility that Zeno's arguments truly establish that nothing really moves, but until I can show where his argument fails, I cannot claim a complete understanding of what motion *is*. In the practical case, the task is more urgent. I take it that what Anscombe thinks would be provided by a proper account of virtue, which she thinks we are very far from having and even, Socratically, implies may be beyond our reach, is the kind of grounding for, for example, the traditional understanding of the virtue of justice, whose current unavailability provides people like Callicles and Thrasymachus with at least the appearance of, at best, an intellectual alibi.

Second, the idea that Callicles's conception of "natural" justice is a counsel of ethical despair, or would undermine any worthwhile human cooperation, so that the whole inquiry into ethics must be premised on the rejection of it, is sheer complacency. We only have to take a couple of steps back and take in the wider context to see that Callicles was quite wrong to lament the widespread subscription to the "conventional" conception as blocking the implementation of his bold and ruthless program. I refer to the institution of slavery, not uncommon in human history, ubiquitous in the ancient Greek world, and still visible, from an appropriately "globalized" perspective, as a continuing foundation of life *in the West*. There could hardly be a clearer case of one group (the strong) dominating and exploiting another (the weak) simply because they can. Far from destroying beneficial social cooperation, this paradigm of Calliclean justice was believed by many Greeks, perhaps rightly, to be its absolutely necessary precondition.

"Virtue ethics" in the Greek sense, then, makes no mention of a special category of the *moral,* and so avoids the problems associated with it. McDowell's version still looks vulnerable to the skeptical question, "But *why* should I acquire *those* qualities?" On the Greek conception, such questions can get no purchase. As P. T. Geach puts it, appropriating "the powerful arguments, in the spirit of Aristotle, . . . developed by Mrs. Philippa Foot," "Moral virtues, she argues, are habits of action and avoidance; and they are such as a man cannot rationally choose to go without, any more than he can rationally choose to be blind, paralytic, or stupid; to choose to lack a virtue would be to choose a maimed life, ill-adapted to this difficult and dangerous world" (1969, 122–123).[10]

And as Christopher Coope wrote, in a similar vein,

> To spend money on something one enjoys is to spend it *on a good cause* (not in every case of course, but in the vast majority of cases in the ordinary run of life). This is a satisfactorily unimpressive thought. Yet the connection between simple rationality of this kind and goodness tends to be obscured by conventional altruistic expectations. Rosalind Hursthouse's chosen example of "acting well" involves giving someone a present. *That* is what gets "the tick of approval" as she puts it. It is however completely misleading in any virtue ethics worthy of the name to cling to such "virtuous" examples. We should be giving the tick of approval to the opening of a can of beans. And if we must continue to talk of "moral reasons," then *in order to make one's supper* must be allowed to count. (2006, 25)

"Egoism" and the Whig Interpretation of the History of Morality

Before we go any further, I would like to issue some clarifications about what is meant here by "egoism."

I said earlier that my dumbfounded undergraduate response to reading MMP reflected how deeply the moral vocabulary is embedded in our culture, to the extent that it has come to seem to many to be simply coextensive with, or even *equivalent to* the ethical (where "the ethical" concerns fundamental questions about how to live and what to do). That this is a misconception can be seen, I think, for the primary reason Anscombe herself gave: that Aristotle (and, by extension, the Greeks[11]) got by without it:

> Anyone who has read Aristotle's *Ethics* and has also read modern moral philosophy must have been struck by the great contrasts between them. The concepts which are prominent among the moderns seem to be lacking. . . . Most noticeably, the term "moral" itself . . . just doesn't seem to fit. . . . If someone professes to be expounding Aristotle and talks in a modern fashion about "moral" such-and-such, he must be very imperceptive if he does not constantly feel like someone whose jaws have somehow got out of alignment: the teeth don't come together in a proper bite. (MMP, 1–2)

Various attempts have been made to show that the Greeks did have the notion after all. I argue against a number of these attempts later. But, all argument aside, and in a spirit of putting my cards on the table, I must say that I profoundly agree with Anscombe here. It seems very clear to me that the concept (in the sense of "intension") of *morality* is not to be found among the Greeks. If we assume for the moment that my arguments are sound, and Anscombe and I are correct on this point, that the moral notions are *clearly* absent from ancient ethics, this raises an important question: If it *is* in fact clear, why are there eminent scholars arguing vigorously (Irwin 1977, 1986, 2006), or even, still, assuming without acknowledging any need of argument (Annas 1993), that it is false? There is circumstantial evidence here, I believe, for what I say about the distortively conditioning effect of the moral notions' being so deeply embedded in our own thinking. "The Greeks just *must* have had the concept of morality! It is what the concept of *ethics* comes to in the end—one might as well deny they had the concept of causality!"[12] Anscombe wanted to dislodge this kind of attitude, but seriously underestimated the difficulty of the task: as I hope to show, just this kind of distorted thinking about the inescapability of the moral concept led to her own paper being very widely and deeply misinterpreted, in ways she cannot have anticipated. Part of my aim in what follows is to present and amplify her skeptical ideas in a way that preempts some of these misinterpretations, many of which provide pretexts for very quick but utterly spurious dismissals of a view that demands serious consideration, precisely because it rejects ideas we are inclined to think of as beyond reproach, so that we have never thought seriously about what would be involved in calling them into question.

The received history of the concept of *morality* is effectively that it *has* no history. Most people think of it as something like a natural kind (a view encouraged among philosophers above all by Immanuel Kant). What sorts of characters and actions and ways of life are taken to fall under the concept vary dramatically from one culture and epoch to another—this is a theme that is elaborated *endlessly*—but in a strange way this encourages us to assume that the concept *itself* endures.[13] This teeming variety through time and across cultures is a variety of conceptions of *the* concept of *morality*. The history of conceptions has culminated, of course, in our own, and it is very difficult for us to resist the idea that this is a genuine culmination, and that its prominently, unprecedentedly altruistic aspirations signify a closer approach to morality's *essence*.

To this way of thinking, the term "egoism" suggests, roughly, the *opposite* of morality. On the natural way of understanding it, it gets a good part of its sense from a contrast with altruism. Since altruism is a concern for others, egoism is, on this way of understanding it, a concern for oneself *as opposed to* others. Egoism as a principle of life is therefore thought to be something we are instinctively and surely correctly inclined to regard as bad. It is even arguable that, if human beings were not perverse, in ways that can lead them to harm themselves, and to harm others, somehow just for the sake of it—that is, without its bringing the agent *any* benefit, even a sadistic enjoyment of cruelty—badness just *would be* egoism.

Now, no governing conception of *morality* could be identified with altruism as such, because "concern for others" can take many forms, and many different principles of conduct and ideals of character are consistent with it. Indeed, this fact is the starting point of a huge proportion of moral philosophy: Which principles of altruism express *the true morality*? Still, most people think that morality is essentially some form of altruism. (There is a minority of dissenters [for example, Gauthier 1987] inspired by an interpretation of Hobbes according to which morality does not, fundamentally, require that one take into account the interests of others *as such*.)

"Egoism" thus has unfortunate associations, to put it mildly. I intend by it a contrast not with altruism but with the distinctive forms of altruism that fall under the purported concept of *morality,* whereby the requirement of taking into account others' interests as such is supposed to have a force that originates in something completely separate from any normative attraction exerted by qualities of character that make one good at being a human being—good, that is, in a sense that does not presuppose *morality*—and that one therefore cannot rationally wish to lack.[14]

In the end I want "egoistic" to be coextensive with something like *acting from intelligible reasons.* If Anscombe is right—as it seems so clear to me that she is—that the Greeks lacked the concept *morality,* in my sense, "egoistic reason" for the Greeks would just mean "intelligible reason." Insofar as altruism is intelligible—and why shouldn't it be?—it is compatible with what I mean by "egoism." My use of the word would not be necessary if it were not necessary to distinguish the true basis of ethics from one that, on the hypothesis it is my business here to promote, makes no sense.

So it is only if the Anscombe view I here present and (qualifiedly) defend is incorrect, and *moral* is a fully legitimate concept, that "egoism" in the sense meant here is open to immediate criticism on ethical grounds. Most of the distinctively moral reasons were supposed to be sui generis reasons having to do with "what we owe to each other" *as such*—that is, not *legal* reasons, or reasons having to do with *integrity,* or reasons stemming from an aspiration to be an admirable specimen of humanity, or anything of the sort. "Egoism" as meant here merely rules out the sui generis *moral* reasons. What are left are *the reasons we had anyway,* and among these there may be any number of kinds of reason underlying robust conceptions of what we owe to each other. In other words, if "egoism" is open to criticism on ethical grounds, those must be specifically *moral* grounds; and it follows directly from Anscombe's main thesis that all such grounds are spurious.

I deny, then, that eudaimonistic-virtue reasons should be identified with reasons that have to be articulated in terms of egoism as opposed to *altruism.* The core idea of eudaimonism is that it makes sense to do something, or to acquire a disposition to do a sort of thing, if and only if this contributes to one's *eudaimonia,* which is to say, it contributes to or manifests one's being good at being a human being.[15] But although being good at being a human being is in one's interest (and, in a way, nothing else is), so that the picture is in *this* sense egoistic, what counts as being good at being a human being is completely up for grabs. That is not to say that we can just let the category of the *moral* in again by the back door, as a kind of mode of *eudaimonia*. The objection to the sui generis category of the *moral* is central to the view. We shall see later on that that objection implies a rejection of the moral notions as *not even concepts*.

But one could, and presumably should, make a case that a very important constituent of being good at being a human being is this: that one be sensitive to the legitimate claims of others on one's practical attention.[16] There is nothing in the idea of *eudaimonia* that is inconsistent with the legitimacy of such claims: on the contrary, the suggestion that one could be good at being a human being while ignoring or denying the categorical reality of claims of others on one's practical attention is prima facie bizarre. It is not, however, immediately self-contradictory, which is why Callicles can mount a coherent challenge to Socratic (and "conventional") ethics. So the import of egoistic eudaimonism here is something like this: the bindingness, the authority of the claims of others derives from the idea that sensitivity to those claims and an acknowledgment of their authority are essential components of *eudaimonia*—that is, of being good at being a human being; and a *philosophical* account of why these claims are inescapable would be an account of why this should be so—that is, of why anyone good qua human being has to acknowledge these claims. That would be an account of the reality of these requirements: presumably someone good qua human being is going to be someone who acts in light of the reasons and sources of value there really are in the human world. But these are not fundamentally sui generis requirements that somehow *don't have to be* vindicated, even in an account that aspires to philosophical adequacy, via a conception of *eudaimonia*. But just this exemption from eudaimonist vindication is, uniquely, supposed to be close to the essence of sui generis morality. Whereas in fact, their fundamental character as reasons is the same as that of all other reasons: acknowledging their authority is a matter not of *Moralität* but of *Menschlichkeit*. So egoistic eudaimonism amounts to something like a commitment to the fundamental *homogeneity* of human reasons. To deny a *fundamental* distinction between egoistic and altruistic reasons is not to say that all our deepest, categorical reasons are "*really* egoistic," any more than it is to say that they are all "*really* altruistic": both of those claims would depend on a residual acknowledgment of a distinction that a true virtue ethic, in its rejection of the concept *morality,* aspires to transcend.[17,18]

1.6   The Misconception of the Moral Notions as Ubiquitous and Unavoidable Encourages and Is Encouraged by the Misattribution of the Notions to the Greeks

The tendency to think of the Greeks' vocabulary of virtue as simply their way of characterizing the realm we call *moral* is still very widespread, and very strong, indeed. Before it became an error in the appropriation of Greek ideas in current moral philosophy, of course, it had to be an error in the history of philosophy. In his recent book on Plato's later ethics (2002), Christopher Bobonich tried to characterize a certain "strand of Greek ethical and political reflection that is disturbing and profoundly alien to us," common to Xenocrates, Plato, Aristotle, Plutarch, and Plotinus:

> On this view, only a philosopher can genuinely live well and only a philosopher can lead a truly happy and flourishing life. All other human beings, no matter what else is true of them, go badly astray in their lives and actions; their lives inevitably fail to be happy and are incomplete or warped. For Xenocrates and [Aristotle's] *Protrepticus,* ethical virtue itself is restricted to philosophers. Only the philosopher, Xenocrates assures us, voluntarily acts virtuously or finely; everyone else acts as virtue requires only under the compulsion of the law, like dogs under the whip. For the *Protrepticus,* the philosopher . . . is the only person whose actions are right and fine, that is, virtuous. In Plotinus, we find a radicalization of these tendencies. Our true goal or good is to become divine, that is, to lead the contemplative life of the gods. Only the philosopher can live such a life and this requires transcending or leaving behind civic or ethical virtue. (1–2)

"To see how alien these views are to us," Bobonich continues, "consider the following characterization of modern moral philosophy offered by one of its most distinguished historians:

'The new outlook that emerged by the end of the eighteenth century centered on the belief that all normal individuals are equally able to live together in a morality of self-governance. All of us, on this view, have an equal ability to see for ourselves what morality calls for and are in principle equally able to move ourselves to act accordingly, regardless of threats or rewards from others. These two points have come to be widely accepted—so widely that most moral philosophy now starts by assuming them. In daily life they give us the working assumption that the people we live with are capable of understanding and acknowledging in practice the reasons for the moral constraints we all mutually expect ourselves and others to respect.'" (1–2)[19]

This sequence of thought illustrates very well how tenacious is the myth of Greek morality. It presents, entirely up front, all the ideas required to dispel it, yet still cannot bring itself to take the final step. The Greek discourse of virtue is explicitly presented as essentially concerned with the virtuous person's happiness. The modern concept of morality is explicitly presented (via J. B. Schneewind) as essentially concerned with the constraints we can expect each other to observe as making social cooperation possible. Yet the ancient restriction of virtue to philosophers and the modern presumptive extension of morality to all competent agents[20] are presented as radically different construals of the same fundamental concept!

In a way, the fact that the shift in question runs much deeper than Bobonich imagines makes it much less amazing than he finds it. Once the fundamental disagreement is identified as *conceptual,* the ancient outlook stands revealed as much less distant, disturbing, and alien with regard to the issue of how things are actually taken to be. For the closest thing the ancients have to morality is not virtue in general but what Callicles calls the conventional understanding of justice, according to which it involves taking into account others' interests (which is why its status as a virtue is a huge philosophical problem). And the citizens of a well-regulated democratic Greek *polis, including the philosophers,* probably did believe, roughly, that all normal fellow citizens were equally able to live together in accordance with the basic precepts whose observance is required by the virtue of justice in this sense. Indeed, this would seem to be a precondition of democratic political community. All citizens, on this view, have an equal ability to see for themselves what justice calls for and are in principle equally able to move themselves to act accordingly, regardless of threats or rewards from others. At least, this is about as plausible as Schneewind's corresponding claim about morality since the Enlightenment, especially given the leeway afforded by his expression "in principle." The main difference is the restriction in the Greek case to fellow citizens of a *polis,* but this is more a matter of radically different prevailing basic political conditions of human life than anything else.

Conversely, the closest we have to the ancient conception of complete virtue is the rare, impressive person who has figured out how to live a successful, flourishing life that acknowledges and accommodates all or very many of the things she credibly and creditably supposes to be important and valuable. Now it is true that we would find it ridiculous to limit this status to philosophers, or even to extend it to many of them. But this would be because we are taking the category of philosopher at face value, as, roughly speaking, institutionally given. In that sense, Plato himself has Socrates explicitly and emphatically affirm, in the course of an argument for distinctively Platonic theses, that most philosophers are vicious (*Republic* 487c–487d; cf. Simmias at *Phaedo* 64a10–64b6). This goes a fortiori for the Socrates of the shorter "Socratic" dialogues, who explicitly identified philosophy precisely with inquiry into the question, "How should I live?" the real answer to which he conceived not as a set of theses but as a well-lived life.

So once we look at the small print that comes with the concepts of *virtue* and *philosopher* that go to make up the ancient tradition Bobonich identifies, it no longer seems so alien and disturbing that it should restrict virtue to philosophers. It looks instead rather like, for *them,* a conceptual truth, which indicates not that the Greeks had a radically different take on how things stand with respect to transhistorically stable and given categories of virtue, philosophy, and (*per impossibile*) morality, but that deep *conceptual* shifts have taken place in the interim, for complicated historical reasons, which (it will turn out) have a lot to do with the rise and fall of Christianity as a cultural force.

Since the Greek concept of virtue is of a quality that makes one good at being a human being, as I mentioned previously, putting the concept at the center of ethics enables one to sidestep from the start skeptical questions about *why* one would want to acquire the virtues. The problem of motivation, however, has simply been traded in for another problem, the one pressed by Callicles: Which qualities *are* the virtues? In particular, how do we know they aren't the qualities that enable one to dominate and deceive one's fellows? What is it about lacking the traditional virtue of justice (what Callicles calls "conventional" justice) that makes one bad qua human being?

2

The Invention of "Morality" and the Possibility of Consequentialism

2.1 Anscombe's Historical Account of the Rise of the "Law Conception" of Ethics; Explanation of Hume's Views as a Corollary

Why were the Greeks egoist-eudaimonists? Why did they lack our concept of morality? These are the wrong questions. The right ones are, Why aren't *we* egoist-eudaimonists? Why do we *have* our concept of morality, with its notion of obligations that seem to make no reference to our interests? And the answer is Christianity; or, perhaps, its demise. As Anscombe observes, Christianity derived its ethical conceptions from the Torah, and so conceived ethics in terms of divine commands. It is significant that Aristotle has no blanket term for wrongdoing like "illicit"; he would need an extended circumlocution to express it (MMP, 6). (Note that this would not amount to an Aristotelian account of *morally wrong,* but merely his most general conception of *what is not to be done.* As the case of Blackburn illustrated, the ideology of morality tends to make us think, mistakenly, that this most general conception simply must amount to "morally wrong.") On this "law conception of ethics," as Anscombe calls it, what is required for conformity to the virtues ("failure in which is the mark of being bad *qua* man") is required by divine law. "But if such a conception is dominant for many centuries, and then is given up, it is a natural result that the concepts of 'obligation,' of being bound or required as by a law, should remain though they had lost their root; and if the word 'ought' has become invested in certain contexts with the sense of 'obligation,' it too will remain to be spoken with a special emphasis and a special feeling in these contexts" (6).

Here Anscombe gives an especially interesting diagnosis of David Hume's view of moral obligation as based on a sui generis sentiment, difficult of explication:

> It is as if the notion "criminal" were to remain when criminal law and criminal courts had been abolished and forgotten. A Hume discovering this situation might conclude that there was a special sentiment, expressed by "criminal," which alone gave the word its sense. So Hume discovered the situation in which the notion "obligation" survived, and the notion "ought" was invested with that peculiar force having which it is said to be used in a "moral" sense, but in which the belief in divine law had long since been abandoned: for it was substantially given up among Protestants at the time of the Reformation. The situation, if I am right, was the interesting one of the survival of a concept outside the framework of thought that made it a really intelligible one. (MMP, 6)

Relatedly, she agrees with Hume that a *"moral* ought" cannot be inferred from indicative sentences—even those whose main verb is "owes" or "needs"—because "this word 'ought,' having become a word of mere mesmeric force, could not, in the character of having that force, be inferred from anything whatever" (MMP, 8; I return to this passage later). At this point she gives her clearest and most forceful expression of her second thesis:

> I should judge that Hume and our present-day ethicists had done a considerable service by showing that no content could be found in the notion "morally ought"; if it were not that the latter philosophers try to find an alternative (very fishy) content and to retain the psychological force of the term. It would be most reasonable to drop it. It has no reasonable sense outside a law conception of ethics; they are not going to maintain such a conception; and you can do ethics without it, as is shown by the example of Aristotle. It would be a great improvement if, instead of "morally wrong," one always named a genus such as "untruthful," "unchaste," "unjust." We should no longer ask whether doing something was "wrong," passing directly from some description of an

action to this notion; we should ask whether, e.g., it was unjust; and the answer would sometimes be clear at once. (8–9)

Anscombe is now in a position to give a fuller response to Louden's objection, which she anticipates, and gives in more detail than Louden himself. That objection was, briefly, that to characterize an action as (for example) *unjust* is not to characterize it as not to be done unless one adopts a *further* principle, to the effect that *injustice is wrong*—for otherwise one might concede that it is unjust but not see why one ought not to do it. So (the objection goes) we can't adopt Anscombe's suggestion that we get rid of "morally wrong" in favor of the unmediated vocabulary of virtue and vice.

> In this argument [effectively Louden's, of which she has just given a rather more detailed version] "wrong" of course is explained as meaning "morally wrong," and all the atmosphere of the term is retained while its substance is guaranteed quite null. Now let us remember that "morally wrong" is the term which is the heir of the notion "illicit," or "what there is an obligation not to do"; which belongs in a divine law theory of ethics. Here it really does add something to the description "unjust" to say there is an obligation not to do it; for what obliges is the divine law—as rules oblige in a game. So if the divine law obliges not to commit injustice by forbidding injustice, it really does add something to the description "unjust" to say there is an obligation not to do it. And it is because "morally wrong" is the heir of this concept, but an heir that is cut off from the family of concepts from which it sprang, that "morally wrong" both goes beyond the mere factual description "unjust" and seems to have no discernible content except a certain compelling force, which I should call purely psychological. And such is the force of the term that philosophers actually suppose that the divine law notion can be dismissed as making no essential difference even if it is held—because they think that a "practical principle" running "I ought (i.e. am morally obliged) to obey divine laws" is required for the man who believes in divine laws. But actually this notion of obligation is a notion which only operates in the context of law. And I should be inclined to congratulate the present-day moral philosophers on depriving "morally ought" of its now delusive appearance of content, if only they did not manifest a detestable desire to retain the atmosphere of the term. (MMP, 17–18)

Her Third Thesis: Unacknowledged (Because Unnoticed) Radical Break with Tradition on the Part of All Recent Ethicists

Her third thesis depends on her classification of all recent (as of 1958) moral philosophy as *consequentialist,* that is, holding that there is no sort of action that could not conceivably be justified by appeal to its likely consequences. (Stronger forms, also common, maintain that the likely consequences are all that is relevant to the moral evaluation of an action.)[1] Of the discussions of minute conceptual matters typical of recent moral philosophers, she writes,

> Such discussions generate an appearance of significant diversity of views where what is really significant is an overall similarity. The overall similarity is made clear if you consider that every one of the best known English academic moral philosophers has put out a philosophy according to which, e.g., it is not possible to hold that it cannot be right to kill the innocent as a means to any end whatsoever and that someone who thinks otherwise is in error. . . . Now this is a significant thing: for it means that all these philosophies are quite incompatible with the Hebrew-Christian ethic. For it has been characteristic of that ethic to teach that there are certain things forbidden whatever consequences threaten, such as: choosing to kill the innocent for any purpose, however good; vicarious punishment; treachery (by which I mean obtaining a man's confidence in a grave matter by promises of trustworthy friendship and then betraying him to his enemies); idolatry; sodomy; adultery; making a false profession of faith. The prohibition of certain things simply in virtue of their description as such-and-such identifiable kinds of action, regardless of any further consequences, is certainly not the whole of the Hebrew-Christian ethic; but it is a noteworthy feature of it; and if every academic philosopher since Sidgwick has written in such a way as to exclude this ethic, it would argue a certain provinciality of mind not to see this incompatibility as the most important fact about these philosophers, and the differences between them as somewhat trifling by comparison. (MMP, 9–10)

The key point of transition here is Sidgwick, who made consequentialism look much more plausible by putting into circulation the idea that "it does not make any difference to a man's responsibility for an effect of his action which he can foresee, that he does not intend it. Now this sounds rather edifying; it is I think quite characteristic of very bad degenerations of thought on such questions that they sound edifying" (MMP, 11).

Thus the dispute between consequentialists and their opponents concerns not only the nature of value but also the nature of action, and more specifically the relation of the agent to the results of his actions that he foresees and intends.[2]

2.3   Connection between Thesis (2) and Rise of Consequentialism

The consequentialism of our time alluded to in thesis (3) is *made possible by* the survival of the special category of moral obligation beyond the demise of the framework of concepts that gave it meaning mentioned in thesis (2):

> If a procedure *is* one of judicially punishing a man for what he is clearly understood not to have done, there can be absolutely no argument about the description of this as unjust. No circumstances, and no expected consequences, which do *not* modify the description of the procedure as one of judicially punishing a man for what he is known not to have done can modify the description of it as unjust. Someone who attempted to dispute this would only be pretending not to know what "unjust" means: for this is a paradigm case of injustice.
>
> And here we see the superiority of the term "unjust" over the terms "morally right" and "morally wrong." For in the context of English moral philosophy since Sidgwick it appears legitimate to discuss whether it *might* be "morally right" in some circumstances to adopt that procedure; but it cannot be argued that the procedure would in any circumstances be just. (MMP, 16)[3]

The Hebrew-Christian law conception is of course strongly deontological or "absolutist." But—and this is less often realized—so is the Aristotelian virtue conception: not through and through, but insofar as certain aspects of the virtue of justice can only be understood in deontological terms. So within those ethical conceptions it is conceptually impossible to suggest that (for example) killing an innocent man to placate the mob could be "permissible" (Hebrew-Christian) or could be just (virtue); such a killing is a paradigm case of the sort deployed in teaching the meanings of "impermissible" and "unjust." But once the law conception adopts a notion of *morally right* that has no conceptual ties to the deontologically structured pronouncements of the Jews' and Christians' God, then—and, Anscombe implies, only then—it becomes conceptually possible to suggest precisely that such an action may be morally right, because justified by its consequences.[4]

It is not clear, however, that this suggestion presupposes the concept *moral,* so it is not clear that the emptiness of that concept by itself invalidates the suggestion.

That would be a very strong conclusion—on this account, in fact, if Anscombe's thesis (2) is right, the suggestion that judicial murder might be *morally* OK would only have been *given the appearance* of conceptual possibility. If *moral* is a pseudo-concept, this is not really a suggestion; it doesn't really express a thought. But it seems that consequentialism need not presuppose the sort of concept of *morality* we are required to regard as discredited by the dismal history of confusion Anscombe narrates. For we certainly don't need that concept in order to formulate the idea of a *good,* or *better,* or *best state of affairs,*[5] and consequentialism can then be cast in the form of an account of the virtue of justice, along the lines of *a commitment to bringing about the best state of affairs,* with various qualifying clauses gesturing at epistemic and psychological realism. It is true that judicial murder, which might be required by this virtue of "consequentialist justice," would work as a paradigm case in teaching the meaning of "injustice." But if *Callicles's* conception of natural justice as a virtue doesn't run afoul of the concept of a virtue as a trait that benefits its possessor, it's hard to see how that concept could rule out "consequentialist justice." This is why Callicles took such pains to distinguish "natural" justice, which he took to be a true virtue, from "conventional" justice, which he thought could not possibly benefit anyone with a strong, talented nature. Judicial murder is only a paradigm case of "conventional" injustice. If Anscombe supposed that the point about paradigmatic injustice showed that the virtue standpoint provided a more secure prohibition on judicial murder than the concept of *morality* does, she would effectively be relying on the same false presupposition that Socrates makes so often in the shorter Socratic dialogues: that "conventional" justice, insofar as this essentially involves taking others' interests into account, is guaranteed to benefit its possessor, as if simply by our habit of *calling* it a virtue.

Consequentialism cannot be discredited on the basis of a rejection of the *moral* alone. Still, the attempt to recast consequentialism as a virtue-based theory looks very dodgy. Socrates's question of what counts as a good human life is given a very flat answer, at bottom in terms of a single, easily specified disposition to facilitate the goodness, primarily, of *other* human lives. But this latter goodness must be of a much more complicated and interesting, because *unmoralized,* kind—a much more plausible answer to Socrates's question than consequentialism's, which is given entirely in terms of a *duty.* If we have abandoned the idea of the *moral* as a sui generis category, why should the richness and susceptibility of endless elaboration we expect from an account of a well-lived human life apply *entirely,* as it were, to the ethical *patient,* and not at all to the *agent?*[6] And why should we be obliged to further the *eudaimonia* of people who, when it comes down to it, should really be conceiving of their own *eudaimonia* in terms of our flatly specifiable consequentialist duty, so that the business of being happy is endlessly deferred?[7] After all, it is *very nearly always* true that there is someone worse off than yourself! It looks very much as though the implausibilities of this kind of view do stem from conceiving of ethics in terms of *morality,* with its characteristic obsession with duty. "Virtue ethics" properly understood—that is, with egoist-eudaimonism at its center—puts strong constraints on the *content* of an account of ethics, and not just on its form.

3

The Misguided Project of Vindicating Morality

Can "Moral Rationalism" Legitimate the Moral Vocabulary?

Might there not be some secular account of norms that affords us a way of rescuing the idea of moral obligation? Anscombe herself perhaps unwittingly encourages some such idea: "Those who recognize the origins of the notions of 'obligation' and of the emphatic, 'moral,' *ought,* in the divine law conception of ethics, but who reject the notion of a divine legislator, sometimes look about for the possibility of retaining a law conception without a divine legislator. This search, I think, has some interest in it" (MMP, 13).

This is a slip. For earlier she *defined* a law conception as one on which "what is needed for conformity with the virtues failure in which is the mark of being bad *qua* man . . . is required by divine law. Naturally it is not possible to have such a conception unless you believe in God as a law-giver; like Jews, Stoics, and Christians" (MMP, 6).[1]

It is not mere pedantry to point out this inconsistency, I think.[2] It is not that much could depend on whether we define *law conception of ethics* in a way that rules out a secular version of that conception. Anscombe is not wavering on any matter of import here. But her juxtaposition, in the later passage (page 13), of the reminder that the moral "notions" have their "origins" in the divine law conception, with a very clear indication that a *secular* law conception cannot be ruled out a priori, was to prove *momentously* misleading to nearly all readers of MMP. For this gave a very strong impression that a law conception—now either religious *or, maybe,* secular—and the moral notions stand or fall together, so that a secular version of *the moral notions* could not be ruled out a priori. And when this idea is then read back into the earlier passage (page 6), it yields an equally strong impression that a religious version of (not just a law conception but) *the moral notions* had been OK, but (returning to page 13) there was at least a *question mark* about a secular version. The impression is very much reinforced when, even in the midst of her most ringing denunciation of "the moral ought" as utterly empty, she speaks of it as "having *become* a word of mere mesmeric force," which "*no longer* signifies a real concept" (8; my emphases; I return to this passage later). Upon inspection, her exclusive concern with *the word* as opposed to anything it could be said to represent could not be clearer; yet somehow it has been easy to miss. The result has been a profuse type of hopeless misunderstanding of her real view, as I shall try to make clear. To anticipate, her real view is this: a law conception is one thing; the moral notions are another. The original home of the law conception was religious ethics. There is perhaps conceptual room for a secular version of the law conception (I will take issue with this, sort of). The moral notions did not have this original home: they were *unthought of* in religious ethics and are now thought of as essentially secular. But there is no more conceptual room for secular moral notions than for religious ones. For the moral notions are not concepts at all. They are *utterly chimerical.*

In recent years, since the publication of Thomas Nagel's *The Possibility of Altruism* (1970) and John Rawls's *A Theory of Justice* (1971), the most popular candidate for the source of a secular *analogue* of a law conception of ethics (as we must describe it if we are to avoid Anscombe's contradiction of her own definition) is practical reason, thought of as generating principles of conduct, often, following Kant, via some abstract version of the idea of a contract (Korsgaard 1996a, 1996b; Scanlon 2000). This approach might seem especially well suited to vindicating an analogue of a law conception, if that is thought of as originating with the Torah. According to Alan Donagan, the Hebrew-Christian tradition is already in a way *secular,* in that most of its spokesmen—until the Reformation, anyway—supposed that most of what God commands with respect to the human realm (that is, "natural law" as opposed to rules of religious observance) is independently discernible by means of practical reason alone, that is, unaided by revelation (Donagan 1977).

This fact (as I take it to be) about the tradition is the starting point of Donagan's *Theory of Morality* (1977), the most sustained and detailed attempt to rebut Anscombe's case against the category of the *moral* that is known to me. In the preface to that work he describes his reaction to Anscombe's paper when it appeared in 1958:

> At last, somebody writing in a philosophical journal had affirmed the traditional moral position I had found in Orwell, and with a like clarity and force. At the same time, however, she had expressed a disturbing doubt whether an adequate philosophical justification of the morality she described is possible, as distinct from a religious one.
>
> Her reason was that the conception of moral law implicit in that morality is religious not only in origin but essentially. Exploration of the concept of practical reason may yield a theory of moral virtue like Aristotle's, but not a theory of moral law. In so concluding, she dismissed Kant's contributions to the theory of practical reason as tendentious and muddled. Had I not become persuaded she was mistaken . . . , I could not have embarked on the present study. What Aquinas wrote about natural law . . . , confirmed me in this. (xiv–xv)

This summary of Anscombe's thesis contains an especially tangled combination of misunderstandings, some of which I have already tried to correct.[3] As we have seen, Anscombe's main point is wholly missed if she is thought to be recommending a theory of *moral virtue*. By itself such an attribution might be defended by appeal to a more expansive sense of "moral" whereby what Aristotle was up to might be called moral philosophy; but in this passage the expression "moral virtue" is coordinate with "moral law," and the latter to be understood as, in its secular form, the main object of Anscombe's attack. But "moral virtue" in this sense of "moral" is no better off (in Anscombe's view) than "moral law," and it is anyway radically anachronistic to ascribe any such conception to Aristotle.[4] The contrast between these coordinately understood conceptions of "moral law" and "moral virtue" is, I argued earlier, largely the relatively inconsequential one of the theorist's preferred form of expression: Do we define the qualities of character in terms of the rules they dispose one to observe, or the rules in terms of how someone with the qualities of character would act? This sort of contrast is too superficial to sustain the idea that a theory of practical reason might vindicate one but not the other.

Anscombe's contrast between the "moral law" and virtue *tout court* is a deep one—the latter is, as the former is not, essentially concerned with *eudaimonia,* for example.

When Donagan writes of Anscombe's affirmation of the "traditional moral position," he must surely have in mind passages like this, from the final two sentences of MMP:

> The present Oxford moral philosophers [that is, in 1958] . . . teach a philosophy according to which the particular consequences of [the judicial punishment of the innocent] *could* "morally" be taken into account by a man who was debating what to do; and if they were such as to conflict with his "ends," it might be a step in his moral education to frame a moral principle under which he "managed" . . . to bring the action; or it might be a new "decision of principle," making which was an advance in the formation of his moral thinking . . . to decide: in such-and-such circumstances one ought to procure the judicial condemnation of the innocent. *And that is my complaint.* (19; my emphasis)

This traditional, absolutist conception is what Donagan says Anscombe doubts can be given a philosophical justification as opposed to a religious one. But if he thinks that she supposed that "exploration of the concept of practical reason may yield a theory of moral virtue like Aristotle's, but not a theory of moral law," he must think that the prohibition of judicial murder, for example, is a matter of law *as opposed to* virtue. But, as we have seen, this is a false opposition: judicial murder might be contrary to the virtue of justice *in virtue of* violating an exceptionless precept, adherence to which is a necessary part of that virtue. Anscombe's quarrel is not with the idea of putting an ethical (ultimately virtue-based) requirement in the form of a precept, but with the supposedly very special *practical modality* with respect to which the *moral* precepts are supposed to express *necessities.*[5] This modality has a certain broadly logical profile: precepts to which it attaches always override claims on our practical attention couched in the language of any other modality, for example, and the reasons we have to conform to the precepts are themselves alleged to be of an equally distinctive, desire-independent kind. This profile in turn marks the modality as essentially and uniquely distinctive of commands having the status of law. The quarrel then is with the version of a secular *law conception* to which the moral notions aspire, and on which, absent divine command, the precepts' binding force has nothing to do with their observance being necessary for the acquisition or maintenance of a virtue, where *that* is understood as a quality no one could intelligibly want to be without. If Anscombe expresses a "disturbing doubt" as to whether exceptionless precepts like that against judicial murder can be given "an adequate philosophical justification . . . , as distinct from a religious one," this is a doubt about whether the necessary work in the philosophy of mind can be done to give us an adequate theory of *virtue* that would underpin such precepts. When it comes to giving an "adequate philosophical justification" of the exceptionless precept understood in accordance with the secular "law conception" of *morality,* that is, independently of the ideas of virtue, *eudaimonia, and* divine command, what she expresses is not a disturbing doubt but a conviction of the impossibility of legitimating a "concept" that has no content.

This idea that the target of Anscombe's critique is really just the rule-like form of moral precepts is part of the standard reception of MMP. What goes missing is the dimension that puts her in the skeptical company of Schopenhauer, Nietzsche, Freud, and Bernard Williams, for all that she doubtless abhorred their outlooks in other ways.

The target of this tradition of ethical critique is largely *morality* in the sense to which Anscombe objects: a mode of ethical theory and practice that inculcates a badly mistaken view of what is important in human life. These other critics emphasize, as Anscombe does not, that morality *makes us unhappy;* but they thereby anticipate Anscombe's proposed alternative, as the only secular hope, of some broadly eudaimonist revival. Freud weirdly neglects this tradition, although it is one to which psychoanalysis itself clearly belongs,[6] but Nietzsche and Williams plausibly conceive of eudaimonism as more or less just what ethics looks like when stripped of its "moral" accretions, and their enduring fascination with the Greeks had a lot to do with a conviction that anyone concerned to think through a properly post-Christian ethic could not fail to learn a great deal from a highly evolved pre-Christian one. The distortions induced by morality, on this kind of view (and this is the main point of contact with Anscombe), are largely structural and therefore unobvious—for example, a fixation on a particular form of obligation—and reflect its origins in particular religious traditions. We are now largely oblivious to these origins and, in large sections of the West and especially among our intelligentsia, increasingly profess indifference to the traditions. Morality in any case essentially aspires to be independent of the traditions, and of religion generally; but given these origins, this aspiration only multiplies confusion, and infects our ethical thinking with wishful fantasies that constitute a kind of unwitting repetition of the "repudiated" religious forms. The almost unanimous insistence of the philosophers on the special character of the *moral* as sui generis, overriding, and the rest is only a symptom of a completely general cultural amnesia about these matters. No cultural moment was ever more aptly captured by the expression *bad faith*. So speaks this skeptical tradition—and with them, Anscombe.

3.2   Kripke on Unicorns: The Moral Vocabulary Cannot Be Redeemed by Rationalism, or by Anything Else

Saul Kripke said in *Naming and Necessity* that, given that stories about unicorns are myths, even if we discovered fossils or other remains of horselike animals with horns growing out of their brows, this wouldn't show that there had been *unicorns*. If unicorns are mythical, in his view, they are *essentially* mythical (Kripke 1980, 156–157).[7] Anscombe, it will turn out, maintains a similar thesis about "moral" precepts, if we find that they coincide with what's required by practical reason: we should just call them precepts of rationality; the word "moral" still imports a spurious atmosphere of special obligation. In fact, we shall see that her view implies a complete generalization of this thesis: every attempt in "first-order moral theory" to give an account of what the correct moral norms are can at most discern which norms we have most reason to observe; calling these norms "moral" is a meaningless distraction. Relatedly, every attempt in "metaethics" to say what it is for a norm to *be* a moral norm is simply a wild goose chase, seeking an answer to a pseudo-question.

Concerning Hume's thesis that it is impossible to infer "morally ought" from "is" sentences, she writes,

> This comment, it seems to me, would be correct. This word "ought," having become *a word of mere mesmeric force*, could not, in the character of having that force, be inferred from anything whatever. It may be objected that it could be inferred from other "morally ought" sentences: but that cannot be true. The appearance that this is so is

produced by the fact that we say "All men are ϕ" and "Socrates is a man" implies "Socrates is ϕ." But here "ϕ" is a dummy predicate. We mean that if you substitute a real predicate for "ϕ" the implication is valid. A real predicate is required; not just *a word containing no intelligible thought*: a word retaining the suggestion of force, and apt to have a strong psychological effect, but *which no longer signifies a real concept at all*. (MMP, 8; my emphases)

She also describes the moral "ought" as a "notion" in which Hume showed "*no content* could be found" (MMP, 8), and later describes the effect of modifying "wrong" with the adverb "morally" thus: "all the atmosphere of ["wrong"] is retained while *its substance is guaranteed quite null*" (17; my emphasis).

On the basis of these remarks, we should certainly understand Anscombe not as claiming that *moral* is a defective (for example, inconsistent) and so uninstantiated concept, but as denying that it is a concept *at all*. As we shall see, however, nearly all readers of MMP understood her to mean not only that *moral* is a concept but that it had been intelligible and so presumably not self-contradictory, and even *legitimate*, in the premodern era when philosophers and others believed in divine command.

Since she took pains to emphasize that *moral* is not a concept at all, the question naturally arises of how such a misreading, if that is what it is, took hold. The answer is that, early in the paper, Anscombe expressed herself on this point in a way that was especially liable to what has become an almost universal misinterpretation. She considers the culture encountered by Hume, in which (as for ourselves) "the notion 'ought' was invested with that peculiar force having which it is said to be used in its 'moral' sense," and gives the following characterization of it: "The situation, if I am right, was the interesting one of the survival of a concept outside the framework of thought that had made it a really intelligible one" (MMP, 6). This makes it look very much as though she held that *moral is* a concept after all, and although now it is an "unintelligible" one, there had been a time, when the relevant "framework of thought" was in place, when it *was* intelligible. Indeed, this troublesome sentence seems flatly inconsistent with her insistence elsewhere in MMP on the nonexistence of a concept of morality, and raises the possibility that that insistence is somehow halfhearted or equivocal.

Since her insistence on that point is so much more extensive and emphatically expressed than the troublesome sentence, if Anscombe *is* consistent in this matter, it is very likely that it is this one sentence, which seems to accord it the status of a concept, that has been misunderstood. If the sentence can be given a different but tolerably natural interpretation on which it fits with the other extensive and emphatic pronouncements, such an interpretation is very likely to be correct.

It turns out that there is such an interpretation, which not only squares the sentence with those other pronouncements but fits very well with other things she says in MMP. On the interpretation in question, the concept the sentence describes as surviving "outside the framework of thought that made it a really intelligible one" is not the "concept" of morality at all, but something more abstract, of which the moral vocabulary aspires to express a version: a conception of the fundamental form of ethical necessity as *being categorically bound* or *obliged.*

A page earlier she says quite clearly that the word "ought" (as well as other deontic modals) *in itself* need not bring along with it this idea of being bound or obliged; and this is obvious enough anyway from examples like "Someone ought to oil that squeaky gate," which does not even imply that any particular person is in question, and usually implies there is not. But the word *can* have such a sense, and this is the sense of which the "special moral *ought*" is *intended* to be a variety:

> The ordinary (and quite indispensable) terms "should," "needs," "ought," "must"—*acquired* this special [moral] sense by being equated in the relevant contexts with "is obliged," or "is bound," or "is required to," in the sense in which one can be obliged or bound by law, or something can be required by law.
>
> How did this come about? The answer is in history: between Aristotle and us came Christianity, with its *law* conception of ethics. . . . In consequence of the dominance of Christianity for many centuries, the concepts of being bound, permitted, or excused became deeply embedded in our language and thought. (MMP, 5; first emphasis mine, second Anscombe's)

The really important *explanans* in Anscombe's genealogy of morals is not, as so many accounts of MMP suppose, the demise of Christianity, but its *rise.* It is only because Christianity set off throughout the West a kind of explosion of the Hebraic conception of divine command embodied in the Pentateuch that "ought" and other deontic modals, as used in the context of ethics *as such,* acquired *any* connotation of "being bound" at all; and *that* is what is absent from Aristotle and pagan ethics generally.[8] I say "in the context of ethics *as such*" because of course there were contexts *within* ethics in which the Greeks, for example, would use words like δεῖ or χρῆ with the relevant connotation, as when particular divine or human (for example, military) commands (see, for example, Plato's *Apology* 28d–30b; cf. Doyle 2012, 42–48), or the requirements of a binding contract, were specifically at issue. But even here the overarching framework that ultimately made ethical sense of binding obligations to a god or to a mortal was a catalogue of virtues in which *piety* (ὁσιότης) and *justice* (δικαιοσύνη) featured prominently (Doyle 2012, 47–48). There can be no question of any sense of "being bound," as by law or contract, attaching to these modal words in a way that marked them off for ethical application *generally.* Anscombe is simply right about this and, as I hope to show in more detail later, all the subsequent attempts to establish that no, the Greeks really *did* have the "the concept of morality," are futile because they make no contact with this point, which is the one that matters for Anscombe's overall argument. That the Greeks believed in some sense that one "ought" to acquire the virtues and act in accordance with them cannot be denied, but the relevant modality, as I have argued elsewhere (Doyle 2012, 52), is not that of duty or "binding obligation" but of *need:* these are the qualities one *needs* if one is to be good at being a human being and so the leader of a life worth living, as Socrates puts it; that is the point of the concept of *aretē.*

Why has it generally been thought that when Anscombe wrote of the "survival of a concept outside the framework of thought that made it a really intelligible one," she was alluding to *morality,* which, it was therefore supposed, she was treating as a concept, and indeed as one whose history stretches back beyond the secular age? To be fair to the many readers of MMP who have misunderstood the "troublesome sentence" on page 6 in this way, Anscombe is unclear here to such a degree that one might almost think she was deliberately trying to mislead the reader. The sentence in question concludes the paragraph quoted in Chapter 2 (section 2.1), which begins with her comparison with the survival of the notion *criminal* after the disappearance of juridical institutions. The concepts of immorality and criminality having such a strong natural affinity, the idea that the notion *moral* is intended as the other term of the comparison was doubtless virtually irresistible for most readers. But if we look closely and read slowly, Anscombe leaves us in no doubt as to what the notion *criminal* is really being compared to:

> *It is as if the notion "criminal" were to remain* when [juridical institutions] had been abolished and forgotten. A Hume discovering this situation might conclude that there was a special sentiment, expressed by "criminal," which alone gave the word its sense. *So Hume discovered the situation in which the notion "obligation" survived, and the notion "ought" was invested with that peculiar force* having which it is said to be used in a "moral" sense. (MMP, 6; my emphases)

Thus when Anscombe describes the introduction of a new vocabulary of "morality" consequent upon the demise of Christianity as a vital cultural-intellectual force in the West, as "the survival of a concept outside the framework of thought that made it a really intelligible one," the concept in question is that expressed by "ought" and other deontic modals, in the context of ethics as such, and intended to be understood as carrying that special connotation of duty, obligation, and being bound. We might call this the concept of an *ethically sovereign "ought."* I say "ethically sovereign" because some duties—including some necessities expressed by deontic modals such as *ought* used in a weighty, binding sense—can be canceled, for example by certain sorts of emergency—even some duties whose neglect would ordinarily count as a serious ethical lapse, as Socrates conceived of his duty as an Athenian to do the bidding of his fellow citizens (*Apology* 29d). But the *ought* conceived, in the Hebrew-Christian tradition, as expressing the precepts of their ethic of divine command can never be canceled. The same is in general true of divine command as the Greeks understood it; but such commands did not express for them an *ethic:* the relevant *ought,* for them, did not characterize the ethical realm *as such;* it was continuous with other sorts of duty (for example, military duty, cf. *Apology* 28d–29a) but distinctive merely in overriding other duties and never being overridden by them. The command of the god, as Socrates understood it, instanced the unique kind of emergency in which his duty to his fellow Athenians lapsed ("I shall obey the god rather than yourselves," 29d2). For the Greeks, such commands were particular orders, often addressed to particular people and by their nature rare. They also had a conception of divine law; but it was rather vague and contested and very far indeed from defining for them in any detail the business of how to live, and how to conduct themselves in relation to each other, to people of other *poleis,* and to other peoples.[9] For the Hebrews, by contrast, the Mosaic law was called "law" because it was promulgated to them all as a people. According to rabbinical Judaism and the mainstream of the Christian tradition, there is a core set of precepts to be found in this law, which are discernible by human reason and so applicable to human beings generally (*ST* IaIIae, Q100 A1; Donagan 1977); yet their status as precepts of practical reason does not detract from their status, where promulgated, as *law,* and so also appropriately characterized by the ethically sovereign *ought.*

The concept of this ethically sovereign *ought,* then, involves the existence of a divine legislator as a fundamental presupposition of its applicability qua law; and *this* is the concept Anscombe describes as having survived "outside the framework of thought that made it a really intelligible one." She is not, therefore, speaking here (or anywhere else) of a "concept of morality."

Moral aspires to be a particular version or determination of such a sovereign "ought" but, for the lack of anyone to whom we may conceive ourselves as being obliged or bound, the aspiration is doomed to fall into nonsense in its very attempt at self-expression. The version or determination of such an "ought" as grounded in the sovereign will of God, by contrast, is fully coherent, inasmuch as if its presuppositions are true, the relevant "oughts" are binding as advertised.

Indeed, while the ideology expressed in talk of the "moral ought" is not so much as aware of the criteria of coherence implicit in the concept of which it could only be understood as a variant if, *per impossibile,* it could be understood at all, it is no coincidence that that concept is fully realized in the law of the Hebrews, since it is a concept that would never have been dreamt up in the first place had the relevant conception of a divine lawgiver not held sway in the souls of those among whom it gained currency. Anscombe's genealogy is an object lesson in the directionality of time: that the Greeks lacked the concept is a fact of the same sort, and embodying the same sort of necessity—although transposed into a world-historical register—as the fact that one does not suffer a hangover *before* a bout of drinking.

Thus the question, frequently pressed, "Does the historical evidence bear out Anscombe's theory?" largely misses the point. As far has her "theory" is concerned, most of the action is to be found in the analysis of the relevant concept of an ethically sovereign "ought." If she is right about *that,* the attempts to undermine her case by sifting through the Greek and Roman corpus for intimations of *morality* are rather like scrutinizing one's dissolute friend for signs of a bad head as a means of predicting whether he is about to embark on a binge.

In any case, equipped with such an understanding of the concept of an ethically sovereign "ought," we are free to understand Anscombe's treacherously misleading sentence on page 6, and the rest of MMP, in full accordance with her vigorous denials that any such concept as *morality* even exists, beginning two pages later with her denunciations of "moral" as "a word of mere mesmeric force" that "no longer signifies a real concept at all."

(As we shall see, the correct understanding of the treacherous sentence has other significant implications. Most notably, since Anscombe does after all consistently deny that *morality* is a concept, and holds that even its spectral half-life as a pseudo-concept does not begin until Christianity has receded, we have a *doubly* a fortiori assurance that she does *not* hold that *the concept of morality was in good order when people believed in divine command,* as accounts of MMP almost invariably report [Donagan 1977, xiv–xv; Baier 1988, 128; Richter 1995, 74; Winch n.d., 10; Leftow 2013, 81n10; Pigden 1988, 33–34; Irwin 2006, 326; Stern 2014, 1098; Darwall 2006, 115n45; and many others; see also note 17]. When people believed in divine command, the relevant "special" sense in which something *ought* to be done was *God has commanded this.* This is not a sui generis, irreducible sense of *ought* at all, and so does not have any of the relevant kind of conceptual continuity with the secular, "moral" *ought.* See the discussion later.)

We can see, then, that Anscombe's view is not that the concept of morality is fatally defective—for example, inconsistent. She clearly denies the very existence of such a concept, and we are now in a position to understand her denial as completely consistent and unequivocal. But what does this distinction, between a defective concept and a pseudo-concept, really amount to? One might have thought that an inconsistent concept, for example, can play no legitimate role in our thinking, or in our "language-games," and so *might as well* be a pseudo-concept.[10] This would be a mistake, however. Whatever its merits as a definition, it is surely true and potentially illuminating to characterize *zero,* as Frege did, as "the number which belongs to the concept 'not identical with itself'" (1953, 88e). Frege observes that he could have used in his definition *any* concept under which no object falls, and so any concept containing a contradiction, which is why the latter are "not so black as they are painted": "To be of any use," he admits, "is the last thing we should expect of them" (88e)—and yet it turns out they *are* of use.[11]

The distinction, then, between a self-contradictory or otherwise empty-because-defective concept and a fake one is sound; and only if we keep it in mind can we really take the measure of Anscombe's skepticism. For the problem with "morality," according to her, runs deeper than its not *applying* to anything in the world or even in any possible world. It is simply not in the business of determining an extension at all. The concept *non-self-identical,* according to the plausible Fregean way of thinking about such things, *is* in that business. *Moral,* on Anscombe's view as I understand it, does not have the empty set as its extension; it has no extension of any kind, since it is not a concept.

Another way of bringing out the depth of the deficiency is to observe that on Anscombe's view, *moral* cannot perform one of the basic functions of concepts, namely, the facilitation of inferences. As she says of the syllogism, "A real predicate is required; not just a word containing no intelligible thought." But self-contradictory concept-words *are* real predicates: they can play a perfectly legitimate role, for example, in the course of *reductio* arguments, and so they do express real concepts. *Moral,* on this view, has no such employment, and so in this respect can be assimilated to a popular account of what is wrong with pejoratives (Dummett 1973, 397, 454), and indeed with that ne plus ultra of unfitness for inferential purpose, A. N. Prior's invented pseudo-connective, "tonk."[12]

There is then an important difference between "mere" self-contradiction and failure to make sense, and, on the reading of Anscombe's diagnosis I have just argued for, the candidacy of the *moral* for concepthood is in far worse shape than that of the merely self-contradictory: the illusion, for her, is not so much a matter of an unnoticed inconsistency as of a spurious kind of psychological "atmosphere" or "force" seeking—hopelessly—conceptual expression.

If I am right about Anscombe and Anscombe is right about *moral*, it follows that you don't legitimate the *concept* of morality by defining a distinct, fully intelligible concept that determines reasons, considerations, principles, issues, and so on that are *coextensive* with what we would call the moral ones. If morality really is a bogus concept, then to point to the rough coincidence of (what people take to be) its extension with that of some form of practical rationality (Donagan) or even with some category defined in terms of virtue itself (McDowell 1979; Hursthouse 1999) is neither to legitimate the category of the moral, which is *ex hypothesi* impossible, nor to enhance, to the slightest degree, the plausibility of the rationalist or virtue-ethical theories in question, since all one has demonstrated is that they more or less meet a bogus criterion.[13]

Donagan claims in his preface to have *answered* Anscombe's skepticism about morality. What he misses is that her skepticism was really about the *intension* of "moral," where the *intension* of a predicate is that by which it determines an actual or possible *extension,* and so secures for the predicate the status of what Frege called a *concept-word.* So when Donagan claims that moral precepts derive their content and authority from their status as precepts of practical reason, Anscombe's retort would be (or should be—see the later discussion) that this is all happening too late in the dialectic. Since there is nothing coherent for a category of the moral to be, there is nothing coherent for that species of precept to be, for which Donagan claims the status of precepts of practical reason. There are just the precepts of practical reason. Similarly, if McDowell or Rosalind Hursthouse purports to demonstrate, or even, like Terence Irwin (1986), maintains that *Aristotle* purported to demonstrate, that *moral* reasons are best understood as the reasons the virtuous person has, if Anscombe is right, the virtuous person's reasons are being invoked to give an account of nothing at all. There are just the virtuous person's reasons; and *these* are to be understood, in the end, in terms of *eudaimonia.*

The basic point here holds whether our candidate *explanantia*—principles of practical reason, requirements of virtue, or what have you—are intended as capturing the extension of "moral," or (in addition) as giving the *meaning* of "moral." Now, someone might concede the point in the former case, but resist the preemption of all *semantic* analyses of "moral," on the ground that it proves too much. Any attempt to vindicate the moral concept in the face of Anscombe's critique must presumably put forward some explication of it, for how else might one establish that it has content? But if Anscombe's claim is that the term "moral" expresses no concept at all, it looks as though she can dismiss any such attempt out of hand. For any explication, having the form of an identity, "The category *moral* is *xyz*," will inherit the meaninglessness of the disputed word, for the subject-term cannot be so much as dignified as a nonempty referring expression, on pain of begging the question. Surely Anscombe's opponent's cards cannot be so easily marked in advance?

Anscombe's position is indeed that the subject-term lacks a referent, but it does not license such a high-handed way with any attempt to specify one. Rather, the author of such an attempt is faced with a dilemma. For if a strict identity of intension is meant, and if "*xyz*" expresses a concept in good standing, he has already given up on the feature of the *moral* concept to which Anscombe is best understood as objecting: that *moral* is a distinctive, sui generis, irreducible category. This is what most philosophers take it to be, at least with respect to its *intension,* since even the most doctrinaire utilitarian, for example, is not going to deny that his thesis that a morally good action is one that maximizes happiness (or whatever) is surprising or at least informative. But since Anscombe does not take it to be such a category (or any sort of category), she can have no principled objection to anyone's refitting the word as an abbreviation for some other, unobjectionable concept. The expression "*xyz*" would then not give an *analysis* of *moral,* but something like a stipulated definition, so that no competent user of the two expressions could fail to be aware of their equivalence. On the other hand, if the identity is supposed to amount to anything more newsworthy than this, the challenge would be to say what more this could be.

"Isn't the Praise Vulgar?"—In Particular, There Can Be No Divine Command Theory of Morality

If Anscombe's line of thought is fatal to these metaethical theories, it is fatal to the metaethical project as such, if this is thought of, as it so often is, as the project of giving a semantics for the moral vocabulary. Here we run up against perhaps the most common and tenacious misunderstanding of MMP. For if its skepticism is as corrosive as *that,* there can be no special exemption for the "divine command theory of morality" itself. Yet, as we have seen, it is *very* commonly assumed that Anscombe takes the concept of morality to have been in good order before the idea of divine command was abandoned. Kurt Baier spoke for nearly all her interpreters when he described her as objecting to moral notions on the ground that they "presuppose a *moral* legislator whose authoritative say-so creates the *moral* norms by reference to which *moral* wrongs, duties, and obligations are determined" (Baier 1988, 128; my emphases).[14] This misreading, which became, and remains to this day, standard, illustrates well how deeply the concept of morality as simply *given* is now embedded in our culture and thinking: the idea that the concept might be spurious *period*—and so always was—seems often not to be recognized as even the remotest possibility. The prominent role assigned in Anscombe's genealogy to the idea of divine command and to its abandonment has given to many readers the illusion of a kind of last-minute reprieve of the moral concept, enabling them to think that it at least *used* to be legitimate, and so to persist in a total repression of the idea that there might simply never have been anything to it at all. But Anscombe takes the idea of morality to be essentially secular. It is not a preexisting concept deprived of legitimacy by the abandonment of the idea of divine command; it is a *new* concept (or rather pseudo-concept) *generated* by that abandonment. "Morally wrong" is really not a concept but merely a *"term"*—a term that, furthermore, "is the *heir* of the notion 'illicit,' or 'what there is an obligation *not* to do'; which belongs in a divine law theory of ethics" (MMP, 17; my emphases). "The *heir*" of the divine command notions, notice—*not,* that is, the same concept deprived of application by new circumstances. One and the same concept might at one time be in good order and then, at a later time, come to lack any instances—but how could new circumstances strip the *same* concept of its status *as a concept?* It is true that with *practical* concepts the question of survival is more complicated. Many archaic practical concepts, such as various versions of *honor,* for example, no longer have a *point* for us (Tenenbaum 2000) and, further, *could not* have a point, because their practical relevance depended on social forms that have long since disappeared, and so the original, primary routes to the practical intelligibility of these concepts are forever closed off to us. But they are still *concepts!* There are, as we might say, *secondary* routes to their practical intelligibility, discernible, sometimes with great difficulty, by the historical imagination.

Since there is nothing for the concept *moral* to be a concept of, there can be no more question of its being legitimated by appeal to divine command than of its being legitimated by appeal to virtue, or to practical reason, or to anything else. Therefore we should not think of the time when God's commandments were regarded as the most general, automatically overriding, categorical ethical requirements as a time when there *were* moral requirements, promulgated and enforced by God. There were just the commandments of God. The authority of these did not depend on their status as "moral requirements"; it was just an aspect of the authority of God, which was thought to derive in turn from basic facts about His nature and His relation to human beings—most prominently, that He made us, He loves us, and He is just. The idea, assumed by many as effectively axiomatic, that the most general, automatically overriding, categorical ethical requirements simply are ipso facto moral requirements is merely ideological.

Anscombe is actually quite clear in her rejection of the idea that the vocabulary of morality might be legitimated by divine command. She supposes that the modal vocabulary of which morality purports to give us a distinctive version—*ought*, in contexts that give it the special sense of *owing* and being *obliged* or *bound*—always brings with it the additional correlative concept of a *verdict* on what has been done, and that the special senses of *ought* and so on are really, although less obviously, at bottom no less legal-juridical than this latter concept. The confused origin of the moral vocabulary is therefore more effectively brought out by reference to the idea of a verdict or ruling to which it is implicitly committed:

> For [the] suggestion [of the "moral ought"] is one of a *verdict* on my action, according as it agrees or disagrees with the description in the "ought" sentence. And where one does not think there is a judge or a law, the notion of a verdict may retain its psychological effect, but not its meaning. Now imagine that just this word "verdict" *were* so used—with a characteristically solemn emphasis—as to retain its atmosphere but not its meaning, and someone were to say: "For a *verdict*, after all, you need a law and a judge." The reply might be made: "Not at all, for if there

were a law and a judge who gave a verdict, the question for us would be whether accepting that verdict is something there is a *Verdict* on." This is an analogue of an argument that is so frequently referred to as decisive: If someone does have a divine law conception of ethics, all the same, he has to agree that he has to have a judgment that he *ought* (morally ought) to obey the divine law; so his ethic is in exactly the same position as any other; he merely has a "practical major premise": "Divine law ought to be obeyed" where someone else has, e.g., "The greatest happiness principle ought to be employed in all decisions." (MMP, 8)

The confusion lies not just in the attempt to hang on to a concept after the disappearance of the necessary conditions of its practical application—the conditions of its being a concept one might *live with*. This by itself would be confusion enough: the hero of Jim Jarmusch's film *Ghost Dog* might be doing something intelligible, but he is *not* in any literal sense *following the way of the samurai*—this is deeply impossible in a modern urban context. But the confusion about *morality* is much more serious: the independence of its distinctive *ought* from any legal-juridical framework is thought to be *essential* to it, so that even the reappearance of such a framework would leave its "meaning" (if it had one) entirely untouched, and a fortiori could not endow it with a meaning it previously lacked. Neglect of this deeper confusion gave rise, in turn, to the confusion of almost all of Anscombe's interpreters, which might be thought of as a confusion about *scope*: they thought that the problem about "morally *ought*" she was trying to bring out was that it was supposed to mean "legally *ought*," but independently of any legislator; but the real problem she had with it was that it was supposed to mean "legally *ought, but independently of any legislator*."[15] That is, the problem is not that external circumstances have rendered the specified concept inapplicable; the problem is that something has gone badly wrong with the attempted specification itself. The reappearance of a legislator might restore the first meaning, but not the second. In fact, "moral" requirements are by their purported nature accorded an authority so exalted that the edicts of any *actual* legislator are automatically subject to it—even the edicts of God, as in the argument against the divine command theory "so frequently referred to as decisive."

Thus Brian Leftow wrote a paper, "God's Deontic Perfection," about whether God is "morally perfect," and thought he had evaded Anscombe's critique because, after all, the existence of God *was* being assumed. "[Anscombe's] point was just that [the notion of the moral 'ought'] was a survival from a theistic context and made no sense outside it. Thus even if she is correct, and even if secular ethicists have nothing legitimate to do with the notion, theists thinking about morality do have a right to it" (Leftow 2013, 81n10). But since the moral "ought" is supposed to give us an *intension* essentially distinct from that expressed by the divine "thou shalt" (and presumably Leftow is not merely insisting that theists may avail themselves of the concept of divine command!), theists have no more "right" to it than atheists do.

Charles Pigden (1988) maintains that "if Christianity is to play its explanatory role" in Anscombe's account "as the cause of the psychological impetus of Ought," then "being commanded by God was built into the meaning of the *moral* Ought, and provided what content was not merely mesmeric" (33–34; my emphasis). He does not explain why, if the Ought in circulation prior to the abandonment of the idea of divine command had no nonmesmeric content over and above "being commanded by God," we should not think of "This ought to be done" as meaning at that time nothing more nor less than "*This is commanded by God*"; nor why we should suppose that such an injunction involved any additional *mesmeric* pseudo-content of a sort that Anscombe invokes the *abandonment* of the idea of divine command to explain. He then presents as an "obvious objection" to her account the fact that "some Christian writers, notably the British intuitionists of the 17th and 18th centuries, have distinguished between the concepts of being right, obligatory or what ought to be done, and being willed or commanded by God" (34). But if the bogus "*moral* ought" is thought to be essentially secular, as on my interpretation Anscombe maintains, and in my view is generally true, the insistence of Ralph Cudworth, Samuel Clarke, Richard Price, and others on distinguishing its force from that of divine command is exactly what we should expect.

Irwin, in a similar vein, supposes that Anscombe's view is that *moral* obligation is legitimated by the theistic framework—whose *demise* she in fact identified as the decisive moment in the *invention* of moral talk: "Aquinas should [if Anscombe's account is right] have the legal conception of ethics that *makes sense of moral obligation*" (Irwin 2006, 326; my emphasis). But what reason do we have to suppose that a divine law conception of ethics should be understood as "making sense of moral obligation," where the latter is conceived of as distinct from the legal conception of ethics that "makes sense" of it? If Aquinas's view is (as it seems to have been) that precepts of natural law are commanded by God as well as discernible, by the reasoning of the wise, as required for the cultivation of virtues necessary for the attainment of *eudaimonia* (now interpreted as the beatific vision)—what grounds do we have to complain that such a system of ethics is incomplete if we fail to give all this the further function of legitimating a sui generis modality of *moral obligation*? More to the point, how could Aquinas himself understand this modality as having a distinct intension from any that could be specified in terms of divine command and the virtues, and, even if he could have given a satisfactory account of this, what could he have hoped his ethical theory might gain from the introduction of such a distinctive deontic modality? Are the commands of a God whose essence is conceived of as infinitely perfect goodness, together with those portions of Aristotle's virtue-theoretic ethical framework Aquinas adapted to fill in the psychological details of how these commands should shape human life, somehow not enough?

Similarly, Robert Stern, in a preface to his recent discussion of Stephen Darwall's response to Anscombe, summarizes what he takes to be her position thus: "Anscombe argues that this new [Judeo-Christian] picture of ethics as involving moral duties rather than the virtues makes sense as long as one is thinking in theistic terms, with God as the lawgiver.... However, once the idea of God has been lost ... then it does not make sense any longer, as such laws need legislating, and only God has the characteristics necessary to operate as the legislator of the *moral* law: for only he has the requisite power, knowledge, authority and so on" (Stern 2014, 1098).

Darwall himself implicitly ascribes to Anscombe the same picture of a prelapsarian era of a moral vocabulary legitimated by the idea of divine command, and records his own endorsement of it in a concessive spirit: "I agree with Anscombe that morality is inconceivable without the idea of addressable demands" (2006, 115n45). He goes on to argue that, since we can address the relevant kind of demands to each other, Anscombe herself should have acknowledged that there can be moral requirements even without the backing of divine legislation—not realizing that she refused to acknowledge the requirements even *with* such backing.

All of these writers, and very many more,[16] have completely missed the point of Anscombe's characteristically scornful response to Sidgwick's allegation that, according to "the best theologians" ("God knows whom he meant," she remarks parenthetically), God should be obeyed "in his capacity as a *moral* being": "*ἢ φορτικὸς ὁ ἔπαινος;* one seems to hear Aristotle saying: *'Isn't the praise vulgar?'*" (MMP, 10–11; my emphases; cf. Aristotle 1920, 1178b16).[17] We witness here a powerful irony in the history of ideas: a hollow pseudo-concept unwittingly generated as a by-product of our newly Enlightened self-confidence is picked up and deployed as one of the very Names of God, as if it redounded to His glory.

4

The Futility of Seeking the Extension of a Word with No Intension

4.1 The Discourse of Morality More Erroneous than "Error Theorists" Imagine

Semantic metaethical theories of a "descriptive" kind—that is, which presuppose that *moral* is a regular predicate that yields truth-apt statements when combined with appropriate subjects—whether structured around Victorian virtue, practical reason, divine command, some kind of maximization, or whatever else, all assert, in effect, something of the form "*Moral* precepts, reasons, and so on are best understood as . . . ," where ". . ." is filled in by categories supposedly less obscure than *moral;* so that "Murder is *morally* (as opposed to prudentially, aesthetically, and so on) wrong" is explained as *meaning* that it is contrary to certain precepts of practical reason, or something the virtuous person would never do, or forbidden by God, or whatever. But the whole of this sort of account of course presupposes that we have some handle on the category of the *moral before* we are presented with the explanation of it. Otherwise we would have no grip on *what it was* that was being claimed to be best understood as ". . . ," and we would be incapable of evaluating the proposals. There can be no reasons for saying, for example, "It's hard to believe that *moral* precepts, reasons, and so on are really best understood as . . ." that do not depend on some prior conception of what the category of the *moral* amounts to.

Nevertheless, accounts of this sort are supposed to be conceptual analyses without remainder; so they seem to imply that the concept *moral* is *not* sui generis after all. The theories are not in any strong sense *empirical:* they typically assert some necessary identity—a logical equivalence—between the concept *moral* and the *explanantia* in question. If *moral* is logically equivalent to these better-understood concepts, in what sense is it sui generis? The question is important because, as we have seen, it is only as an aspiring concept that aspires to be sui generis that Anscombe objects to *moral.*

The problem is quite general. It concerns how conceptual analyses, of the sort that have long been thought to be *the* characteristic product of philosophy, can be *conceptual* without being *trivial.* If they assert necessary identities between concepts, how can they be informative? The possibility can only be explained by appeal to a way of individuating concepts that is finer-grained than logical equivalence. That is, in the case under discussion, we must be thinking of *moral* not as a (candidate) intension but as what people in semantics call a *hyperintension:* something like a mode of presentation of an intension (sense, concept), as an intension might be thought of as something like a mode of presentation of an extension (individual, set of individuals). This in itself is no ground for suspicion: there must be hyperintensions if mathematics, for example, is to be informative, and if there is to be more than one inconsistent proposition (Cresswell 1975; Jespersen 2001). But the word is cumbersome, so I shall continue to speak of *moral* as aspiring to the status of an intension, on the understanding that since it purports to be sui generis, the status must be, strictly speaking, that of a hyperintension.

Anscombe's claim, then, is in effect that there is no such adequate conception (hyperintension) answering to *moral:* it does not determine an intension, and so is not to be associated with an extension in any possible world.[1] In accordance with this, she should also say that these metaethical theories are not really saying anything—and we have seen that, contrary to the standard reading of MMP, this is exactly what she does say. The situation is not like the investigation into heat that revealed it to be best understood as molecular kinetic energy. It is like the investigation into phlogiston that revealed it to be unreal, and explained the things *it* had been invoked to explain by appeal to better-attested items. This latter investigation did not conclude that phlogiston was really these items all along; and the judgment that it was *not* these items depended on a prior, independent conception of what phlogiston was supposed to be. The correct form of a virtue-ethical theory does not give an account of morality but wholly supplants it.

It is important to resist a certain temptation to misunderstand this analogy, in a way that domesticates Anscombe's position. Phlogiston, what turns out to be nothing, does not stand, in the analogy, for the moral obligations, reasons, considerations, and so on that "moral realists" wrongly suppose to populate the world. That would amount to an analogy illustrating J. L. Mackie's famous "error theory" about moral properties, according to which statements ascribing such properties are one and all false, on account of the total absence of such properties from the world (Mackie 1977). The sort of rationalist or virtue-theoretic or "divine command" attempts to vindicate the category *moral* we have been considering do pose a challenge to error theory: moral properties *are* real, they maintain, because they are identical with, or constituted by, or supervene on, or bear some other such intimate relation to, properties explicable in terms of practical reason or virtue or divine command. But Anscombe's view is not a form of error theory. It is more radical than that. It is not challenged by these attempts to vindicate morality: rather, it challenges their presupposition that there is anything there to vindicate. Phlogiston in the analogy stands, not for moral properties, reasons, and so on, but for the (purported) *concept* of the moral, in the sense of the intension of the word.[2] The problem, for Anscombe, is not that it determines a null extension in the actual world. To repeat: it's that it can't be in the business of determining any extension, in any world, at all.

These rationalist, virtue-theoretic, and divine command responses miss the point because they don't see that Anscombe's real objection to their sorts of theory derives from this thoroughgoing eliminativism about the *concept* (or rather, "concept") of the moral (as opposed to merely its purported instantiations). Her view is more skeptical than error theory, because when Mackie maintained that there were no such things as moral values in the world, so that our ordinary moral talk, as well as all "realist" theories of it, were radically in error, he was not going so far as to deny that the idea of the *moral* made any sense at all. Quite to the contrary: as with all error theories, he *presupposed* the meaningfulness of the propositions it was the point of his theory to deny. On Mackie's account, the moral vocabulary expresses concepts that are *at the very worst* self-contradictory and so, as Frege maintained, "not so black as they are painted," since they still have a legitimate use, and so must be accounted meaningful. For Anscombe, Mackie's claim that all talk presupposing the reality of "moral values" was false in the end makes no more sense than the realist's claim that some of it is true.

Mackie would suppose that his criticisms of moral realism apply equally to the virtue picture. It too is supposed to ground objective facts about what we should do, so the norms associated with the virtues, no less than *moral* norms, are supposed "to have to-be-doneness built in to them," as he puts it, and so are equally "queer." But Mackie's critique seems to have much less bite here, once we have abandoned the "moral" conception of virtue. Anscombe's own arguments show that you don't have to be a thoroughgoing Humean about reasons to find something fishy in the very idea of what "moral values" are supposed to be—and to anyone not already committed to the relevant Humean ideology, it is very far from clear that her diagnosis doesn't express better than Mackie's the uneasiness we might have felt about "moral values." The idea that *what counts as a fine specimen of humanity,* understood as a source of reasons, is in the end just an expression of the evaluator's "brute attitudes"—not themselves up for objective evaluation—is, to anyone not already in the grip of an ideology, on the face of it much less plausible than the same line on what we take to be *moral values,* as understood from the distinctive perspective of morality.[3]

Can an Apparent Concept-Word with a Well-Established Use Nevertheless Lack an Intension?

In this section I address a particular difficulty with the idea that *moral* might lack an intension.

I have argued that, although Anscombe doesn't quite put it this way, one of the main problems with the vocabulary of *morality* is that it presupposes a special kind of reason for action, which is just not there. This is a corollary of a broader point she does emphasize: that the vocabulary is descended from one that took its meaning (and so its reason-giving force) from a surrounding framework of ideas, institutions, and practices concerning God and his commands. It is a *descendant* of that vocabulary: it is not just the same vocabulary ripped out of the context that gave it sense; this is why the widespread view that Anscombe would accept *moral* as a legitimate concept if only it were "reinserted" into the relevant theistic form of life is mistaken. It is of the essence of *morality*, as most people purport to understand it, that its special kind of normativity *not* have its source in divine command: the special autonomy and sui generis nature of the moral notions ensure that it will make sense to ask of any actual commands, even those of God, whether they express *moral requirements* and, more generally, whether we are *morally required* to obey them.

I have also claimed that, if this debunking genealogy is correct, the sentences typically intended to express *moral precepts* are best thought of not as false but as senseless—and that this is how Anscombe herself thought of the matter. To get clearer about what this claim involves, and why it might seem especially implausible, let us look again, more closely, at Anscombe's own comparison between the uprooting of the ethically sovereign *ought* of obligation from its native Judeo-Christian soil, and how things would stand if the vocabulary of *criminality* were similarly wrenched from any context of recognizably juridical institutions: "It is as if the notion 'criminal' were to remain," she wrote, "when criminal law and criminal courts had been abolished and forgotten" (MMP, 6).

So let us imagine that scenario in a bit more detail, fleshing it out, if we can, in a way that sheds light on what Anscombe takes to be the analogous case of *ought*. Suppose that all institutions associated with the state administration of justice have withered away, but people keep applying the word "criminal" to actions, people, and so on; and suppose, further, they apply it to *roughly* the sorts of thing that fell under the old, legitimate concept expressed by the word: generally disapproved-of behaviors like theft and murder—although it is not unanimously agreed that any of these should *always*, that is, in all circumstances, count as "criminal." "Criminal" is emphatically a word of disapprobation: virtually no one will freely acknowledge "criminal" behavior or profess indifference to being deemed a "criminal." But suppose also it is taken to be part of the word's meaning that it can have no essential connection to actual or possible juridical institutions. Beyond this, *criminal* is widely believed to be a sui generis category, such that we risk failure to respect its special autonomy if we try to define it without remainder in terms more familiar to us. A number of philosophers, we may imagine, have nevertheless proposed a variety of analyses of *criminality*, many of them exhibiting an alarming degree of conceptual complexity and sophistication. These analyses would perhaps be regarded as eccentric and even denounced as subversive, but few people outside the philosophers' circles are aware of them.

Before we ask whether such a term could have an established use, let us ask how things could stand in respect of its meaning—which is to say, in line with our interest in the analogy with the case of *morality,* in respect of questions of intension and extension.[4]

There seem to be four relevant options: we might think of the new use of "criminal" (and, analogously, the "moral *ought*") (i) as having an intension that determines a nonempty extension in the (envisaged) actual world; (ii) as having an intension that determines the empty set as its extension in the actual world, but a nonempty set in some possible worlds; (iii) as having an intension that determines the empty set as its extension in all possible worlds; or (iv) as having no intension at all.

(i) looks like a nonstarter: given what we know about how the word is used, nothing in the imagined world could count as "criminal" given that the word is *supposed* to imply very strong reasons against doing the things that qualify. For no such reason has been given; it is essential to the term's use that no such reasons can be conjured out of imagined, or merely possible, juridical institutions and processes; and there is a strong, widespread animus against understanding "reasons of criminality" in any kind of reductive spirit, in terms of kinds of reason more familiar to us. Similar considerations tell against (ii): since the term's users are adamant that no *possible* institutional arrangements could provide the right sort of reason for observing the norms associated with "criminality," it is hard to see how anything really counts in any possible world as *criminal,* if the "concept" is understood as, *as such,* aspiring to the status of a source of intelligible reasons. (Notice that *moral* norms, which might otherwise seem the obvious candidate *explanantia,* are as unavailing as any other kind: the "concept" of the *criminal* is sui generis and irreducible, notwithstanding the various, widely ignored, elaborate reductive or semireductive theories of the philosophers.)

If (ii) isn't right, the natural response is to opt for (iii). In the case we are really concerned with, that of the moral terminology, we have seen that most readers of Anscombe have understood her position as analogous to (ii), our "criminal" case modified to exclude the clause about no actual or possible juridical institutions making the word intelligible: if Western intellectuals, like those of medieval times, generally accepted unargued appeals to the agreed-on existence and nature of a divine law-giver in their ethical inquiries, then, they suppose, Anscombe would have no quarrel with the term "moral" as expressing a legitimate and instantiated concept in philosophy after all; and if hoi polloi accepted, as a rather large proportion of them in fact still do, an ethic descended from the Torah, on the basis of its supposed divine promulgation, then the vocabulary of *morality* in their mouths would be perfectly OK as well. I maintain of course that this is not Anscombe's view at all.

So I find myself arguing against a further possible misunderstanding of Anscombe—that her position is analogous to (iii)—that perhaps very few of her readers have even fallen into, since most have got stuck at the even more wildly erroneous view that she believes some analogue of (ii). But I suspect that even someone prepared to grant me that Anscombe takes *moral* to have no extension in any possible world would be much happier at this point to ascribe to her a (iii)-type view, which would make *moral* something like a self-contradictory concept, than they would be to read her as holding the even more radical (iv)-type view that *moral* determines not a null extension but *no* extension, and is not in fact a concept at all.

I anticipate such resistance to my interpretation on the basis of interpretative charity toward Anscombe. My reading may well seem terminally afflicted by a particular sort of implausibility.

An anonymous referee of an earlier version of my account of MMP took particular exception to the idea that *moral* might lack an intension and so be literally senseless, because it clearly has an established use. "You can argue that 'moral' and the moral 'ought' are confused, ambiguous, or contradictory, or that neither of them corresponds to anything real," he or she wrote, "but the idea that they are literally *senseless* is just about as obviously false as a philosophical thesis can be. They've got a well-established use: hence they have a meaning."

This objection has force on the face of it, and needs to be addressed. "Just about as obviously false as a philosophical thesis can be" seems a bit strong, however. It is not *obvious* to me, at all, that a population could not come to use a term in the kind of regular, patterned way that normally marks a genuine concept-word, even though the word in question has literally no meaning. In fact, something very like this seems to me to be true of quite a few widely used terms *besides* "moral." But admittedly such situations call for special explanations.

Presumably part of the difficulty arises in this way: if *moral* is not a concept, it cannot be, as Frege would put it, a constituent of a thought. What we take to be thoughts about morality, or thoughts that something is or is not moral, will then be "thoughts" about nothing, or "thoughts" that ascribe no property to what they are supposed to be about—which is to say, they will not be thoughts at all. We might find this perturbing, but it is certainly not impossible. There is no question that someone can falsely think they are having a thought; falsely, that is, in that the thought they think they are having is no thought at all. (Of course such a person is thinking, and is having *a* thought, to the effect that they are having some other thought—the possibility in question is that this second "thought," the one they think they are having, is not a thought.) One might think, for example, that one is having the thought that someone at a certain location at that moment is thinking something false, without realizing that the only person at that moment at that location is oneself. In such a case, as I believe has been shown by A. N. Prior (1976, 174–175), the purported thought one takes oneself to be having cannot be supposed to be true, nor to be false, without leading to contradiction. The purported thought is therefore not something that can be true or false, and so is not a thought at all. So there is no *logical* difficulty in the idea that, if *moral* is not a concept, then many of what we take to be thoughts involving "morality" are not really thoughts.

Furthermore, a recognition of the meaninglessness of *moral* as an irreducibly sui generis concept will not wreak anywhere near as much havoc in our ethical discourse as we might at first fear. A salient question in this connection is: If *moral does* have an intension, why can no one agree on what it is? Uses of the term by those who take it to be *extensionally* equivalent to something like *productive of the best consequences* may charitably be supposed to mean by it, *in part,* something like that, since that is the extension they are explicitly claiming for it; those who think of *moral* precepts as a species of precept of practical reason may be understood *at least* as meaning that; when the term is used by the dwindling band of divine command theorists, we may concede that they do succeed in signifying something about the law of God, even though they are mistaken in thinking they mean more; and so on.[5] Many other uses are clearly intended to convey, inter alia, ideas of justice, of benevolence, or of some other virtue pertaining to our dealings with each other. As I remarked earlier, the upshot of Anscombe's skepticism in these cases should be thought of in this way: in the end, *there is only what is productive of the best consequences, or the precepts of practical reason, or the laws of God, or the virtues,* combined in each case, as these ideas may be, with the thought that the totality of our reasons favor acting with the idea in question as our guide. The meaninglessness, the illusion, pertain to what the term "moral" is supposed to bring along *over and above* whatever more familiar concepts it is being claimed to overlap or coincide with. To put the point paradoxically: in many contexts, the term "moral" may *in a way* be credited, pragmatically and charitably, with a kind of extension, *even though it lacks an intension.* In any such context, the effective extension is that of whatever more familiar concepts are being *anointed* with the supposedly unique chrism of *morality;* the illusion lies in thinking that *this* rite can have any meaning: that the disputes among the advocates of the various ideas could ever concern the contours of any concept more distinctive than that of *what we have most reason to do.* The component reasons we may weigh, or ignore, or regard as always taking precedence, and so forth, in our thinking about *what,* individually or in the context of whichever collectivities we may help to constitute, *it would be best to do*—these component reasons may be aesthetic, or reasons of state, or of expediency, or compassion; they may have to do with God, or with a conviction that there is no God, or with other forms of veneration, of our ancestors, say, or of the earth, or of cultural achievement, or with the repudiation of any forms of veneration; they may be whimsical or frivolous, for a well-lived life need not be marred, and may be enhanced, by elements of whimsy or frivolity—there are endless varieties of reason making some at least initially minimally plausible claim on our practical attention. What Anscombe insists is that there is no class of such reasons we can informatively call *moral.*

But what about the highly regimented pattern of use? What could sustain that, if not an intension—something that puts the word *in the business* of applying to things, even if, like *the ether* or *non-self-identical,* it never succeeds in doing so? Relatedly, if the word really is senseless, on what grounds could anyone maintain, as I did earlier, that "if I have a virtue in the modern 'Victorian' [that is, "*moral*"] sense, this is, by definition, good news for other people, but it is an open question whether it is good news for me," or anything else of this sort? As my referee put it, "since the 'modern "Victorian" sense' certainly presupposes 'morality' and perhaps the moral 'ought' (which is what the author has just been arguing) the author has managed to derive a conceptual truth from what he claims to be a non-concept. No concept; no conceptual truths and conversely. Conceptual truths require a concept to generate them no matter how silly or non-referential that concept may be."

Well, looking back, "by definition" was perhaps not the happiest expression to use here. But the idea of definition, which certainly does imply conceptual truth and so a concept, is entirely dispensable relative to the point I was, and am, really concerned to make. The important idea here is simply *what may be predicted on the basis of someone's sincere use of a certain terminology.* The essential claim is that someone who has qualities people *call* moral virtues may generally be expected to act with some regularity in a way that takes into account their conception of others' interests. There may be any number of plausible justifications for such an expectation. I see no reason at all why they must all concede that the vocabulary whose sincere use forms the basis of the expectation must express bona fide concepts. Why should a certain kind of talk not form the basis of reliable predictions about how those who engage in it will behave, merely because that talk is, unbeknownst to them, strictly meaningless?

After all, as we know, *words are deeds* (Wittgenstein 1980, 50e).[6] The pattern of a word's use may express that use's reliable efficacy as a type of deed, even if the words *as words* have no meaning at all.

Consider in this connection the famous denunciation, in an anonymous 1936 *Pravda* editorial generally known, even at the time, to have been written at the behest of Stalin, of the "bourgeois formalism" of Dmitri Shostakovich's opera *Lady Macbeth of the Mtsensk District.* It seems to me implausible to suppose that *bourgeois formalism* is a concept, that is, has a legitimate intension such that musical works as such might be determined as falling under it or not. The function of the expression was not to pick out a kind but to express disapproval and perhaps convey a threat, like a bullet in a mailbox. A system or pattern of use for an expression can be perfectly well held in place by functions of this kind. Other Soviet composers repudiated and condemned "bourgeois formalism" as a means of distancing themselves from Shostakovich and avoiding Stalin's frequently fatal disapproval. There was nothing the slightest bit random about the consequent use of *bourgeois formalism:* lives depended on it. But it was not, I think, a concept-expression. No doubt it was inadvisable to inquire too insistently into what *bourgeois formalism* really amounted to. One might even thereby make oneself vulnerable to charges of *bourgeois formalism*. Such patterns of use of meaningless phrases, partly enforced by a kind of secondary deployment as a means of denouncing and so evading critical scrutiny of themselves, are especially common when people's actions are massively constrained, as they frequently are, by bullying, threats, and intimidation or, again, inspired by mysteriously infectious grandiose notions, as in some of the crusades, or, especially, when the two sorts of factor are combined, as in the Cultural Revolution.

Few words have proved so versatile, in circumstances of this kind, as "moral." Surely philosophers should be a bit suspicious when, as does happen, the charge of immorality itself is laid against a too-assiduous inquiry into the credentials of *moral* itself as a concept. When confronted in this spirit with the idea of an unanswerable "moral necessity," there is a lot to be said for the insouciant response of which, according to reports, Anscombe herself was fond; namely, the peremptory question, "What if I don't?"[7]

The point is not that the vocabulary of morality is simply an instrument of bullying—although it certainly can be that—but that a *purported* concept-word does not need to be in the business of determining an extension for a stable pattern of use to be held in place; my referee's "[The moral terms] have got a well-established use: hence they have a meaning" is simply a non sequitur. Nevertheless, the forces by which the highly systematic use of the moral vocabulary is sustained may have rather more in common with bullying, and kindred phenomena, than might at first appear, because that sort of basis can be disguised very effectively by various processes of *internalization*. The psychosociological questions here are large and complex, and this is not the place to investigate them in any detail; but the basic idea may be illustrated by reimagining the case of Stalin's excursion into musical criticism: What if composers had been brought to *believe*—by various means including inculcation from the earliest age—that there *was* such a musical-aesthetic phenomenon as *bourgeois formalism*, and that this was the worst musical vice a composer could fall into? This may sound fanciful, but it may well have been the actual condition of *some* Soviet composers of the period.

Another source of illumination of these matters is provided by the Socratic dialogues of Plato. In Plato's *Gorgias* (Plato 1959, 1997), for example, Callicles criticizes Polus, Socrates's previous interlocutor, for succumbing to "false shame" in refusing to acknowledge that committing injustice is not only more advantageous but less shameful ("by nature") than suffering it (482e). He is certainly right that norms of shame can distort discussions of, among other things, what the true norms of shame prohibit, in such a way that people may be inhibited from saying what they really think—much as *moral* norms might distort conversations about, among other things, the force and authority of *moral norms*. But if we look back at how Polus and his even more conventionally minded predecessor Gorgias behaved in conversation with Socrates, it is clear that neither of them could give anything approaching a coherent account, even of an elementary kind, of what sort of authority the norms of justice are supposed to enjoy, or how those norms stand in relation to what is and is not advantageous, and what is and is not genuinely shameful. It is not just that Socrates, as usual, leads them into contradiction—this is only a symptom of something deeper: they do not have an inconsistent conception of justice; it is more that, as their conversations with Socrates proceed, we slowly realize that in apparently talking about justice, they *don't know what they're talking about* (see Doyle 2010). Plato's point is not that there is no genuine concept of justice—it is of course the burden of the main argument of the *Republic* to show that there is such a concept, which is in fact a virtue worthy of our allegiance—but that in the mouths of the many of Socrates's interlocutors who, in accordance with Socrates's and Plato's never-relinquished view of hoi polloi, are not even aware of the alternative to an unexamined life, their talk of justice *might as well* be like the idle wind.

Something very similar is going on, I submit, in many other Socratic dialogues: the interlocutor's real problem is often something much more serious than its primary manifestation—inconsistent beliefs about some central practical-ethical concept. Ion, Euthyphro, Meno, and others are revealed by Socrates's interrogations as having trained themselves to use a word in the systematic way characteristic of a genuine predicate, which nevertheless remains for them, did they but know it, nothing more than a *word*. The regularity of this result strongly implies that few of their fellows are in much of a stronger epistemic position. And yet, in every case, the word in question—piety, virtue, or whatever—conforms to a pattern of usage so regular and agreed-on that it looks for all the world as though it expressed a regular, bona fide concept.

It may seem that some of the reasons I have given for supposing it possible that a term lacking an intension may yet exhibit a regular pattern of use are equally reasons for looking on the word in question not as lacking meaning altogether but as having a meaning of a radically different kind: namely, the kind characteristically ascribed by *expressivist* accounts of the words in question, whereby their semantic function is to express a nondoxastic attitude of the speaker rather than to represent or refer to something in the world. Such a function seems not to involve an expression's being associated with an extension at all; in fact, insofar as an expressivist account of an expression is the appropriate one, it seems the expression *cannot* have an extension, at least if we assume that part of the point of such an account is to deny that the expression in question can function as a predicate in genuinely truth-apt judgments. For what can it mean to say of an expression in predicate position in an atomic indicative sentence that it has an extension, if not that, if what is picked out by the sentence's subject-term is *in* the predicate's extension, then the sentence is *true*? Whereas if an expression lacks an extension—where this is to be distinguished from having the empty set as its extension—nothing about it can *determine* one; that is, it will therefore lack an intension too. But to call it *meaningless* on that account is too quick; such a verdict would merely reflect the application of criteria of meaningfulness not appropriate to the word's true semantic function.[8]

Perhaps Anscombe's best-known devotee in ethics, in extending what he takes to be Anscombe's critique of *moral* to the Bloomsbury group's fixation on G. E. Moore's account of *good*, takes something very like this line: "An acute observer at the time . . . might well have put matters thus: these people take themselves to be identifying the presence of a nonnatural property, which they call 'good'; but there is in fact no such property and they are doing no more and no other than expressing their feelings and attitudes, disguising the expression of preference and whim by an interpretation of their own utterance and behavior which confers upon it an objectivity that it does not in fact possess" (MacIntyre 1984, 16, quoted in Teichmann 2008, 105).

In the case we are concerned with, that of the vocabulary of *morality,* one might wonder more generally whether at least some of Anscombe's skeptical arguments intended to expose that vocabulary as meaningless are effective (to the extent that they are) only on the assumption that any meaning it has would have to be *cognitive.* As she herself said of her imagined case, in which use of the vocabulary of *criminality* outlives the existence of juridical institutions, "A Hume discovering this situation might conclude that there was a special sentiment, expressed by 'criminal,' which alone gave the word its sense" (MMP, 6). How confident can we be that the *real* Hume was *wrong* to reach the same conclusion about "moral"?

This response would, however, only push the problem back. For suppose that, as the emotivists and expressivists hold, the function of the vocabulary of *morality* really were to express the speaker's attitudes of approval and disapproval, or endorsement and rejection. If the attitudes in question were merely whichever of the speaker's prejudices, whims, and so on happened to be seeking expression at the time, as in Alasdair MacIntyre's description of the Bloomsburyites, I see no particular reason why Anscombe herself could not go along with this, consistently with what she says in MMP. For *moral* would then lack not only an extension but any remotely objective criteria of application, and the expressivist construal provides no defense against her charge that it has "no intelligible content."

Those who would resort to expressivism to defend the *legitimacy* of the vocabulary would have to make a case for its expressing attitudes of a sort that can underwrite relatively robust, systematic, and shareable conditions of appropriate application. But even supposing that such a case has been made, they still cannot be absolved of the task of presenting an account of *moral* as a special category. For if the expressivist's case is not to be dismissed on grounds of simply changing the subject, *moral* approval must still be understood as sui generis, just as much as "*moral* reason," "*moral* defect," and the rest were essentially sui generis for those who construed the vocabulary in traditional, "realist," descriptivist fashion. Just as a *moral* defect, if the self-image of "morality" is to be given its minimal due, must be distinguished in its essence from an aesthetic or some form of technical defect, so must the specifically *moral* dimension of evaluation be explained as fundamentally different in kind from the dimensions that interest, for example, connoisseurs of the many varieties of artwork and craftsmanship. But accounting for this sui generis essence of the *moral* was the main problem Anscombe has been raising all along. After all, even if the distinctively modern framework of subjectivist ideas presupposed by expressivism were available to Aristotle, it would be no more plausible to ascribe to him the concept of *moral* evaluation than, on Anscombe's persuasive account of the matter, it is to ascribe to him the concept of a *moral* reason, defect, consideration, virtue, and so on. And we would then be faced with close analogues of our old questions: *Why* does Aristotle, as an agent, lack this mode of evaluation and, as a philosopher, the concept of it? And what, exactly, is he thereby *missing* in his apprehension of the ethical realm that we, to our advantage, can discern?

Even if we grant the expressivist a sui generis mode of approval and disapproval, it is hard to see how the kind of disapproval of *injustice* one might encounter in the ancient world could be made out to be a *different* mode. So if, as we are now supposing, the particular category of the *moral* was not available in ancient culture, the expressivist account of moral judgment in terms of the expression of attitudes of approval and disapproval will not discriminate among *kinds* of approval finely enough to give us a distinctively moral flavor. If, instead, the expressivist claims that there is a generic mode of disapproval, which the ancient expresses toward what is *unjust,* and we might express toward what is *immoral,* expressivism is presupposing the distinction between these categories, and so is no help in understanding it.

There are many ways in which populations come to subscribe to systems of norms generated by seemingly autonomous processes of evolution, systems they do not realize they do not understand and perhaps cannot be understood—that is, are strictly meaningless. These phenomena seem to me undeniable but still little understood, in spite of the invaluable contributions to their elucidation provided by many great works of literary fiction and philosophical anthropology.[9]

5

What's Really Wrong with the Vocabulary of Morality?

Divine Command and "Morality" Again

We have seen that nearly all readers of MMP have misunderstood the historical account of the origins of "morality" Anscombe gave in support of her claim that the vocabulary of morality was fundamentally unintelligible. The basis of that claim seems to be that the vocabulary presupposes a divine legislator but, at the same time, effectively presupposes that there is *no* divine legislator. On the standard reception of the account, this is held to imply that the full-fledged divine command ethic of the Jews, the Christians, and the Muslims *did* give us a coherent account of morality. For the problem with the secular conception was precisely that it was secular: it tried to make do without God. So Anscombe was read as supposing that if God were *put back in*, the result would be a *legitimate* conception of morality.

The main problem with this standard reading is its assumption that the vocabulary of morality, when "made intelligible" by the reinsertion of the divine legislator, remains in any sense at all a version of *morality*. For morality was supposed to be a distinctive, sui generis, irreducible concept, widely believed for *Euthyphro*-style reasons to be *essentially* independent of the divine. Those reasons were not extrinsic to what the notion of morality aspired to be. Rather, they were supposed to fall out of an elucidation of the concept itself: anyone who didn't see that something's being *morally required* could not depend on its being *commanded by God*, for example, had simply misunderstood the sort of concept *moral* was supposed to be.

The reason we regain intelligibility with the readdition of the idea of God, then, is *not* that we now have an intelligible version of the idea of *morality* but that we have simply reassembled the wholly familiar idea of *divine command*. That idea was, as per Anscombe's definition, that what is required for virtue is also required by divine law: "To have a [*divine*] *law* conception of ethics is to hold that what is needed for conformity with the virtues failure in which is the mark of being bad *qua* man . . . is required by divine law" (MMP, 6).

The idea that morality is vindicated in this context is therefore multiply confused. Since morality was supposed to be essentially secular, it gets no support from being placed alongside divine command; and even if it were *not* still unintelligible in this context, it is very unclear what the idea could add to that of what is already required *both* for virtue *and* by God.

This all seems to me to be correct as far as it goes; but we have as yet no detailed understanding of what it is about the vocabulary of morality that is supposed to make it unintelligible. Recall that Anscombe intended a very strong reading of this claim: the vocabulary is unintelligible *as opposed to merely self-contradictory*. Her real target was not Mackie's: the supposition that anything falls under the concept *moral*. What she denied was the *intension* (or hyperintension) of *moral*: she held that it is not in the business of determining an extension at all; that is, that it is not a concept.

This skepticism certainly has to do with *something* about the nature of divine command ethics. But *what*, if it is not that the unintelligibility of morality can be remedied by reintroducing God into the picture? The idea is that divine command ethics has a certain *distinctive character* that is *essentially bound up with*, but not *identical to*, its presupposition of a divine legislator. She holds that the vocabulary of morality is an attempt to reproduce that character but *essentially independently of* that presupposition. The fall into incoherence then reflects the deep impossibility of retaining the character without the presupposition. The character cannot simply *be* the presupposition, or the absurdity of the moral vocabulary would simply be too apparent; the centuries-long confusion would be completely inexplicable. But if Anscombe's view is right, the relation between the character and the presupposition—this *"essentially bound up with"*—must be of a kind that makes sense of the strikingly uncompromising form of her skepticism—her denial that *morality* is so much as a concept.

The place to look, then, for this distinctive character of the divine command conception is in what that conception *adds* to what was already there; that is, what it adds to the ethics of *virtue*. Anscombe seems to hold that virtue gives us the only intelligible conceptual framework for ethics other than divine command; at any rate, if she is right about the bankruptcy of the vocabulary of morality, it is the only alternative the Western tradition has to offer.

Historically, the rise of the Hebrew-Christian version of divine command ethics consisted in its being conjoined with a preestablished ethic of virtue, in accordance with the definition of Anscombe's I quoted just now. Aquinas's ethics is a very clear illustration of this. As is well known, he takes over the virtue-ethical structure of Aristotle's ethics, as of so much else in Aristotle, virtually entire. And yet if anyone counts as a divine command ethicist, Aquinas does. Now certainly Aquinas's ethics, being Christian, includes on the basis of revelation significant prohibitions, for example of certain sexual activities, and requirements, for example of loving enemies, which the pagans did not observe and in some cases found completely baffling. Some of these precepts exclusively concerned religious observance and could only be based on what was deemed to be revelation; many of the rest, however, were overdetermined, in that Thomas was conforming to the dominant tradition in Christian ethics in holding that they were both revealed and discernible by practical reason independently of revelation, for all that the pagans seemed oblivious to them (see Donagan 1977).

Thomas's ethics conforms to Anscombe's definition of a divine command conception, in that he held that every offense against the law of God—that is, every sin—was contrary to some virtue or other (for example, *ST* IaIIae, Q71 A4 Ad 1, Q72 A2 *sed contra*, A4 Resp, Q77 A1 Resp). What Aquinas adds to Aristotle, then, does not involve a radical departure from the structure of virtue ethics, for this is not affected by his expanding the class of virtues to include the explicitly and exclusively religious qualities of faith, hope, and charity, and newly revealed components of classical virtues.

Rather, his innovations[1] are to be found in his imparting to the requirements of *all* the virtues, classical and Christian, the additional deontic necessity that attaches to divine law, whatever that amounts to.

But what *does* that amount to? This was our question, whose answer was supposed to be the clue to the alleged incoherence of morality. If Anscombe is right, morality, while essentially secular, must equally essentially exhibit some kind of aspiration to this additional necessity, which must yet be *essentially bound up with* the idea of a divine legislator, in a way that dooms that aspiration to be frustrated, to a degree that leaves morality literally unintelligible.

5.2   What's So Special about Divine Command?
(I) The Circumstantial Account

How might the element of divine command transform the character of virtue ethics? Well, first we have to get clear on the prior question: What is the character of virtue ethics? What sorts of reason does it articulate for acting as it recommends or requires? And what sorts of recommendations or requirements does it issue? What sort of *necessity* does it attach to ethical norms?

We have seen that eudaimonism is the point of virtue ethics: it relates right conduct to what an agent needs in order to flourish, or to be good at being a human being. This is why the motivational question gets sidestepped from the start: it can't make sense to fail to want what one needs in this way, provided of course one knows one needs it.[2] This is surely one reason why the concept of virtue is supposed to hold out the prospect of an intelligibility the moral vocabulary lacks: it is designed to provide a kind of reason-giving content that is, at bottom, familiar. If we ever *can* do what Anscombe insists we currently *cannot* do, and explain what sort of characteristic a *virtue* is without debunking the whole idea, our explanation will include an account of why we *need* the virtues (cf. Geach 1977). If our picture is to avoid the mysteries of a wholly sui generis category of the kind morality aspires to be, then at some point it must connect up with reasons of a sort with which we are familiar. Reasons for securing what we need in order to flourish are not distinguished by being radically different in kind from those we invoke outside ethical contexts, but only by their highly *general* character. Thus, when Aristotle says that *eudai-*

monia is the most *teleion* (complete or end-like) end, he is not thinking of it as somehow generating its own distinctive "moral" hierarchy of ends; he is assigning it to the supreme position among ends of the sort we already took ourselves to have *anyway*.

What can we conclude from this about the kind of necessity imputed to ethical norms when we think about them in terms of virtue? Eudaimonistic virtue ethics is structured around a certain *natural* species of necessity, in a sense of "natural" that is so far vague and intuitive but will be made more precise later. This kind of necessity is mentioned by Aristotle in book 5 of the *Metaphysics* (1015a19–1015a26) but has subsequently been largely neglected, as Anscombe remarks in some of the various places in her own works where she seeks to revive interest in it. Purely for convenience I will refer to this as "Aristotelian necessity." It is the necessity that attaches to something without which some good cannot be obtained, or some harm avoided. So *just* actions and habits of mind, for example, whatever else might be said in favor of them, are necessary in this way for the agent's *justice*, which, we are assuming, is a genuine (that is, non-"Victorian") virtue, and so an indispensable ingredient of the agent's good. This is how Plato's "Socratic" Socrates, for example, often talks of the reasons for acting virtuously. To act unjustly is to make oneself less just, that is, *worse;* but who wants to harm himself? As Aquinas makes especially clear, however, Aristotelian necessity can play a much larger role in an account of the virtues than the one Socrates typically accords it; one that enables us to say much more than Socrates did about why we should acquire them. Thus, this necessity attaches to *courage* in connection with the goods of overcoming dangers, carrying through with one's projects, and defending one's city; to obedience to military commanders in connection with the good of coordinated military action, to honesty in connection with the good of well-ordered social life, and so on. Of course, in the secular Greek context the connection between some of these goods and the *individual's eudaimonia* becomes less clear, and it is typically reestablished by invoking the peculiar dynamics of the admirable (*kalon*) and the shameful (*aiskhron*).

Thus eudaimonistic virtue ethics gives us a particular account of the reasons we have for acting virtuously. One promising way of thinking about what is distinctive about the ethics of divine command looks to the impact it has on this account, whereby a certain transformation of virtue ethics is effected. For once divine command enters the picture, we have significantly *more* reason to act as virtue requires. That is, even if the Aristotelian necessity was sufficient reason, the divine commands provide additional *incentive*—in the case of Christianity, the greatest incentive one could imagine: avoidance of eternal damnation and attainment of eternal beatitude. Divine command, as we have seen, also makes possible new ethical requirements—such as the commandment of universal love—for which there is no clear rationale within secular virtue ethics.

We might call this the *circumstantial* account of the difference divine command makes to virtue ethics. It does not change the form or structure of the ethic: the fundamental basis of ethical requirements remains the Aristotelian necessity of the required conduct for the agent's good. It changes instead (the agent's conception of) the circumstances in which he is deciding what to do and how to be, in a way that might make a radical difference for his conception of what is necessary for *eudaimonia*.

What are the implications for the moral vocabulary? *Moral* is supposed to be a *practical* concept, as the words for virtues and a great many others, including "fun," "evil," and "pleasant," give us practical concepts. This means that its interest is supposed to lie not just in its determining an extension but also in the life we live with it. Although I have no commitment to *kashrut,* I could become an expert in the business, which can be pretty complicated, of identifying which foods are *kosher* and which not. But, obviously, the concept *kosher* would not have for me anything like the significance it would have for an observant Jew. Perhaps the word "kosher" doesn't even mean the same thing in my mouth, and I can mean it only in a distanced, "inverted commas" sense (Tenenbaum 2000).[3] In any case, the concept just doesn't have any traction with me, and seeing why not brings us straight back to the issue of *reasons*. Kashrut doesn't figure in my reasons for doing this or not doing that, in the way that it does in the reasons of an observant Jew. If Anscombe is right, *everyone* is in something like this position with regard to the concept *moral*—even believing Jews and Christians, oddly enough, because the concept actually presupposes precisely the commitment Anscombe claims deprives it of any legitimacy, to an entirely secular grounding. On Anscombe's account, the true situation is significantly more bizarre than my expertise in identifying kosher food or even her imagined case where "the notion 'criminal' were to remain when criminal law and criminal courts had been abolished and forgotten." To make the latter parallel more complete, we would have to imagine also that if anyone tried to reestablish a connection between the judicial vocabulary and real or imagined laws and courts, she would be widely criticized for missing the point of the concept. Some might even retort, in the manner of Blackburn, that arguments similar to those found in Plato's *Euthyphro* prove that the true concept of *criminal* cannot depend on any such institutional arrangements.

"Criminal," in the imagined case, might still *in a way* determine an extension: people might agree, by and large, on which actions were to count. And they might produce very subtle arguments, in the hard cases, about whether the special, irreducible sentiment associated with *criminality* properly attached to the actions in question. But they would be like the inhabitants of Plato's cave vying with each other in their demonstrations of detailed knowledge of the shadows on the wall: their minute disputes would lack any *point* because they would not connect up with anything that could be supposed to *matter*: again, they would not connect up with *reasons* for doing one thing rather than another (cf. Teichmann 2008, 106). In the absence of the institutional infrastructure, we have no reason to fear punishment. Similarly, when the ancestor of *moral* was conceptually connected to the prospects of the beatific vision and eternal damnation (or prosperity from generation to generation and the wiping out of one's line, as parts of Hebrew scripture have it), it figured in the most intelligible reasons we could imagine for doing God's will. Cut off from those prospects, the category of the *moral* loses all reason-giving force. Morality dispenses with the Aristotelian necessity of virtue ethics, whereby ethical norms could play an obvious role in deliberation, but it doesn't replace this with anything else that secures in any obvious way the right connection to what we might take ourselves to have reason to do.

One plausible rationale for Anscombe's thesis (2), then, would be this: the concept *moral* should be jettisoned as harmful because, although it has a convincing appearance of playing an essential role in our reasons for doing and not doing various things, in reality it can play no such role; and both the appearance and the reality can be explained by reference to cultural history. For I take it that this is an important upshot of Anscombe's critique: that to call an act, person, consideration, or whatever "moral," as opposed to calling it "just," "brave," and so on, cannot in itself contribute to our deliberations about what to do. Morality aspires to a kind of *pure altruism* that cannot be understood in eudaimonistic terms. A eudaimonist will find it plausible to explain this as an unwitting attempt to preserve what was a distinctively Christian ethical ideal—the self-sacrificing ideal of charity—while cutting it off from the only thing that could give it sense (that is, make it *consistent* with eudaimonism): the prospective rewards and punishments of a divine legislator.

5.3   The Inadequacy of the Circumstantial Account

For a long time I thought that this circumstantial account was the best way of understanding the difference divine command made to a preexisting ethic of virtue—and so the best way of making sense of Anscombe's claim that the modern vocabulary of morality is a hopeless attempt to combine the distinctive character of an ethic of divine law with rejection of the idea of a divine legislator. Eventually, however, I came to see it as unsatisfactory.

Although Anscombe says some things in MMP that seem to point in the direction of the circumstantial account, it is not a case she explicitly makes. Her own description of the difference made by divine command is very hard to understand: "[In a divine law theory of ethics] it really does add something to the description 'unjust' to say there is an obligation not to do it; for what obliges is the divine law—*as rules oblige in a game*" (MMP, 17–18; my emphasis).

What on earth can this mean? The bindingness of rules in a game looks very different in many ways from the bindingness of divine law, particularly if we are inclined to think of the matter, in line with the circumstantial account, in terms of reasons. To take the most obvious difference: that something is forbidden by the rules of some game gives us in itself *no* reason not to do that thing, whereas according to the relevant religious traditions, if something is forbidden by God (Yahweh, Allah), that gives us about as strong a reason for not doing it as anyone could ever hope to have for not doing anything.

It was the obscurity of this remark, among other things, that drove me toward the circumstantial account. Conversely, when I finally began to understand it, I came to see why the circumstantial account, while there is certainly something to it, was not in the end adequate as a characterization of the relevant difference made by divine command or, therefore, of what went wrong when the vocabulary of morality was introduced.

The inadequacy of the circumstantial account can be seen, however, without yet going into the meaning of Anscombe's mysterious comparison, which I will discuss later on. The fundamental problem with the circumstantial account is that, because it remains within the bounds of Aristotelian ethical necessity, it leaves out precisely the *command* (or *law*) element of divine command ethics. For imagine that the agent's circumstances were changed from the natural context of human life that characterizes, say, the virtue ethic of Aristotle not by the jurisdiction of a divine lawgiver, as on the Hebrew-Christian conception, but by some impersonal "natural" mechanism that somehow has the same upshot in terms of Aristotelian necessity: some maximally good consequence for those who act in accordance with the requirements of virtue, and a maximally bad consequence for those who do not. Or, alternatively, imagine that these posthumous consequences are credibly promised and threatened by some kind of superhuman gangster figure, merely because it fits in with *his* plans, which have nothing to do with the agent's good.

The circumstantial conception cannot distinguish these ethical predicaments from the Hebrew-Christian dispensation, since the "payoff structure" of the circumstances remains unchanged. The Aristotelian ethical necessities are identical: acting virtuously is required to secure this maximal good and avoid this maximal harm. But what makes divine law *law* is precisely what distinguishes it from any impersonal mechanism or the credible threats and promises of a gangster, and that is *legitimate authority*, or the *right to be obeyed*.

That this is an important essential feature of divine command comes out in its making possible the application of a number of new concepts of great ethical significance: *defiance*, for example, as expressed in the *non serviam* of Milton's Satan or the mutinous soldier, and which rejects a purported *right* to be obeyed; similarly *rebellion*; conversely, the genuine acknowledgment of authority, as opposed to the various personae of Caliban: terrified hatred, power worship, servile ingratiation, or gritted-teeth acknowledgment of merely natural necessity.

The reasons those who believed in the divine commands took themselves to have for acting in accordance with them cannot be understood entirely in terms of Aristotelian necessity, precisely because reasons for obeying commands are of a very distinctive kind: they essentially involve the thought that, in addition to any bad consequences of noncompliance, the command must be obeyed simply *because* it is a command, because its being a command as opposed to (for example) a threat is a matter of the one who issued it having a right to be obeyed. Someone who takes himself to be subject to an authority thereby takes himself to be guilty, if he refuses to comply with an order in the absence of any excusing conditions,[4] of a wrong of a very particular sort, namely, *disobedience*. We cannot think of disobedience simply as the result of going against some Aristotelian necessity, that is, as some kind of bad consequence incurred or good consequence forgone by refusal to comply; for the disobedience *is* the refusal to comply.

Once we see this, the possibility opens up of a very different way of thinking about the distinctive nature of divine command ethics by which it transforms the character of virtue ethics. For while a command's having been issued by an acknowledged authority certainly gives rise to a new kind of reason for compliance, this is derivative: the reasons only count as being of a new *kind* in virtue of a more fundamental innovation at the level of the *nature of the ethical necessity* by which the agent is now constrained. This is no longer the natural, Aristotelian necessity that attaches to that without which some good cannot be obtained or harm avoided. It is a new kind of necessity that is in an important sense *nonnatural*. If this is the relevant new feature of divine command ethics, then the real basis of Anscombe's charge of incoherence against the vocabulary of morality will be that it tries to preserve this distinctive *form of necessity* independently of the divine authority that alone can give rise to it, and that is therefore a condition of its intelligibility.

We will see that Anscombe's comparison of divine law to the rules of a game is an allusion to precisely this new, nonnatural necessity at the heart of divine command ethics, and so points to just this objection to the vocabulary of morality. Her elucidations of the comparison, in work subsequent to MMP, also make clear the point of calling this necessity *nonnatural*.

5.4 What's So Special about Divine Command? (II) The Generation of Nonnatural Deontic Necessity

The key to Anscombe's comparison between divine command and the rules of a game lies in subsequent papers of hers in which she discusses rules, contracts, rights, commands, and—above all—promises (Anscombe

1969, 1978b; cf. Anscombe 1976, 1978a). There is a special kind of modality that attaches to these institutions or practices, which cannot be understood in natural terms—that is, in terms of Aristotelian necessity. This nonnatural modality is philosophically very puzzling, as Hume was the first to point out. Anscombe discusses the issues in some detail in connection with promises, but essentially the same puzzles arise for commands and laws. There are two such puzzles that, in those latter cases, take the following form: (i) How is it possible for someone to put me under an obligation merely by telling me to do something? Normally, if someone tells me to do something and I refuse, I might be being uncooperative, but I am not being *disobedient*. How is the special obligation of obedience generated? The fact of the authority's attaching to this person when he speaks in this capacity is supposed to consist in *what is said* then restricting what I may do: for now, I must *either* do what he has said *or* be guilty of disobedience. In the relevant context, it is simply what the authority says that is supposed to impose this restriction; but how can it be part of the *meaning* of what is said that I must conform my behavior to *it,* on pain of being guilty of a distinctive kind of wrong? (ii) How is this obligation itself to be characterized without circularity? As I mentioned previously, to say that I am obliged to obey legitimate authority is to say that if I don't, I will be guilty of some *distinctive* wrong. What wrong? Why, as we have seen, the wrong of *disobedience*—which is to say, of disregarding legitimate authority? The mention of authority seems to be essential to characterizing the wrong—disobeying authority—but characterizing the wrong seems to be essential to an account of what authority is—a source of imperatives, noncompliance with which constitutes disobedience.

It is a great virtue of Anscombe's overlapping treatments of the cluster of questions of which these are a part that she made it very clear that they are much more puzzling than they had generally been thought to be, even by Hume, whose own solutions are clearly unsatisfactory. Her solution (which I shall not expound except in outline) gives a plausible account of how *coercive power* and the *utility of the practices* providing the context of the command play an essential role in the proceedings, as they surely do. I will summarize how her picture applies to commands, in a way that brings this out, since it will be important for our understanding of the distinctive conceptual shape of divine command ethics, and therefore of why the idea of a legislator is essential to it, so that any attempt to impose this shape on a secular ethic is inevitably quixotic.

It is important for the account that it describes the advent of the distinctive necessity in two separate stages, on the supposition, which the account itself makes plausible, that only in this way can the process be made intelligible. The account of the first stage sounds peculiar, because it posits as indispensable a kind of "prototype" necessity that is in an important sense *groundless*. One thing that hampers us in our understanding here is an assumption that everything must be intelligible to the practitioners *all at once*. But at the prototype stage, the only form of "nonnatural necessity" involved—that is, over and above coercion, which introduces a version of natural Aristotelian necessity—is that illustrated, in the case of a game, by my saying, "I say 'ping,' and you have to say 'pong'" (Anscombe 1969, 74). In the case of the first phase in the emergence of promising, it consists in the establishment of some special way of describing a future action—say, prefacing it with the exclamation "Bump!" or writing it in green ink—whose significance consists in the one who issued the description reliably foreseeing that he will incur criticism from others if he does not conform himself to it. But it is an important fact about this phase that there is no question about these others having a *right* to criticize, or of the criticism being *deserved*. For then our explanation would fall back again into circularity, since *right* and *desert* clearly belong to the family of normative concepts we are in the process of trying to understand:

> What I have sketched here is what Wittgenstein usefully and intelligibly called a "language-game," and we may say that it is a fact of nature that human beings very readily take to it. We can see at once that one whose "Bump" has been received *has* created *a* restriction for himself: namely on his possibilities of acting without danger of getting reproached, and pressed to act; and since it is inglorious to be reproached and annoying to be pressed, we can see that he has created for himself a reason for doing what he "bumped" to do, when there is any danger of detection if he does not. But this is not yet to say that he has created a restriction either on his possibilities of doing well (as opposed to *faring* well) or on his possibilities of acting without *deserving* reproach. For the content of the reproach is simply "you did not do what you bumped

to do" and nothing has yet been said to show why this is a reproach he needs take account of beyond the inconvenience attendant on incurring it. (Anscombe 1969, 71)

Anscombe does not indicate in comparable detail how this sort of story would go for authoritative command; but it is natural to suppose that what would there be analogous to this first stage would simply involve the threats and coercion that generate an Aristotelian necessity with respect to compliance, exactly as the natural mechanism or the all-powerful gangster generates such necessity in the cases I described earlier, to illustrate the inadequacy of the circumstantial account of divine command.

In the second and final phase (returning for now to the case of promising), the distinctive *obligation* to keep promises is generated via the Aristotelian necessity arising from the enormous utility of the as-yet-groundless practice:

[The language-game of "proto-promising"] is an instrument whose use is part and parcel of an enormous amount of human activity and hence of human good; of the supplying both of human needs and of human wants so far as the satisfactions of these are compossible. . . . Then not to "go along with it," in the sense of accepting the necessity expressed by "Now you've got to . . ." after one has given the sign, will tend to hamper the attainment of the advantages that the procedure serves. It may be asked: "But what is this necessity?" The answer is given only by describing the procedure, the language-game, which as far as concerns the "necessity" *expressed in it* does not differ from this one: "I say 'ping' and you have to say 'pong.'" . . . There is clearly no answer to "Why do I have to?" and so initially with the language-game: "You have to do it if you say Bump! I'll do it." But if the procedure has the role of an instrument in people's attainment of so many of the goods of common life, the necessity that people should both actually adopt the procedure . . . and also go along with [it] . . . is a necessity of a quite different sort: it is the necessity that Aristotle spoke of, by which something is called necessary if without it good cannot be attained. And hence it comes about that by the voluntary giving of a sign I can restrict my possibilities of acting *well* and hence it can lead to my deserving, as well as receiving, reproach. (Anscombe 1969, 74–75)

We might think of the overall picture as an extension of the familiar understanding of the groundlessness of such customs as driving on the left to cases that we are not used to thinking of as groundless at all. Thus, in the British Isles, for example, there is nothing *inherently* wrong with driving on the right, as there is inherently something wrong with murder; but once the custom is up and running, the derivative wrong of driving on the right is obvious. This is much harder to see in the case of promising, for although (on this account) it shares the "inherent groundlessness" of driving on the left, it does not share its *arbitrariness*. There seems to be nothing in the promising case that is analogous to the equally practicable alternative, in the driving case, of driving on the right. That it should be the custom to *break* one's promises is not even intelligible. The driving case encourages us to conflate groundlessness and arbitrariness; the case of promising, seen for what it is, shows that these features are importantly distinct.

Anscombe presents her account of promising as an instance of a more general account type, which can also be adapted for the cases of rules and rights. In the case of rights, this presumably amounts to treating the "You have to / must not [take this object, sit in this seat, kill this person]" that defines a right as playing the role of "You have to keep your promise [or 'do what you've bumped']" in the story about promising.

Thus, in the first instance, one is reproached or perhaps punished for not "respecting a right" even though there is no justification for this. We think of this as starting off as a groundless game. Take property rights: they begin as *purely* conventional. "You can't take that; that's *his*" is initially on a par with "You have to say 'Pong.'" *Then* the convention is seen to have great utility so that failure to play the game really counts as, for example, *theft*, and subject to *legitimate* censure. (Like the groundlessness of promising, the conventionality of systems of property rights tends to become invisible; see Donagan 1981, 1982.)

It is characteristic of the vocabulary of morality that its claim to a special sui generis status is partly bound up with the categorical form of its norms: *thou shalt* and *thou shalt not*—"forcing" and "stopping" modals, as Anscombe calls them (1978b). It is a further virtue of Anscombe's account of the nonnatural practical necessity generated by promising and related practices that, like Philippa Foot's (1972) comparison with the rules of etiquette, it helps us to see that this form tells us nothing about the kind of force the norms carry: there is nothing distinctively ethical about categorical requirements. Their categorical form is no basis for treating such requirements as different *in kind* from other, utterly mundane norms; in this regard, Anscombe's initially mystifying comparison with the rules of a game was quite apt. As Roger Teichmann puts it, "Just as you may not castle twice in chess, you may not take another's property without his consent: the same modal, 'may not,' occurs in both cases. It is the Aristotelian necessity of our having the institution of property that makes the second example a moral example, rather than any special 'moral' sense of the phrase 'may not.' (The stopping modals used in explaining property or promises are not a special 'moral' kind, any more than are the stopping modals used in explaining chess a special 'boardgame' kind)" (Teichmann 2008, ch. 3, sec. 3).

The Unintelligibility of Morality

In this way we arrive at an account of the practical concept of legitimate authority, since this is equivalent to *a right to be obeyed.*

The Hume-Anscombe account of promising as an irreducibly "nonnatural" phenomenon has of course been challenged, notably by Thomas Scanlon (1990). The whole issue seems to me to be extraordinarily vexed. Fortunately, I need not take a position on it here since, even if Scanlon and others are right that the institution of promising and the obligations to which it gives rise can be understood antecedently of human conventions, it does not seem plausible that the institution of *legitimate authority* can be understood in the same way. At any rate, I shall assume that it cannot.

Presumably, this style of account, in the case of institutions of legitimate authority, would go somewhat as follows. In the first phase, the commander issues an order and it is "part of the game" that its recipient does as he's told. He is liable to be reproached and perhaps punished if he does not comply; this phase is deontically indistinguishable from the threatening gangster or the natural mechanism mentioned earlier. But then the convention is seen to have great utility. And the substance of the idea of *disobedience* is this: noncooperation with the institution of commanding and complying tends to block access to the goods that institution makes available. But the disobedient person is reproached *for disobedience,* not for "blocking access to goods"—for the convention *is* to see *this* as wrong-doing; similarly with breaking promises. And so it must be: for the securing of the benefits partly depends on *not* seeing the obligation to obey commands (keep promises) in any particular instance as conditional on its securing any benefit in that instance. And this necessity, of regarding the fact of having promised, or the status of the one who commands, as the repository, as it were, of the obligation, combined with the convention of compliance's clearly not being *arbitrary,* inevitably tempts us into a kind of *obligation fetishism,* whereby we take what is conventional for natural. The conditional ground of Aristotelian necessity requires its own effacement; and by a process akin to transference we conceive a new, unconditional necessity: "*That* necessity which is the first one to have the awful character of *obligation,* is a tabu or sacredness which is annexed to this sort of instrument of human good," as Anscombe puts it. "It is like the sacredness of ambassadors and serves the same purpose" (1969, 75). No doubt these deceptive appearances play their part in smoothing the path toward the illusions of morality.

Thus the difference between the legitimate authority and the gangster consists in the transition to the second stage, whereby the person commanded accepts the right of the commander to command. He is still subject to coercion; yet it is not *mere* coercion.

This account gives a very clear sense to Anscombe's remark in MMP that "the concept of legislation requires superior power in the legislator" (2). There can be no hope of implementing stage one, whereby compliance is secured without the claim of any right, unless the commander has the coercive power to ensure compliance. This plays an *essential role* in the account, much as the reproach and "being pressed to act" on the part of other people in general is essential to the parallel account of the origin of promising.

None of this is to say that in any *particular case* of legitimate authority can we see two distinct stages in its emergence: the explanandum here is how the *concept* of legitimate authority can have arisen. There is no question of this evolution taking place in each instance, any more than we must suppose the analogous process whenever a promise is made. Thus, while the fascinating accounts in Genesis of how Abraham, Jacob, Moses, and others came to acknowledge God's identity and authority shed important light on the concepts of acknowledgment, authority, and indeed promising, the "nonnaturalistic" account of authority is prior to all this: it is rather an account of *what it was* that the patriarchs were acknowledging.

Morality, in the sense deemed objectionable, is supposed to be essentially distinct from any system of norms based on virtue as originally, that is, eudaimonistically, construed; equally, its special force is supposed to be essentially distinct from that attaching to divine command. Yet the *form* taken by supposedly *moral* norms is unmistakably a distinctive deontic modality that claims for itself a distinctive kind of binding authority. But outside the moral domain, the only instances we can find of such practical necessity, in terms of which we have to make sense of the moral case if it is to be made sense of at all, attach to such customary practices as rules of a game, promises, conventional rights, and the acknowledgment of a legitimate personal authority. Now, a good proportion of the norms called moral also belong to the virtue of justice; and many of these, in turn, pertain to the observance of such nonnatural obligations as are incurred in making promises and contracts, implicit or explicit. But the obligation in those cases, what is *owed,* is to the other party, to whom one is, as we say, *bound* by the agreement. The basis of these norms cannot plausibly be extended to cover the many purportedly moral precepts that give no appearance of grounding in custom, such as the prohibition on murder. That is, so long as God is out of the picture, there can be no hope of making out the ethically salient feature of murder as being the breaking of a covenant or disobedience to authority or anything of that kind. So the deontic linguistic forms of morality have no place. They do not misrepresent the ethical situation, for they don't represent any possible situation: they have no intelligible application.

6

Assessing "Modern Moral Philosophy"

6.1 Philosophy and Its History

In our time the study of philosophy and the study of its history increasingly diverge. Quite a few philosophers regard the history of philosophy (often with the interesting ad hoc exception of the history of early analytic philosophy) as having little more to do with their own activity than the history of physics has to do with the ongoing researches of the physicists. At the same time, the preoccupations of historians of philosophy are becoming more antiquarian. The meanings of the old texts must of course be discerned before the question of their truth can be framed. And sometimes that question does not arise; many philosophical ideas from the past are no longer live options for us, especially metaphysical doctrines that prove hostage to advances in scientific knowledge.

Still, there are plenty of ideas and doctrines going back even to the pre-Socratics, properly philosophical even by the standards of current debates, which, on plausible interpretations, cannot be ruled out immediately as unworthy of consideration, and on the face of it may well be loaded with philosophical interest. Of course we must always be on the lookout for the snares of anachronism: that is one of the main themes of MMP, and so of Part 1 of this book. All the same, historical distance does not make texts even from the distant past a priori inaccessible or irrelevant to our concerns. Yet the possible relevance of the texts to current debates seems to be of less and less interest to historians of philosophy in recent decades; and so the possible relevance of the work of the historians to current debates is not merely neglected by philosophers but, increasingly, *justifiably* neglected. Demand for stimulation from history shrinks further; supply dwindles accordingly.

In this climate, MMP provides an instructive example of the vital relevance of the history of philosophy, and of the history of culture more generally, to philosophical practice here and now. It was not really incongruous in its own time, in the way it is in ours, since Anscombe belonged to a generation of philosophers, many of them products of the peculiarly classics-oriented philosophical curriculum of Oxford, for whom it still went without saying that the Greeks could be a source of living philosophical insight (medieval philosophy, then as now, suffering scandalous neglect). But even in its own time, MMP stood out as an exceptionally bold illustration of the philosophical relevance of the distant past; for in essence it claimed that the philosophical ethicists of the last few centuries, largely through a deficient historical consciousness, had failed to realize that they had literally been talking nonsense. Of course, Anscombe's account has been challenged on all sides. Much of Part 1 of this book has been concerned to show that nearly all of these challenges fail, usually due to more or less basic misunderstandings of what she is really arguing. But it is important to realize that MMP would demonstrate the general point about the relevance of the past *even if Anscombe were wrong.* For even if the history of philosophy, religion, and culture more generally did *not* play out in the way Anscombe recounts, we cannot know this a priori, without inspecting the history. It *could* have happened this way; and if it *did,* then generations of ethicists have been barking up entirely the wrong tree. We cannot know in advance that something similar is not true of any number of other "current debates" in philosophy—especially in ethics, in which the central concepts have a particularly tangled and enduringly relevant history, but not only there. Any number of philosophers might be spending their time on landscape painting, when they should really be studying geology.

A Problem in MMP: Could There Be a Secular "Law Conception" of Ethics?

At the end of Chapter 5, I remarked that the deontic linguistic forms of morality have no intelligible application. This might look on the face of it like an outrageous a priori dismissal of all current metaethical theories, since they purport to give substance to, precisely, the authority claimed for moral norms. But to understand my words this way would be to ignore one of the main argumentative burdens of Chapters 3 and 4, that the predicate *moral,* in the relevant use, is unintelligible as the bearer of an *intension* (hyperintension). Contractualist and other construals of morality are not shown to be pointless by this finding; it is just that they must instead be understood as construals of *something else.* My favored candidate would be *requirements of the virtue of justice* or, equivalently, *norms structuring the social operation of practical reason.*

Anscombe herself seems to take a harder line. When she says that, in the context of a divine law theory of ethics, "it really does add something to the description [of an action as] 'unjust' to say that there is an obligation not to do it" (MMP, 17), the clear implication is that, *outside* such a conception, it adds nothing at all. But at this point her picture is rather murky and smudged, and some of its lines need to be reconstructed. She seems to confirm the idea that there is no place for a distinctive, ethically sovereign "ought" of any kind outside of divine command conceptions in her very definition of "law conceptions of ethics": "To have a *law* conception of ethics is to hold that what is needed for conformity with the virtues failure in which is the mark of being bad *qua* man . . . , is required by divine law. Naturally it is not possible to have such a conception unless you believe in God as a lawgiver; like Jews, Stoics and Christians" (6).

But as we saw earlier (section 3.1), this is flatly inconsistent with something we read a few pages later: "Those who recognize the origins of the notions of 'obligation' and of the emphatic, 'moral,' *ought,* in the divine law conception of ethics, but who reject the notion of a divine legislator, sometimes look about for the possibility of retaining a law conception without a divine legislator. This search, I think, has some interest in it" (MMP, 13).

Anscombe's interest turns out to be somewhat limited. After dismissing various candidates, she remarks, "Just possibly, it might be argued that the use of language which one makes in the ordinary conduct of life amounts in some sense to giving the signs of entering into various contracts. If anyone had this theory, we should want to see it worked out. I suspect that it would be largely formal" (MMP, 14).

The difficulty here, however, does not concern her take on the prospects for contractualist metaethics in particular, but rather her acknowledgment of even the conceptual possibility of a secular law conception of ethics at all, given her definition back on page 6.

If we are operating without a divine legislator, how could there be any prospect of retaining a law conception of ethics if that is supposed to be distinguished—as it seemed to be by definition—from a virtue conception? If the point of a virtue conception is egoistic eudaimonism, in keeping with the rejection of the moral vocabulary, mustn't its associated reasons simply be the reasons we have *anyway*? And if ethical norms could be derived (Anscombe's pessimism notwithstanding) from nature, or from some conception of an implicit contract, would not adherence to those norms just take its place among the reasons we have according to whatever is the correct virtue conception? If such adherence does not contribute to our *eudaimonia,* we are surely left with no answer to Anscombe's question, "What if I don't?" We have already seen that what distinguishes a "law conception" must be more than just exceptionless precepts, and that Anscombe herself sees some such precepts—the one forbidding, for example, judicial murder—as inseparable from the virtue of justice. Norms deriving from *contract* seem especially directly to belong to a virtue conception, since abiding by contracts will presumably be central to anything she will recognize as justice, so that such norms will be only as compelling as the reasons supplied by that virtue. I cannot see how, by her lights, it could "add something to the description 'unjust' to say that there is an obligation not to do [some action]" (MMP, 17), if that obligation is supposed to have its origin in a contract, however implicit or abstract. But if no additional force or meaning is procured by speaking of obligation or "ought," in what sense do we have a "law conception"—even if this is *not* by definition supposed to be distinguished from virtue?

Ethics of Virtue and of Divine Command Not Really Distinct

It is not at all clear that the "virtue / law" distinction between ethical conceptions goes all the way down. We saw that a full-fledged divine command conception yields ethical norms with a distinctive logical profile, which depend for their very intelligibility on the reality of a divine legislator with the requisite coercive power. This was the real basis of Anscombe's critique of the vocabulary of morality: it purports to express norms with just this logical profile, but in a "version" that violates these preconditions of their own intelligibility. But can we not maintain, consistently with all this, that the necessity attaching to divine command can be accommodated within an overarching "ethic of virtue"? After all, obedience to divine command is *itself* central to virtue—piety, primarily, but also often courage, as Socrates brings out especially clearly in Plato's *Apology* (28d6–29a4), and no doubt many others too, in varying proportions. And what I called previously "the most intelligible reasons we could imagine" for doing God's will provide the needed connection with *eudaimonia*.

It is true that obedience to divine command as such involves a kind of subjugation of the will, so that the obedient subject cannot conceive of her own reasons for compliance as entirely rooted in piety, understood as just one more virtue conducing to *eudaimonia*. Action expressing this kind of piety is not so much an exercise of autonomous choice as a renunciation of it. Its characteristic form of reason is not (as Socrates sometimes seems to suppose) "because it is pious, and so virtuous, and therefore serves my interest," but simply "because *He* commands it."

However, something similar is true of that part of justice that consists of fidelity to promises and observance of customary rights. It is characteristic of the virtuous person that, under normal circumstances, the fact of a promise is a *fully sufficient* reason for the action that keeps it. Someone who, when asked why he kept a promise, would trace a chain of reasons back to the benefits to himself of cultivating virtues like honesty and justice would be entertaining, as Williams might put it (1981, 18), several thoughts too many. (In fact the same goes for the virtues generally: only in exceptional cases does a specification of the relevant virtue enter into the reasons one would give for acting virtuously.) And if, as we have been intermittently assuming, Anscombe's account of the normativity involved in promising and rights is along the right lines, then the form of practical necessity involved in promises, and the form involved in customary rights, have much in common with that involved in obedience to legitimate authority: they are all to be understood as species of "nonnatural" obligation, dependent for their intelligibility on prior frameworks of language-involving beliefs and practices and, in different ways, betokening a kind of *binding of the will to a certain rule.* That is, the deontic modality, as I called it, that characterizes the ethical as such on a divine command conception is a species belonging to the same genus as other species that play a prominent role in any ethic whatever.

In short, the parts of Anscombe's view that really matter fit together much less awkwardly if we simply drop any supposedly deep distinction between law-based and virtue-based conceptions of ethics. At least, I cannot see what is lost, except gratuitous confusion, if we suppose that *all* conceptions are ultimately virtue based, that among those that involve exceptionless norms, an important *species* of these is distinguished by the norms being commandments of God, this species *alone* comprising all and only the various versions of the law conception, so that the search for a secular law conception has *no* interest in it. The problem with the moral vocabulary is then that its "obligations" mark it as aspiring to the status of a law conception, but this is made into nonsense by those "obligations" being supposed essentially to float free of any legislative source, human or divine. But (and this is the important point here) the form of practical necessity to which "moral requirements" aspire, and to which commands of God, if there are any, attain, are *not* distinctive of a kind of ethic radically different from one based on virtue: for the form involved in obedience to authority is kin to those involved in the ethically inescapable phenomena of contract, promise, and customary right.

There is more than one layer of falsifying simplification, then, underlying the standard reception of MMP. Much of Part 1 of this book has been concerned to explain why Anscombe did not think that morality was all very well before its "basis in divine command" was removed. But, independently of that misconception, many ethicists still seem to think that (leaving consequentialism aside) ethical theories can be divided into "law conceptions" and "virtue conceptions," each with their distinctive accounts of ethical reasons and of the form of ethical norms. On this picture, Anscombe's main objection to morality was that it tried to retain a form of practical necessity characteristic of *law,* but without the divine legislator that was a condition of its intelligibility; we should abandon law conceptions, if we want a secular ethics, in favor of a theory of virtue. But now we can see that that is also a misrepresentation—of Anscombe's critique, to an extent, but also, more importantly, of the actual conceptual terrain. What was wrong with the vocabulary of morality—with the idea of a secular law conception—was not that it persisted in imposing on ethics a form of practical necessity characteristic of *binding rules.* For that form is also to be found in other, ubiquitous ethical phenomena, like rights and promises. Nor did the problem with morality lie in its allegiance to a law conception whose *rejection of an ethic of virtue* only made sense when its laws were thought of as divinely promulgated. For the Jews and the Christians and the Muslims did *not* reject the ethics of virtue. In the first place, they could quite consistently maintain an ethic of virtue alongside their divine law conception, as Aquinas did, overdetermining much of the nonceremonial part of what they took to have been commanded, and perhaps augmenting the catalogue of virtues with distinctively religious ones, as the Christians did with faith, hope, and love. But second, even in their religious ethic, they just subscribed to a very lopsided version of a virtue conception, on which the whole of ethics, in a way, could be subsumed under the virtue of piety. Similarly, what Anscombe in an unguarded moment envisaged as a possible secular, contractualist "law conception without a divine legislator" would really be a conception on which all would be subsumed under the virtue of fidelity to contract.

6.4 The Limits of Virtue Ethics

As I have said, the difficult questions about ethical reasons cannot simply be got rid of by switching to a secular virtue conception: it is effectively exchanged for hard questions about what sort of conduct the virtues, construed eudaimonistically, require. Thus we are faced with Callicles and his ilk, who say that if virtues really do benefit their possessors, then the *real* virtue of justice must comprise the qualities that enable one to dominate one's fellows and expropriate their goods. Here we have to acknowledge that Anscombe's recommendation, that we simply abandon *moral* as a sui generis category, while it might liberate us from a set of powerful, unconscious ethical fantasies, and so put us on the path of undeceived ethical inquiry, does not advance us on that path as much as an inch, if our intended destination is a philosophical vindication of norms that are, collectively speaking, practically necessary.[1] Unlike Socrates in the *Gorgias,* she doesn't want to argue with Callicles—he shows a corrupt mind! Rather, like Socrates in the *Republic,* she restricts the philosophical constituency to the uncorrupted—the heirs of Glaucon and Adeimantus.

"It is clear that a good man is a just man" (MMP, 16)—this has to be an invocation of what Callicles called conventional justice. So Anscombe supposes that the other-regarding requirements of justice as *traditionally* conceived are no less essential to it than its benefiting its possessor. Yet she also finds a "big gap in philosophy" here, which leaves us unable to give "a general account of the concept of virtue and of the concept of justice" (16), and which cannot be filled until we have "equipped" ourselves with a "sound philosophy of psychology" (4)—surely a vast undertaking, as she is well aware, and one whose prospects look even dimmer today than they must have done in 1958. The gap itself appears where there should be a *"proof* that an unjust man is a bad man" (4–5; my emphasis)—bad, of course, simply qua man. And yet, as the mark of an "uncorrupted mind," *practical* confidence in the conclusion cannot possibly be hostage to such a difficult and uncertain philosophical task as the provision of the proof by which it is established—it is *clear* that a good man is a just man. A proof is required, it seems, even though to demand it for the sake of *practical* certainty is to out oneself as corrupted beyond the reach of any ethical argument worth engaging in. As with Bertrand Russell and Alfred North Whitehead's extraordinarily elaborate derivations of the simplest theorems of arithmetic, there is a real question what the point of such a proof would be. I do not mean to suggest, in either case, that the question might not have a perfectly good answer. But it is at least not obvious why anyone inclined to Anscombe's brusque way with serious (that is, Calliclean) ethical skepticism should not rest content with Philippa Foot's one-time vision of the fight "against inhumanity and oppression" as fought not by conscripts of Reason but by volunteers (Foot 1972, 315). More to the point, it is even less clear that we don't *have to* settle for this.

To secure for such a concept a philosophical vindication as opposed to a merely practical one, we would have to show no less than that the conflict between what benefits me and your interest in not being treated unjustly is always, ultimately, only apparent. It is not clear that any amount of further *philosophical* work could do that for us.

PART TWO

No Self: "The First Person" (1975)

If the sense of a name were something subjective, then the sense of the proposition in which the name occurs would also be something subjective, and the thought one person connects with this proposition would be different from the thought another connects with it; a common store of thoughts . . . would be impossible.

GOTTLOB FREGE

"But surely the word 'I' in the mouth of a man refers to the man who says it; it points to himself; and very often a man who says it actually points to himself with his finger." But it was quite superfluous to point to himself.

LUDWIG WITTGENSTEIN

7

The Circularity Problem for Accounts of "I" as a Device of Self-Reference

Anscombe's "Circularity Argument" against
the Possibility of Explaining "I" as a Device
of Self-Reference

In "The First Person" (Anscombe 1975; hereafter FP), drawing on Geach (1957) and Hector-Neri Castañeda (1966), Anscombe argued that the first-person pronoun "I" cannot be elucidated as the device that a person uses to refer to herself, since any such account either fails to capture "I" or presupposes it. She pointed out that it is possible to refer to oneself without realizing it: " 'When John Smith spoke of John Horatio Auberon Smith (named in a will perhaps) he was speaking of himself, but he did not know this' . . . [That's a possible situation]" (FP, 46). "I" certainly can't be correctly used to refer to oneself in cases like that. The objection is obvious and unanswerable, but the equally obvious emendation is to add the condition that the "I" user refer *knowingly and intentionally* to herself. This is where things start to get interesting. Anscombe said that this line won't work either: "For did not Smith knowingly and intentionally speak of Smith? Was not the person he intended to speak of—Smith? and so *was* not the person he intended to speak of—himself?" (46).

The reply here looks obvious too, to anyone who takes a standard line on the behavior of referring expressions in indirect discourse; but Anscombe was convinced that that stock response wouldn't work here, and for a reason that makes the problem suddenly look a lot harder:

It may be said: "Not in the relevant sense. We all know you can't substitute every designation of the object he intended to speak of and keep
the statement about his intention true." But that is not the answer unless
the reflexive pronoun itself is a sufficient indication of the way the object is specified. And that is something the ordinary reflexive pronoun
cannot be. Consider: "Smith realizes (fails to realize) the identity of an
object he calls 'Smith' with himself." If the reflexive pronoun there is
the ordinary one, then it specifies for us who frame or hear the sentence, an object whose identity with the object he calls "Smith" Smith
does or doesn't realize: namely the object designated by our subject word
"Smith." But that does not tell us what identity Smith himself realizes
(or fails to realize). For, as Frege held, there is no path back from reference to sense; any object has many ways of being specified, and in this
case, through the peculiarity of the construction, we have succeeded
in specifying an object (by means of the subject of our sentence) without
specifying any conception under which *Smith's* mind is supposed to
latch onto it. For we don't want to say "Smith does not realize the identity of Smith with Smith."

We only have to admit a failure of specification of the intended
identity, if we persist in treating the reflexive in "He doesn't realize the
identity with himself" as the ordinary reflexive. In practice we have
no difficulty at all. We know what we mean Smith doesn't realize. It is:
"I am Smith." But if that is how we understand that reflexive, it is not
the ordinary one. It is a special one which can be explained only in
terms of the first person.

If that is right, the explanation of the word "I" as "the word which
each of us uses to speak of himself" is hardly an explanation! (FP,
46–47)

A page earlier, she had introduced this "peculiar reflexive": "It is the
reflexive called by grammarians the 'indirect reflexive' and there are languages (Greek, for example) in which there is a special form for it" (45).

So according to Anscombe, any account of "I" in terms of self-reference[1]
either will be inadequate, because it will include in its scope varieties of
self-reference other than that distinctive of the correct use of "I," or, in
seeking to rule out these wrong sorts of self-reference, will end up having
to invoke the special sort of self-reference, distinctive of "I," it was supposed

to explain. This argument of Anscombe's I will refer to as *the circularity argument,* and I will call the problem it raises for standard accounts of "I" as a device of self-reference *the circularity problem.*

In the years since Anscombe posed the problem, which she herself deemed fatal to the prospect of giving an illuminating account of how "I" refers, Lucy O'Brien, Gareth Evans, and Christopher Peacocke, among others, have proposed solutions to it. The circularity problem does not often show up on the menu of live philosophical issues nowadays, so perhaps one or another of these solutions has been widely accepted. In this part of the book I argue that prominent solutions in the literature do not work. For all that these writers have said, Anscombe's circularity problem is still with us. Another solution, proposed by Ian Rumfitt, turns out to be something of an exception. His account of the "I" user's intention by which first-personal self-reference is to be defined is *not,* so far as I can see, vulnerable to Anscombe's circularity argument. The account essentially relies, however, on a construal of reflexive pronouns as nonreferential, and a thought experiment of A. N. Prior strongly suggests that there is no nonarbitrary way of resisting an extension of this construal to the first-person pronoun itself. Since Anscombe's chief purpose in constructing the circularity argument was to support the main thesis of her paper that "I" is not a referring expression, and Rumfitt's chief purpose in trying to evade that argument was to rebut that thesis, he wins the battle—if he does—at the cost of losing the war.

Clearly, Anscombe's circularity argument depends crucially on the distinction between the ordinary and the indirect reflexive. It has become controversial among linguists whether there is such a pronoun as the indirect reflexive at all.[2] I will raise the issue in the course of discussing the views of Rumfitt, who expresses doubts about the distinction, but actually seems required by his position to deny it outright. I will assume the distinction in my discussion of the other authors, who do not question it themselves.

The Depth of the Circularity Problem

If Anscombe's circularity really does vitiate the standard accounts of "I," it runs rather deeper than may at first appear. Even writers who are explicitly addressing Anscombe's argument are apt, in the course of trying to *set out* the problems, to make assertions that, innocent as they sound, cannot be acquitted of fatal ambiguity until that argument has already been dealt with. A recent example is provided by Peacocke in his book *Truly Understood* (2008).

Peacocke sets himself the task of showing that the "I" user's special knowledge that he is a "self-referrer," and other crucial features of first-personal self-reference, can be explained entirely by appeal to the fundamental reference rule for "I," that it denote its user (speaker or thinker). This special knowledge is expressed in (and only in) what Peacocke calls "fully self-conscious *I*-thoughts": "A fully self-conscious use of *I* in thought is one in which the thinker knows he is referring to himself, without drawing on any special information about the case" (2008, 79).

So, for example, if someone knows he is the Chairman of the Company and thinks "It's quite right that the Chairman of the Company be well paid," this is not fully self-conscious thought even though he knows he is thinking about himself*, because his knowledge that he is thinking about himself* depends on the "special information" that he* is the Chairman of the Company. In fully self-conscious thought, one knows one is thinking about oneself* simply by virtue of what is involved in normal conscious judgment, and of one's grasp of the concepts involved in the judgment.

In my paraphrase, I have included asterisks as marks of indirect reflexive pronouns,[3] since this is clearly the meaning Peacocke intends, even though his text gives no such indications; and therein lies the problem.

For of course our subject knows simply by virtue of what's involved in normal conscious judgment, and of his grasp of the concepts involved in the judgment he is making, that he is thinking about *the Chairman of the Company*. The Anscombe point is that it follows that he knows, simply by virtue of what's involved in normal conscious judgment, and of his grasp of the concepts involved in the judgment he is making, that he is thinking about *himself* (ordinary reflexive). For it is a key lemma of the circularity argument that when *himself* is the ordinary reflexive, it picks up the reference of the preceding "he," *without giving any indication of the mode of presentation under which the thinker is conceiving of himself.*

So according to the circularity argument, Peacocke is presupposing "I" (because he is presupposing the indirect reflexive) even in his initial account of what fully self-conscious *I*-thoughts *are.* But if one already understands the special mode of self-reference (if such there be) involved in the use of "I," presumably one *already* understands what "fully self-conscious *I*-thoughts" are. But the special epistemic features of first-personal self-reference were supposed to be explained in part by appeal to such thoughts.

The conditions that one must know oneself to be a self-referrer *simply by virtue of what is involved in normal conscious judgment and of one's grasp of the concepts involved in the judgment one is making* are arriving too late on the scene to effect the necessary disambiguation, for those conditions are already met by our subject's knowledge that he is thinking about *the Chairman of the Company,* and his thinking about the Chairman of the Company *is* a way of thinking about himself and, further, his *knowledge* that he is thinking about the Chairman of the Company is, in a way, knowledge that he's thinking about himself. So the case fits the letter of Peacocke's account of fully self-conscious *I*-thought: our subject, *simply by virtue of what is involved in normal conscious judgment and of his grasp of the concepts involved in the judgment he is making,* does know that he is thinking about himself. The problem is that he does not know, simply by virtue of what's involved in normal conscious judgment and of his grasp of the concepts involved in the judgment he is making, that he is thinking about himself*—he does have this further knowledge, but it depends on the "special information" that he* is the Chairman of the Company. Anscombe's circularity point, adapted to the case, is that we can't explain what it is for him to fail to have knowledge that meets the stated conditions, that he is thinking about *himself*,* without appealing to a prior understanding of "I." For the explanation is that although he has, in a way, knowledge, which meets the conditions, that he is thinking about himself, nevertheless he is not, subject to those conditions (that is, absent his further knowledge that he* is the Chairman of the Company), in a position to say or think, "I am thinking about *myself*"; and his being in a position to say or think *that* is what matters in fully self-conscious *I*-thoughts.

As long as the circularity argument goes unrefuted, furthermore, no specification of the "special information" relevant to any such example, such as the "special information . . . that [the thinker] is Chairman of the Company" (Peacocke 2008, 78), can be relied on to specify the information Peacocke intends, without a disambiguation that again makes essential appeal to an unexplained, distinctively first-personal (and surely, by

Peacocke's criteria, "fully self-conscious") self-reference. For according to the argument, in the last analysis, the only specification truly immune to misinterpretation is this: information our thinker is in a position to express in the judgment *I am Chairman of the Company*.

Similarly, Peacocke writes that fully self-conscious uses of "I" generate a norm of truth—that her thought *I am F* is true only if she herself* is F—knowledge of which puts the thinker "in a position to know that she should judge *I am F* only if she herself is F" (2008, 79). But if the circularity argument is sound, this is almost entirely vacuous: the norm cannot permit Smith to assert, "I have inherited a lot of money," merely because he has learned that John Horatio Auberon Smith, of whose identity with himself* he has not the slightest inkling, has inherited a lot of money. The Anscombe point, again, is that a thinker's knowing that she *herself** is F is *logically equivalent* to her being in a position to judge "I am F." What Peacocke claims the speaker is in a position to know, on the basis of fully self-conscious "I" use, boils down to this: that she should judge *I am F* only if she takes herself to be in a position to judge *I am F*.

Further, in clarifying the challenge he has set himself, Peacocke writes, "The account must explain how it is that a thinker of a first-person thought knows that he is a self-referrer, in the sense that he . . . knows that he has the property λx [x's use of I refers to x]" (2008, 81). The lambda expression is adapted from Evans's attempt to avoid the circularity problem in characterizing the "I" user's intention (Evans 1982, 258–259; see later discussion), but its use here is futile if, as the circularity argument implies, our only way of ensuring there is no misinterpretation is to specify that the knowledge in question must of its nature be expressible by our self-referrer in the judgment *I have the property λx [x's use of "I" refers to x]*.

Of course, Peacocke is not here proposing an explanation of "I" ab initio as a device of self-reference, and so a fortiori he is not vulnerable to the charge of circularity Anscombe makes against those who do propose such explanations. But he certainly is trying to say what "fully self-conscious *I*-thoughts" are. We have shown, by an uncontroversial extension of Anscombe's (admittedly controversial) argument, that Peacocke's attempt to say what these thoughts are presupposes a prior understanding of, precisely, certain fully self-conscious *I*-thoughts as such. So it seems fair to say that in supposing, as he clearly does, that his characterization is informative, Peacocke is assuming, wittingly or not, that Anscombe's argument is unsound. Yet, puzzlingly, he conceives part of his own discussion of fully self-conscious *I*-thoughts as consisting in critical scrutiny of just that position of Anscombe's, that "I" cannot be explained as a word each person uses to refer to himself, for which her main argument is the very one his exposition so conspicuously ignores, in the sense of presupposing, without responding to it or even remarking on it, that it is unsound.[4]

8

Is the Fundamental Reference Rule for "I" the Key to Explaining First-Person Self-Reference?

8.1 O'Brien

Lucy O'Brien puts forward an account of "I" she believes avoids Anscombe's dilemma: it rules out the wrong sorts of self-reference, but without circular appeal to "I"-type reference, or to anything, such as the indirect reflexive, that presupposes it:

> Once it is appreciated that "I" is used *as* a device of reflexive reference or self-reference, that is, that it is used as a term that is understood to be governed by the self-reference rule, we can come to see how that rule is sufficient to deliver the meaning of "I" without involving any straightforward circularity. The rule is sufficient because a subject who uses "I" (understood as a term that refers to the person who uses it) will inevitably succeed in self-referring self-consciously. She will do so because of the fact that a subject who is engaged in producing an utterance, does so self-consciously: A subject knows that she, herself is using a term when she is. Giving an account of how she knows this is another matter. The point for now is that the rule is not circular since it states only that "I" is a device of reflexive self-reference, not that it is a device of self-conscious self-reference. The rule that "I" is a device each one uses to refer to themselves (where "themselves" is read neutrally) is such that if "I" is understood and used in accord with that rule, then it will *in fact* be the case that it is a term each person uses to refer to themselves in the first person way. It is, as it were, the pragmatics of our use of "I"

that provides us with the element that Anscombe feared would render the rule either insufficient or circular. She seems to have thought that that element would be missing if it were absent from the specification of the rule and would be present only if it were included in the specification of the rule. We have come to see that the required element need not be part of the rule, but is rather something that a user of the rule can bring to bear when they use the rule. That required element is: the knowledge that a subject has that they themselves are using a term when they are. (1994, 279–280)

While Anscombe focused on accounts of "I" in terms of the rule that each person use it (knowingly and intentionally) to refer to herself, O'Brien's account defines "I" in terms of the pattern of use that will *in fact* ensue if everyone uses "I" with the intention of conforming to the rule.

I seem to discern two accounts of the rule in what O'Brien says.

(1) She more often supposes that it states "that 'I' is a device each one uses to refer to themselves (where 'themselves' is read neutrally)"; first-person reference is supposed to follow from everyone knowing this. Even if this is not what she intends, it is a suggestion worth looking at: might it be that, if everyone *knows* that the rule for "I" is that each person (each speaker) use it to refer to herself, then each person must intend to use "I" to refer to *herself**? One way of understanding her remarks about the speaker is as giving support to this account: the rule is that the *speaker* use "I" to refer to herself; when one speaks, one cannot fail to know that one *is* the speaker, and so one cannot fail to know that one's uses of "I" refer to oneself*.

(2) At other points, however, she seems to envisage that it amounts to a requirement that "I" be used to refer to *the speaker* (namely, of the word "I"). This may look similar to (1) but, as we shall see, it is very different. Since no one can fail to know that they themselves are using a term when they are, "unwitting" self-reference seems impossible on this specification of the referent, so it is supposed to suffice for first-person self-reference.

We shall examine O'Brien's two proposals separately; we shall see that neither of them determines first-person reference.

On the first proposal, the idea seems to be that the problem cases of "unwitting" self-reference can be excluded not by the content of the rule alone but by the stipulation that each user of "I" intends to use it in accordance with the rule, that is, to use it to refer to herself (ordinary reflexive).

This proposal, however, does not succeed in determining a rule at all. The ordinary reflexive ("'themselves' . . . read neutrally") does not differ from the indirect reflexive by indicating some different way the speaker conceives the referent. The ordinary reflexive, rather, differs from the indirect one in, "through the peculiarity of the construction," not indicating the way in which the speaker conceives the referent *at all*. Account (1) therefore states a condition met by an infinite number of rules, one for each way in which the referent of "I" may be specified, and one of which is the rule given in account (2).

But without the indirect reflexive, we can't stipulate that the rule not be formulated in a way that makes the self-reference it requires unwitting and so not first-personal. "Use 'I' to refer to J. H. A. Smith" (Smith still being ignorant of the identity of J. H. A. Smith and himself*) is an impeccable example of a rule that requires Smith to use "I" to refer to himself. It does not help that the rule applies to the speaker and one always knows one is the speaker. Smith's guarantee that he always knows when is referring to J. H. A. Smith is of no help if he doesn't realize that J. H. A. Smith is himself*.

O'Brien cannot insist that the promulgated rule be "Use 'I' to refer to yourself": "yourself" *means* something the addressee can only understand as "myself." There are as many other formulations that will do the job as there are ways of specifying Smith, and he will not recognize himself* in the vast majority of these.

Can O'Brien's first account be saved by appeal to the generality of the rule? Obviously the rule "Use 'I' to refer to J. H. A. Smith" only yields self-reference when "Smith" follows it, and there doesn't seem to be any circularity involved in requiring that the rule be given the same formulation for all speakers: *each* person is to use "I" to refer to *xyz,* where each speaker's understanding of *xyz* determines as referent someone who happens to be herself. But here too very many referring expressions can take the place of *xyz.*

There may remain a strong temptation to suppose that "Each person is to use 'I' to refer to himself," where "himself" is an ordinary reflexive, *could* be a rule (as opposed to a rule schema), and even a rule that may serve as the basis for capturing "I." Although "himself" cannot by itself determine how each person conceives of himself in using the term to refer to himself, isn't O'Brien right that the knowledge that the rule operates *as a rule* will ensure that "I" gets used in the right way? If I know that *A* is using a term to refer to herself, my ignorance of the way in which *A* conceives of the referent (and therefore of whether *A* realizes that the referent is herself*) leaves my knowledge, that the referrer and the referent are one and the same person, entirely intact. If I know that *each* person is to use "I" to refer to herself, don't I know enough to know that in my case too I must use it to refer to myself*, without needing to inquire about the conception under which everyone else refers to herself in using the term? If I know of the identity of referrer and referent in every other case, how can I avoid knowing that my using the term in the same way requires this identity in my own case too?

This thought is nevertheless an illusion. If I am conceiving of the rule as "Each person is to use 'I' to refer to himself," and reading "himself" in such a way that I can infer straight off that *my* following the rule requires me to refer to myself*, then "himself" as it occurs in the rule is *already* an indirect reflexive. Even if I know that the rule requires everyone else to use "I" to refer to themselves, I cannot know what my following the same rule consists in unless I understand the rule in precisely the way that the ordinary reflexive precludes. From the fact that each person should use "I" to refer to herself, I can only infer that *I* should use "I" to refer to *myself** if a certain possibility is being excluded: this is the possibility that each person should use "I" to refer to herself merely because she should use "I" to refer to someone, conceived in a specific way, who in each case *turns out to be* herself; on this possibility it remains an open question whether what the rule determines as the referent of *my* use of "I" is in fact myself, and a fortiori whether this is someone I know to be myself*. The exclusion of this possibility is what it is to use "herself" as an indirect reflexive. So long as it is an ordinary reflexive, then even if I do know that the rule requires every other speaker to refer to (someone who is in fact) herself, I cannot know that *my* following the same rule will require me to refer to myself* unless I have first checked that the conception under which each other person is referring to herself is one that, in my case too, requires me to refer to myself*. This point, I hope, will become clearer through illustration later.

Returning now to the requirement that the self-reference rule be given the same formulation for all speakers, upon closer inspection it is not at all clear that it does not already involve the account in circularity—unless the rule be something like "'I' designates the speaker," which we have postponed for a separate examination. For it is hard to see how there could be any other reference rule formulated in the same way for everyone that still determined in the case of each speaker that she refer to herself, unless the rule itself made use of some indexical expression that presupposes "I" (for example, "Each person is to use 'I' to refer to whoever casts her* shadow"). Thus it looks as though account (1) is imposing a condition that could not be fulfilled without presupposing "I." But for now let us assume for the sake of argument that a uniform rule could determine self-reference without such a presupposition.

Even granted this assumption, however, the account will not work. For suppose now that everyone is her own worst enemy. Then the rule "Each person is to use 'I' to refer to her own worst enemy" qualifies as a rule requiring each person to use 'I' to refer to herself. But now suppose in addition that no one realizes she is her own worst enemy and, furthermore, that no one has any definite view about who her own worst enemy is. Under the rule that each person use "I" to refer to her own worst enemy, each person will now conceive of the referent of "I" as her own worst enemy, whoever that should happen to be. Since it happens to be herself, each will now use 'I' to refer to herself, but this will not be first-person reference.

Perhaps one might object that this is too degenerate a case of reference, on the ground that the speaker can give no information about who she has in mind as the referent of "I" except what is already given in the description by which the reference is fixed.[1] But now suppose that instead of having no conception of who her own worst enemy is, each person has her own conviction about who her own worst enemy is. Each person identifies the object of her conviction by some name—a different object, and a different name, in each case. In every case, however, the speaker stands to that name in the same semantic and epistemic relation as Smith bears to "J. H. A. Smith" in Anscombe's example: it is in fact a name of herself, but she has no idea it designates herself*. She might nevertheless know quite a lot about this person, to the extent that she is struck by how much she* has in common with her. Of course, in knowing a lot about this person, she thinks she thereby knows a lot about her own worst enemy—

and she is right. Her use of this name and the associated description cannot be impugned as borderline cases of reference. She really is referring to herself when she uses "I" with the intention of conforming to the rule that each person use it to refer to her own worst enemy. But since by hypothesis this is a rule that each person use "I" to refer to herself, her usage, and that of all the other speakers, fits O'Brien's account (1) of "I." But none of these people refers to herself in the right way.

Finally, a defender of account (1) might protest that we have so far ignored the crucial role played by each person's knowledge that the rule is the same for everyone. The idea was that each person knows that the rule requires each person to use "I" to refer to herself. So let us suppose that, as before, each person is her own worst enemy, and that each has her own conviction as to who her own worst enemy is; each person refers to this person, the object of her conviction, using an expression that, unbeknownst to her, designates herself. But now suppose further that each person knows with respect to every *other* speaker what she is ignorant of in her own case, namely, that each of them is her own worst enemy. So every speaker is aware that the uniform rule "Each person is to use 'I' to refer to her own worst enemy" in fact requires each person, including herself*, to refer to herself, and, accordingly, each speaker does use "I" to refer to herself, in conformity with the uniform rule. But no one is using "I" to effect first-person self-reference, for no one uses it with the intention of referring to *herself**. Again, that "a subject who is engaged in producing an utterance, does so self-consciously" will of course not avail the account, since knowing that the speaker is oneself* only suffices for knowing that the referent is oneself* if one knows that the referent is the speaker.

Let us turn, then, to the particular version of account (1) given in account (2). At some points, we saw, O'Brien seems to envisage that the rule specifies the referent of "I" as the speaker (namely, the speaker of these very words). This rather different account of "I" would then run:

"I . . ." is the device each person uses with the intention of conforming to the rule that "I . . ." refer to the speaker (of those very words).

"The speaker (of those very words)" as it occurs in the rule must of course indicate the way in which the referent is to be conceived. If the words are construed in a *de re* manner, so that the rule gives no such indication, this account collapses into the one already considered, since "the speaker (of these very words)" will mean the same as the ordinary reflexive.

The problem with this account is that the very same account seems equally to fit a very different expression:

> "The speaker (of these very words)" is the device each person uses with the intention of conforming to the rule that "the speaker (of these very words)" refer to the speaker (of those very words).

(The parenthetic qualification will be taken as read and omitted from now on.) It seems as though on account (2), we cannot distinguish between the meanings of "I" and "the speaker." Does this matter? It would appear that it does. "The speaker" *fixes the reference* of "I," in Kripke's expression; it does not give its meaning. But what does this amount to? Why can't we treat "I" and "the speaker" as synonyms?[2] This question has been answered especially perspicuously, I believe, by David Kaplan, in a way that may be illustrated as follows.[3] Suppose that A is warm and B is cold, and A says "I am warm." Let us ask, "Suppose that B had said 'I am warm' instead, the other relevant circumstances remaining the same. Would *what A said* in the original case be made true or false by the changed case?" Answer: true. Because the content of what A said is that *A* is warm; this remains true whoever is speaking.

Now suppose A is warm and B is cold as before, but A says "The speaker is warm." Let us ask, "Suppose that B had said 'The speaker is warm' instead, the other relevant circumstances remaining the same. Would *what A said* in the original case be made true or false by the changed case?" Answer: false. For the content of what A said is the same as the content of what B said: that the speaker is warm. Whether that is true in a given "circumstance of evaluation" depends on whether the speaker, if there is one in that circumstance, is warm in that circumstance. In the circumstance as specified where B is the speaker, that content is false.

Thus the fact that "The speaker is warm" is true if A is the speaker but false if B is the speaker should not distract us from the fact that A and B express the *same content*. The difference in truth-value arises from the peculiar fact that A's saying it and B's saying it ipso facto give us not different contents but different *circumstances of evaluation*.

Like "The speaker is warm," "I am warm" is true if said by A but false if said by B. But now A and B, in using "I," are expressing *different contents. The content of what A says is not that the speaker is warm but that A is warm; and what B says is that he*, B, is warm. The relevant circumstances of evaluation are not affected by who the speaker is: only the content is. Since A is warm and B is cold, what A says is true, and the different thing that B says is false.[4]

For an account of "I" to be adequate, it is not enough that it yield the right referent when the term is used in talk about actual states of affairs; it must also conform to the distinctive profile of the first-person pronoun in discourse about counterfactual situations, and no account in terms of the rule that "I" refers to the speaker can do this. That rule fixes the reference of "I," but does not give its meaning. Account (2) does not rule out an erroneous understanding of "I" on which it refers to the speaker qua *speaker*; notoriously, "I" by contrast seems not to pick out its referent under any description at all. The lacuna in account (2) can only be made good by adding the condition that each person uses "I" to refer to the speaker, not thought of *as* the speaker, but thought of simply as *herself**;[5] and once again we fall into circularity.

I conclude, then, that neither version of O'Brien's account can give us an adequate understanding of what "I" means.

Evans

Gareth Evans claimed that a version of the revised account considered by Anscombe, whereby "I" might be understood in terms of *intentional* self-reference, could be vindicated against Anscombe's allegation of circularity, not by relying on any "pragmatic" consideration of the sort O'Brien appealed to but by simply offering a fully adequate specification of the intention with which "I" is used:

> Miss Anscombe does consider the suggestion that we should say that "I" is a device which each of us uses *knowingly and intentionally* to refer to himself. (Oedipus may have referred to himself by the words "the slayer of Laius," but not knowingly and intentionally.) Her reply is, essentially, that the suggestion cannot satisfactorily explain what the relevant intention is supposed to be. The idea seems to be as before: either "*x* intends to refer to himself" simply amounts to "*x* intends to refer to *x*" (which yields "The slayer of Laius intends to refer to the slayer of

Laius"—so that what is special about "I" has not been captured); or else, once again, it can be explained only in terms of the first-person pronoun.

But this does not seem to be correct. It is perfectly possible to ascribe to a subject the intention to refer to himself, in the sense of the intention of bringing it about that he satisfies the one-place concept-expression "ξ refers to ξ." Of course intending to satisfy the one-place concept-expression "ξ refers to ξ" is the same thing as intending to satisfy the one-place concept expression "ξ refers to me" (since "I satisfy '$[\lambda x(x$ refers to $x)]$ ξ'" is logically equivalent to "I refer to me"). But it does not follow that in order to elucidate the intention of satisfying "ξ refers to ξ," we need a grasp of the self-conscious Idea-type that we have of ourselves. Indeed, it seems plausible that the explanatory direction goes the other way: the fully self-conscious use of "I" can be partly explained, precisely, as a use in which the subject knowingly and intentionally refers to himself (satisfies "$[\lambda x(x$ refers to $x)]$ ξ"). (1982, 258–259)[6]

Evans's proposal is ingenious. If the intention with which "I" is used is characterized in this way as the intention to satisfy a concept-expression, it is very hard to see how a speaker could use "I" without knowing that she was referring to *herself**, but neither the indirect reflexive nor any other expression presupposing "I" appears in the account; so it does seem to sidestep Anscombe's "J. H. A. Smith" problem without succumbing to circularity.[7]

The trouble lies with Evans's expression "intending to satisfy the one-place concept-expression 'ξ refers to ξ.'" First, it is an unhappy fusion of mismatched idioms. The Greek letters and the phrase "concept-expression," given Evans's explicitly avowed philosophical allegiances, allude unmistakably to Frege (in particular, [2013, 5])—although to call "ξ refers to ξ" a *one-place* expression is both tendentious and not unequivocally Fregean. Evans takes pains to distinguish between a free variable in an open sentence and an argument-place in a Fregean concept-expression: at 259 he uses lambda-abstraction to construct the concept-expression "$[\lambda x(x$ refers to $x)]$ ξ"—in which a Fregean argument-place rubs shoulders with a free variable—out of the open sentence "x refers to x." It was absolutely essential to Frege's notion of a concept-expression as incomplete that a quasi-sign like "ξ" was *not* to be understood as a free variable, but simply as marking a "gap," so that the concept-expressions in which it "occurred" were not well-formed open sentences but ill-formed incomplete sentences or sentence-schemata (see further Frege [1960a, esp. 24–25]); I assume that the point of Evans's adoption of Frege's notation here is to mark just this contrast with a free variable.[8] Satisfaction, on the other hand, is a relation between objects, or sequences of objects, and open *or closed* well-formed sentences. The point here is not, I think, a pedantic one. If an object satisfies, for example, an open sentence of one free variable, it is not normally thought of as doing so by virtue of combining with some *nonlinguistic* entity for which the open sentence stands, and producing thereby a new nonlinguistic entity expressed by a true closed sentence. But for Frege[9] there can be no question of a semantic relation between an object and a concept-expression that is not routed through the concept the expression expresses (refers to, *bedeutet*), which the object is to be thought of as completing. A consistently Fregean idiom would require Evans to speak here of an intention to *saturate* (or *complete* and so on) *the concept named by "ξ refers to ξ,"* and on this way of speaking his proposal seems to lose the "metalinguistic" character that made it look like a solution to Anscombe's problem in the first place. For the *de dicto* intention *to saturate the concept named by "ξ refers to ξ" (whichever concept that should turn out to be),* under that description, cannot possibly be an intention that characterizes the kind of self-reference we are after (even if our speaker understands English, what if he is indifferent to the expression's meaning?); while the *de re* intention to saturate the concept, *however it is named,* that all and only self-referrers essentially fall under, looks indistinguishable from the plain intention to refer to oneself*, and we again fall back into circularity. I shall therefore eschew the Fregean idiom altogether and (following Peacocke [2008, 83]) rephrase Evans's account in terms of an intention to satisfy the open sentence "x refers to x." (I suspect that a proper investigation of this matter, which I cannot undertake here, would show that Evans's effective reliance on the unadorned idea of satisfying an open sentence makes his account incompatible with Fregean Platonism about concepts.)

Even if we amend the offending expression to "intending to satisfy the open sentence 'x refers to x,'" however, it still conceals the main problem with Evans's account. Evans himself also uses the expression "intention of bringing it about that he satisfies [the open sentence]," and one can only suppose that this formulation was a slip, since of course "he" here must be read as *he**. But then it seems that it is only the *formulation* of the intention-description that is at fault, and not the description itself; for the indirect reflexive is dispensable, as is attested by that other formulation, "intention of satisfying [the open sentence]." It is not as though one could allege that the expression "his intention of walking" makes covert use of the indirect reflexive, on the grounds that its *real* meaning is "his intention of bringing it about that *he** walk." For to walk and to bring it about that one* walks are not necessarily the same thing, and one of the differences between them is precisely this: any use of the indirect reflexive in an elucidation of the intention to walk would be entirely superfluous because the idea that such an intention might go awry by the attempt to carry it out resulting in *the wrong person* walking is not really intelligible.

Someone who intends to *bring it about* that he walks, by contrast, may indeed go astray and bring it about instead that someone else walks: I need an operation if I am to walk, for example, but so does someone else with the same name, and I pay for the other person's operation by mistake, and so on. And the same goes for my intention *to bring it about* that I, or someone else, be in any condition. When it comes to my intention to bring things about with respect to a particular person, be that myself or another, there is normally no logical guarantee that I can't bring the thing about with respect to the wrong person by mistake.

So it looks as though the question whether the indirect reflexive is really dispensable in the specification of an intention turns on whether the intention relates directly to an action, where the action itself may be described without an indirect reflexive, as with the intention *of walking,* or, instead, it is fundamentally an intention to bring about a state of affairs the subject conceives essentially in terms of something's being true of himself*, for example *that he* walk,* which therefore cannot be described without an indirect reflexive. Once we know who has the intention *to* ϕ, there is no further question in *whose* ϕ-ing the fulfillment of the intention would consist. But if all we know is that someone intends to bring about some state of affairs, there is always a question about which person in the envisaged state of affairs he conceives of as himself*, even if the answer is obvious. As Kaplan remarks, "Circumstances of evaluation do not, in general, have agents" (1989, 495). Circumstances may include the presence of agents; but circumstances do not have agents the way *actions* have agents.

But if this is right, it looks as though Evans is off the hook. For is not the intention by appeal to which he seeks to capture first-person reference the intention *to satisfy an open sentence*? And is not *to satisfy* an action?

It is not. "Intending to satisfy an open sentence of one free variable" (as my emendation of Evans has it) looks very much like an intention to do something: satisfying an urge can certainly be an action, since smoking a cigarette, for example, may *be* (that is, may also be describable as) the satisfying of an urge. Yet satisfying a concept-expression is *not* an action. Similarly, enjoying a concert, laboring in the fields, harboring a known criminal, and falling under a bus can be actions; but enjoying immunity from prosecution, laboring under an illusion, harboring doubts, and falling under a concept cannot. Like them, satisfying an open sentence of one free variable is a *condition*—specifically, a relation one bears to the sentence if and only if the sentence is true on an interpretation that assigns *oneself* as the value of the free variable. My satisfying the open sentence "x refers to x" is no more an action than is the number two's satisfying the open sentence "x is a natural number." The verb is entirely univocal across the two cases; but the number two never *does* anything.

To intend to satisfy an open sentence, then, is *fundamentally* to intend to bring about a state of affairs or a circumstance or condition: there is no *proper action, ϕ-ing,* such that an intention to satisfy an open sentence is more concisely, accurately, and aptly specified as an intention *to ϕ.* (Contrast the intention *to bring it about that one* walk,* in a case where this *is* simply an unhelpful underspecification of an intention *to walk.*) Since states of affairs or circumstances "do not, in general, have agents," *who* in the circumstance is (or are) envisaged as bringing it about is a piece of information that must be supplied "by hand."

Thus the expression "the intention to satisfy the open sentence 'x refers to x'" conceals an extra argument-place: a full specification of the intention type must read "the intention to bring it about that A satisfy the open sentence 'x refers to x,'" where A is a language user, a person. The particular subtype Evans means to identify is the special case in which A is the person who has the intention. But not just any specification of this person will do if the right intention is to be captured; for it must be one that the intender, the prospective agent, *recognizes* as referring to *himself**.

That is to say, in effect, the speaker's intention must be to bring it about that *he** satisfy the open sentence "*x* refers to *x*." The indirect reflexive is logically indispensable, and so first-person reference is, after all, presupposed.

So it seems; but might Evans not save his account by taking a leaf out of O'Brien's book at this point? It may be that, logically speaking, the speaker's intention should be specified in a way that brings out the structure it shares with an intention that someone else (or someone believed to be someone else) satisfy an open sentence; but the necessity of such a specification should not obscure the fact that there is a *practical guarantee* that the right person will end up satisfying the open sentence. For the right person is the speaker and, as O'Brien emphasizes, there can be no question of the speaker failing to realize that she* *is* the speaker. Remember that the intention in question is that *with which* the word "I" is uttered: we cannot easily imagine someone saying "I" and, *by that very utterance,* bringing it about directly, or intending to bring it about directly, that anyone other than herself* satisfies the open sentence. The intention is to make it true of someone that she self-refer: how could a speaker conceive of an *utterance* of hers as ipso facto fulfilling that intention, that is, bringing about a self-reference, but on *someone else's* account? Surely her knowledge that the self-reference is effected by her own utterance is sufficient for her to know that if anyone is doing any referring it can only be *herself**; and since the open sentence, to which she is therefore intentionally ensuring she stands in the relation of satisfaction, features two occurrences of a single variable (the concept-expression is one-place, as Evans puts it), she can hardly fail to know that she* is also the referent.

Evans's problem is not a mere "logical technicality," however. For what we are all of us supposed to be in search of here is not just an intention that *accompanies* the use of "I" in its authentically first-personal function— however reliably such an intention may provide such accompaniment, even to the point of its being unimaginable that it could be present without "I" serving that function, or that it could be absent without "I" failing to serve it. What we are after is an intention *by virtue of which* a use of "I" counts as authentically first-personal. And if that is the quest, the intention *that one's utterance bring it about that one satisfy the open sentence "x refers to x"* cannot satisfy us. For since we cannot deploy the indirect reflexive in this description, an intention may fit it that clearly has nothing to do with securing first-personal reference. In fact, if Evans's account does have to rely here on a version of O'Brien's point, that an intentional utterance is necessarily self-conscious, he also runs into a version of her problem, that guaranteeing reference to *the speaker,* so conceived, is not enough. We can imagine circumstances, for example, in which there are a number of potential speakers, speaking is somehow difficult, and it is important for some reason that *one* or another of them bring it about that she satisfy the concept-expression, that is, that one of them should self-refer. We can, further, easily imagine in such circumstances that one such speaker may succeed in referring to herself, with the intention that she bring it about that she do so, but, since the identity of the speaker is in a sense unimportant, that her doing so is intentional under the description that *the speaker* self-refer. Now, it may be deeply psychologically impossible to act on such an intention without performing the very same act with the additional intention that one self-refer qua oneself*, so that authentically first-personal self-reference is, by Evans's criteria, secured. But that is not the point. The point is that, according to Evans's account, the *first* intention, whereby the speaker conceives of herself as the speaker, should already be one by virtue of which the speaker counts as effecting authentically first-personal self-reference; but this is clearly *not* the right kind of intention. Both intentions equally meet Evans's criteria for generating first-personal self-reference; the only possible ground for preferring the second over the first is that it makes use of an indirect reflexive, so the preference cannot be supported without presupposing first-personal self-reference. So Evans's account is circular after all.

Should the reader find the case against Evans weak for the reason that it does not include a clear-cut counterexample to his account, whereby his conditions are all fulfilled but it is obvious that no genuine first-person reference is going on, it may be worth pointing out that a thought experiment presented by Anscombe herself, insofar as it is intelligible, can be adapted for this purpose. (I say "insofar as it is intelligible" because, as other authors have pointed out [O'Brien 1994, 279n1; McDowell 1998, 140–142], it is in some respects unclear exactly what sort of situation Anscombe means to depict, and whether various omitted details can be filled in in a way that makes overall sense.) She describes the case as follows:

Imagine a society in which everyone is labelled with two names. One appears on their backs and at the top of their chests, and these names, which their bearers cannot see, are various: "*B*" to "*Z*" let us say. The other, "*A*," is stamped on the inside of their wrists, and is the same for everyone. In making reports on people's actions everyone uses the names on their chests or backs if he can see these names or is used to seeing them. Everyone also learns to respond to utterance of the name on his own chest and back in the sort of way and circumstances in which we tend to respond to utterance of our names. Reports on one's own actions, which one gives straight off from observation, are made using the name on the wrist. Such reports are made, not on the basis of observation alone, but also on that of inference and testimony or other information. *B*, for example, derives conclusions expressed by sentences with "*A*" as subject, from other people's statements using "*B*" as subject.

It may be asked: what is meant by "reports on one's own actions"? Let us lay it down that this means, for example, reports issuing from the mouth of *B* on the actions of *B*. That is to say: reports from the mouth of *B* saying that *A* did such-and-such are prima facie verified by ascertaining that *B* did it and are decisively falsified by finding that he did not.

Thus for each person there is one person of whom he has characteristically limited and also characteristically privileged views: except in mirrors he never sees the whole person, and can only get rather special views of what he does see. Some of these are specially good, others specially bad. Of course, a man *B* may sometimes make a mistake through seeing the name "*A*" on the wrist of another, and not realizing it is the wrist of a man whose other name is after all not inaccessible to *B* in the special way in which his own name ("*B*") is.

In my story we have a specification of a sign as a name, the same for everyone, but used by each only to speak of himself. How does it compare with "I"?—The first thing to note is that our description does not include self-consciousness on the part of the people who use the name "*A*" as I have described it. They perhaps have no self-consciousness, though each one knows a lot about the object that he (in fact) is; and has a name, the same as everyone else has, which he uses in reports about the object that he (in fact) is. (FP, 48–49)[10]

Each speaker, in Anscombe's scenario, conforms in his use of "*A*" to Evans's account of "I" (as elaborated previously) as a device of self-reference uttered with the intention *of bringing it about that he satisfy the open sentence "x refers to x"*; "he" here of course being an ordinary reflexive: as the speaker conceives the intention, "he" is thought of not as himself*, but as the person of whom he has "characteristically limited and also characteristically privileged views," as Anscombe puts it. Clearly, since the speakers in the scenario lack self-consciousness, a fortiori their use of "*A*" does not amount to first-personal self-reference, and indeed this is Anscombe's main point. I mention this to cast especial doubt on Evans's claim that "the fully self-conscious use of 'I' can be partly explained, precisely, as a use in which the subject knowingly and intentionally refers to himself (satisfies '[$\lambda x(x$ refers to $x)$] ξ')."[11] Unless we *start* with self-consciousness fully in place, no Evans-style account in terms of the speaker's intention to enter into the relation of satisfaction to an open sentence expressing self-reference is going to be of any help in conjuring it.[12]

9
Rumfitt's Solution to the Circularity Problem

9.1 What Does It Mean to Construe a Reflexive Pronoun as a "Surface Trace of a Higher-Order Linguistic Functional"?

Even if Evans's account were not vitiated by such problems, its "metalinguistic" character makes it unfit for purpose as it stands, for it implies that only English speakers can form the intention in whose fulfillment the kind of self-reference effected by the first-person pronoun is supposed to consist. This observation is made by Ian Rumfitt, in the course of his own attempt to identify a flaw in Anscombe's argument and specify the distinctive intention with which properly first-personal self-reference is accomplished (Rumfitt 1994, 633n21). Rumfitt's diagnosis is, as he acknowledges, quite similar to Evans's: Anscombe has overlooked a perfectly adequate way of specifying the content of the intention in question, he alleges, which yet does not presuppose, by recourse to the indirect reflexive, the kind of reference it is supposed to explicate because, according to Rumfitt, the reflexive character of the reference is captured not by a pronoun at all but, as in Evans's account, by the "one-place" *form* of the concept-expression ("predicable," in Rumfitt's terminology) that gives the description under which the self-referring action, if it is to count as securing properly first-personal reference, must be intended. Rumfitt avoids the sort of objection I have made to Evans's account, however, precisely by avoiding its metalinguistic maneuver: the relevant intention is simply *to perform* the action expressed by the one-place predicable in question. To put it in the terms in which I discussed Evans's proposal, the intention *relates directly* to that action; that is, it is only secondarily, if at all, an intention to *bring it about* that the predicable be true of oneself.

Rumfitt presents his account as a kind of technological spin-off from a fascinating program of research into, and elaboration of, Frege's theory of predication. The important aspects of his treatment, for our purposes, are those pertaining to reflexive predications, whereby the subject ostensibly stands to itself in some relation in which it could also stand toward something else. Somewhat surprisingly, Rumfitt holds, with Geach (1968, 1972) as against Evans (1977), that the *ordinary reflexive pronoun,* as it appears in such predications, is not a referring expression. It is, rather, "the surface manifestation of a higher-order linguistic functional . . . that maps a transitive verb form V to a one-place predicable 'Vs himself'" (Rumfitt 1994, 623).

Rumfitt sees in this analysis a way of resisting Anscombe's argument that there can be no adequate noncircular account of "I" as a device of self-reference. If the analysis is correct, of course, all predications involving the predicable "ξ refers to himself" will be subject to it, and "himself" as it occurs in any such predications, including those that are then embedded in ascriptions of intention, will not refer. Yet Anscombe's argument seems to turn on the question of *how* the reflexive pronoun picks up the reference of its antecedent (which, in ascriptions of reflexive speech acts and of intentions to perform them, is the speaker). She sees the question as presenting a dilemma: if the reference is picked up in the manner of an ordinary reflexive, the account of "I" is inadequate because it also fits the wrong (inadvertent) kind of self-reference; but if it is picked up in the manner of the indirect reflexive, the account is circular because no account can be given of that pronoun except in terms of "I" itself. If we suppose, with Rumfitt and Geach, that the reflexive pronoun is not a referring expression at all, Anscombe cannot so much as frame her dilemma.

The evaluation of Rumfitt's argument requires us to quote it at some length, and situate it at the right point in Anscombe's own dialectic. Recall, first, the insistence on the part of Anscombe's interlocutor that the self-reference effected by "I" must be knowing and intentional. She responded with the rhetorical questions, concerning Smith's utterance of "John Horatio Auberon Smith," "Did not Smith knowingly and intentionally speak of himself? Was not the person he intended to speak of—Smith? and so *was* not the person he intended to speak of—himself?" (FP, 47). It is the interlocutor's imagined reply to this that Rumfitt describes as "an identifiable key error in [Anscombe's] argument" (1994, 632). That reply runs as follows:

> It may be said: "Not in the relevant sense. We all know you can't sub-stitute every designation of the object he intended to speak of and keep the statement about his intention true." But that is not the answer unless the reflexive pronoun itself is a sufficient indication of the way the ob-ject is specified. And that is something the ordinary reflexive pronoun cannot be. Consider: "Smith realizes (fails to realize) the identity of an object he calls 'Smith' with himself." If the reflexive pronoun there is the ordinary one, then it specifies for us who frame or hear the sen-tence, an object whose identity with the object he calls "Smith" Smith does or doesn't realize: namely the object designated by our subject word "Smith." But that does not tell us what identity Smith himself realizes (or fails to realize). For, as Frege held, there is no path back from refer-ence to sense; any object has many ways of being specified. (FP, 47)

Concerning this reply, Rumfitt says the following:

> The interlocutor offers to explain the meaning of "I" . . . using a formula among whose instances is
>
> (I) "I" is the word Smith uses when he knowingly and intentionally speaks of himself, and Anscombe supposes that he will resist her *re-ductio* of this explanation, which she reaches by substituting "of Smith" for "of himself" in (I), by protesting that one cannot in general substitute co-denoting terms in a statement ascribing an intention—a protest that leads to the fruitless search for a reflexive pronoun which not only picks out the right object, but picks it out under the right Fre-gean *Bestimmungsweise* [mode of determination (see, for example, Frege 1879, 14)], and does all that without presupposing what one is trying to explain.
>
> However, the reply that Anscombe puts into her interlocutor's mouth evidently presupposes that the semantic function of the *ordinary* re-flexive pronoun in such a statement as (I) is to make a designation; in

Anscombe's own words in the passage quoted, such a pronoun "specifies for us who frame [a sentence containing it] an object." That is to
say, in formulating her own argument and her interlocutor's response
she presupposes the Evansian account of reflexives attacked [earlier in
Rumfitt's paper]. And once Anscombe's imagined interlocutor is alerted
to that, he is in a position to give an alternative, "Geachian," response
to the objection. Of course, he will concede,

(16) Smith intends to refer to Smith

and

(17) Smith intends to refer to himself

can differ in truth value; but that is not because the expressions "Smith"
and "himself" are associated with different Fregean *Bestimmungsweisen*
of the common denotation, the man Smith. Rather, it is because (16) may
be rendered as . . .

(18) Smith stands in the intending relation to A_β (β refers to Smith)[1]

whereas (17) may be rendered as . . .

(19) Smith stands in the intending relation to A_β (β refers to β)[2]

Moreover, for exactly the reason that A_β (β kills Cato) was distinct
from A_β (β kills β), so A_β (β refers to Smith) is distinct from A_β (β refers
to β). There is, then, no need to set off on a wild goose chase, looking for
a peculiar way in which Smith may be "presented" to Smith, in order to
account for any difference in truth value between (16) and (17). (Rumfitt
1994, 632–633)

A Noncircular Account of "I" as a Device
of Self-Reference at Last?

Rumfitt's analysis of the intention involved in first-person reference may
well solve difficult problems by showing how this intention may be understood without recourse to metaphysically or epistemologically ex-
travagant posits, such as the Cartesian ego or Frege's "particular and
primitive way" in which "everyone is presented to himself" (Frege 1956,
298; cf. Rumfitt 1994, 629). For when such reference is construed in
Rumfitt's fashion as a one-place predicable, it becomes possible to specify
the intention to refer without having to specify the referent—as had
seemed necessary—in some way consistent with the speaker's possible

ignorance (by reason of amnesia and anesthesia) of *any* description of it (Rumfitt 1994, 629–630).

There is still, however, the separate and prior question of when such an analysis is appropriate; that is, how do we specify those cases of self-reference that are authentically first-personal? This was the question to which, Anscombe argued, no adequate noncircular answer can be given. And it seems to me that Rumfitt's account of how such reference works leaves this problem completely untouched. For although Anscombe frames her argument in a way that presupposes that the ordinary reflexive pronoun is a referring expression, the *force* of that argument, pace Rumfitt, is completely independent of any such presupposition.

Rumfitt talks of Anscombe's interlocutor conceding that

(16) Smith intends to refer to Smith

and

(17) Smith intends to refer to himself

can *differ* in truth value, and he supposes that, because she construes both the second occurrence of "Smith" in (16) and the reflexive pronoun in (17) referentially, Anscombe thinks that the only explanation of the difference is a difference in sense between those two words, and this leads to the "wild goose chase" in search of an appropriate sense for the pronoun. But it seems to me that Anscombe's argument turns on a case in which (16) (or perhaps, more precisely, (16) amended to "Smith intends to refer to John Horatio Auberon Smith") and (17) are *both true*—the case in which Smith uses the name "John Horatio Auberon Smith," although lacking the knowledge he would express by saying "*I* am John Horatio Auberon Smith." Anscombe says that what makes (17) true in this case is the "peculiar construction" whereby the reflexive pronoun picks up the reference of the subject-term, but without giving any indication of the mode of apprehension of himself under which he figures in the content of his own intention. This, she says, is why (17) is made true by Smith's intending to refer to John Horatio Auberon Smith, even though he has no inkling of this person's identity with himself*.

Now if Rumfitt is right in his "Geachian" construal of the reflexive in (17) as nonreferential, Anscombe's explanation of what makes (17) true must be wrong, since the pronoun then does not "pick up" any reference at all. But that does not affect her argument, which only requires that (17), in such a case, be *true*. And surely it *is* true, *whatever* theory we favor of the semantics of reflexive pronouns. That anyone in Smith's position counts as knowingly and intentionally referring to himself is simply a datum that any semantic theory must accommodate; it is not an entitlement such a theory has the power to grant or withhold.

I find it difficult to make out Rumfitt's position on these matters, but my suspicion is that, partly because he has been misled by his own "paratactic" account of attributions of intention, he is *effectively* assuming that "himself" in (17), and in fact in all cases of what he *calls* the ordinary reflexive, is really the indirect reflexive. I say "effectively" because Rumfitt himself would not accept such a characterization, not only because he calls the pronoun the ordinary reflexive but also because he expresses a doubt, or at least disavows certainty, as to whether there is such a grammatical item as the indirect reflexive pronoun at all (1994, 634, 634n22); but I hope to show that there is a point to my suspicion nevertheless.

My evidence is drawn from the preceding section of Rumfitt's paper, in which he adjudicates the dispute between Evans and Geach about whether reflexive pronouns refer. He considers the attribution (I use his enumeration)

(12) Cato intends to kill himself

which, on his Davidsonian "paratactic" theory of such sentences, "is to be understood as saying" (626)

(13) Cato intends (to do) that (act). Kill himself.

On Evans's "co-referential" account, reflexive pronouns are to be treated in accordance with the rule

(F) If σ is a sentence containing the singular term positions p_i and p_j, which are chained together, and p_i contains the singular term τ and p_j contains the pronoun κ, then the denotation of κ in σ is the same as the denotation of τ. (Rumfitt 1994, 623, quoting Evans 1977, 89)

But according to Rumfitt—and this is part of his case against the co-referential account—

Rule (F) by itself fails to fix the truth conditions of an attribution such as (13). For those truth conditions are not fixed until it is determined which act Cato is said to have intended to perform. And by our account of the individuation of such acts, that is not determined until it is determined which sense the predicable "ξ kills himself" expresses. All that rule (F) tells us, however, is that in the context of attribution (13), the denotation of "himself" is the man Cato. And if, as we have been supposing throughout, Frege was correct to say that co-denoting expressions may express distinct senses, then application of rule (F) alone does not suffice to determine the sense of the relevant predicable. (1994, 626)

It is clear from other things he says that Rumfitt takes a "determination of the sense of the relevant predicable" to yield a determination of "which act Cato is said to have intended to perform," which specifies the *description under which* Cato is being said to have intended to perform it.[3]

However, this is to ignore Anscombe's point (abstracted from her "co-referentialist" assumption) about the distinctive semantics of the ordinary reflexive when it occurs, as here, in the "peculiar construction" of attributions of intention and other contentful states. Even if it is an overstatement to call this point, as I did previously, a "datum," Rumfitt gives no reason for denying it since, to repeat, it is completely orthogonal to the issue of whether the pronoun is a referring expression, which is the issue about which Rumfitt thinks Anscombe mistaken. That point may be illustrated here by bringing Anscombe's example closer to Rumfitt's: suppose that Smith intends not to refer to John Horatio Auberon Smith but to *kill* him (while, again, ignorant of the identity he would express by saying "I am John Horatio Auberon Smith"). The Anscombe point is that in such a case, it will be *straightforwardly true* that

(H) Smith intends to kill himself

By "straightforwardly true" here, I mean that it is not merely "technically" true in the manner of one of those marginal locutions that result from a refusal to respect the usual conventions governing the attribution of contentful states, like "Oedipus wants to marry his mother" or "Lois Lane thinks Superman is a reporter." For what distinguishes the ordinary from the indirect reflexive is precisely its *failure* to indicate, in this case, how Smith conceives of the person he intends to kill, or even whether Smith has any such conception at all (as, according to Rumfitt, in cases of first-personal self-reference he has not). When it comes to the *ordinary* reflexive, Smith's intending to kill John Horatio Auberon Smith makes it the case that he intends to kill himself just as surely as his intending to commit suicide does.

Rumfitt's paratactic construal of (12) as (13) encourages us to overlook this. By isolating the specification of the action, it tempts us to assimilate it to similarly isolated specifications the theory produces when applied to "standard issue" attributions of intention, such as

(P) Smith intends to do that. Kill the president.

Here, "it is determined which act [Smith] is said to . . . [intend] to perform," as Rumfitt puts it, because (P) *does* specify Smith's own mode of apprehension of his intended action and its object: so long as (P) is interpreted in a natural rather than a perverse, "marginal" way, it says that Smith intends to kill the president *under that description*.

(H), by contrast, does not tell us that Smith intends to kill himself under that description because (still assuming that "himself" is the ordinary reflexive) it does not indicate *any* description of such a sort that his action might be intentional under it. (H), and therefore (12), is an *essentially incomplete* attribution, since it is equally made true by "Smith intends to kill Smith," "Smith intends to kill John Horatio Auberon Smith," "Smith intends to kill the man mentioned in the will," "Smith intends to kill himself*," and so on. So it is a mistake to suppose, as Rumfitt does, that "rule (F) by itself fails to fix the truth conditions" of (H)—or, therefore, of (12) or (13); and that "those truth conditions are not fixed until it is determined which act [the intending subject] is said to have intended to perform," if this requires a specification of the description under which the action is intended. For those truth conditions may be thought of as given by an open-ended disjunction of descriptions under which the intending agent may intend the action in question.

On the other hand, Rumfitt may well be right that an adequate account of (H), (12), and (13) does require us to determine "which sense the predicable 'ξ kills himself' expresses." And this must presumably be a *determinate* sense. But a sense for this expression may be perfectly determinate even though it, in turn, determines that an occurrence of the expression in indirect discourse does *not* determine the sense the *agent* attaches to the object of his action—or even whether there is such a sense at all, as on Rumfitt's "Geachian" construal, whereby no such object is referred to, there is not. All of this is consistent with that construal.

Now, as Rumfitt proceeds with his case against Evans's co-referential account of the ordinary reflexive, he remarks, surely correctly, that "himself" in (12) cannot have the same sense as "Cato" there, because

(15) Cato intends to kill Cato

does not have the same sense as (12), or even the same truth conditions, for

> if . . . (12) shared its truth conditions with (15), it would be a requirement for the truth of "Cato intends to kill himself" that Cato know what it would be to kill Cato. Now having *that* knowledge surely involves . . . *knowing who Cato is;* and however vague the notion of knowing who such and such is might be, it is pretty plain that when
>
> (a) Cato is amnesiac, and has thereby lost all knowledge of what Cato has done,
>
> and also
>
> (b) Cato is sensorily deprived, and has thereby lost all knowledge of *how* Cato is now disposed
>
> then Cato *doesn't* know who Cato is, so that attribution (15) must be false. It seems clear, however, that even in these circumstances Cato *could* form the properly suicidal intention ascribed in (12); indeed, his being in the condition described might very well account for that intention. (Rumfitt 1994, 627–628)

Rumfitt then generalizes this argument: the act one intends to perform when one intends to kill oneself cannot be the act specified by $\ulcorner \xi$ kills $\alpha \urcorner$, for *any* denoting expression $\ulcorner \alpha \urcorner$. For given his "conceptual requirement" (1994, 622, 627), the intending subject would have to know what it would be to kill α, which in turn would require a capacity, however fleeting, to identify α, in however "thin" a way. The amnesiac, sensorially deprived Cato has no such capacity, but he can still form the intention to kill himself.

But notice, now, what the conditions Rumfitt has placed on the ordinary reflexive amount to. Our account of an attribution like (12) must *both* determine, in effect, the description under which Cato intends his action *and* be consistent with the possibility of Cato's amnesia and sensory deprivation. Taken together, this amounts to the requirement that at least one of the descriptions under which Cato intends his action include no specification of whom he intends to kill, of a sort that Cato could fail to apply correctly even when amnesiac and sensorially deprived. Thus Cato cannot intend to kill himself unless he is in a position to assert (or think a thought that would be expressed in English by) "I intend to kill *myself*." Against the background of Rumfitt's various requirements on attributions of intention, this follows from his account of what the ordinary reflexive must mean. But if *this* is what the ordinary reflexive must mean, it is not the ordinary reflexive after all. It is the indirect reflexive.

Rumfitt might reply that in a way this is the whole point: the conditions on the attribution of intention are such that no distinction between the ordinary and indirect reflexive can in the end be drawn; it was not assumed at the outset that the pronoun in question was the indirect reflexive. This is why we can conjure first-personal self-reference from the ordinary reflexive, via those conditions:

> Anscombe observes that one cannot simultaneously offer ["the indirect discourse correlate of 'I' in direct discourse"] as a specification of the meaning of "he*" *and* use "he*" in explaining the meaning of "I," and in this she is surely right. If, however, I am correct in maintaining that "I" may be explained using the "ordinary" reflexive pronoun (so long as that pronoun is properly understood), then there is no objection to using "I" to explain what (if anything) is semantically distinctive about Castañeda's pronoun [the indirect reflexive]. There is no circularity here, for the order of explanation is simply: "ordinary" reflexive, then first-person pronoun, then "indirect" reflexive (that is, Castañeda's pronoun). (Rumfitt 1994, 634)

At the very least, one might wonder what the distinction here is supposed to amount to, between the ordinary and indirect reflexives. What does it mean to say that the indirect reflexive is the indirect discourse correlate of "I," if the ordinary reflexive turns out always to correlate with what in direct speech is expressed by "I"? As Rumfitt presents his position, while the ordinary reflexive is accepted on all sides, it is not uncontroversial that the indirect reflexive, which corresponds in indirect speech to what would be expressed in direct speech by "I," so much as exists. Yet it is his view that the reflexive pronoun as it occurs in these sorts of contexts (and it would be arbitrary to resist an extension of the claim to "propositional-attitude" contexts in general) *always does* correspond in indirect speech to what would be expressed in direct speech by "I." So it would be less misleading to describe him as holding that what others, including Anscombe, call the ordinary reflexive pronoun *always* in these contexts amounts to the indirect reflexive.

As for the "conceptual requirement," it is surely true that if someone intends to ϕ, they must know what it is to ϕ. But it does not follow that every true report of what someone intends to do will enable us to construct an unambiguous description under which the action is intended. A fortiori, there is no reason to suppose that we will be able to construct, on the basis of the component sense of "ϕ" in an ascription of the form "S intends to ϕ," the sense that encapsulates what S's understanding of what he intends to do consists in. And this is shown—to return to our central case—by the fact that we cannot construct such a sense on the basis of the ascription "Smith intends to refer to himself." This might be made true by Smith's conceiving of this action in any number of ways, including *referring to John Horatio Auberon Smith*, even when he is not in a position to assert the identity "I am John Horatio Auberon Smith."

As far as I can see, Rumfitt has not given us any argument to show that this cannot count as a case of Smith's intending to refer to himself. And, to repeat, it is hard to see what kind of argument *could* show this, since (as it seems to me) it is simply a datum that it *can* count as such a case. If we abbreviate as ξ *s-refers* Rumfitt's construal of "ξ refers to himself," as a one-place predicable to which the reflexive pronoun maps the two-place predicable "ξ refers to η," then Rumfitt's view is that every case of a person referring to himself is a case of his s-referring, and indeed that "ξ refers to himself" and "ξ s-refers" are logically equivalent and, in Frege's sense, *equipollent*: no one who understands both predications of the same subject apprehended in the same way could take one as true and the other as false. But then if Smith's intention to refer to John Horatio Auberon Smith makes true the ascription *Smith intends to refer to himself*, Rumfitt must regard this as a case of Smith's intending to s-refer. But according to Rumfitt's theory, the intention to s-refer is the intention that marks the use of an expression as an authentically first-personal form of self-reference. It follows that Smith, in uttering "John Horatio Auberon Smith" with the intention of referring to John Horatio Auberon Smith, is referring to himself in the first-personal way. But this is absurd. This is essentially the *reductio* Anscombe herself presented in the passage quoted by Rumfitt, but put in terms explicitly consistent with Rumfitt's own favored construal of the ordinary reflexive as nonreferring. That construal, then, does nothing to deflect the *reductio*.

Filling a Lacuna in the Account

As it stands, then, Rumfitt's account looks incomplete. Its completion, however, might not be such a difficult job.[4] We begin by simply abolishing the distinction between the ordinary and indirect reflexive pronouns. We then explain the ambiguity of the relevant reports of self-reference in terms of a kind of scope ambiguity instead. Thus we paraphrase "Smith intends to refer to himself," where Smith utters "J. H. A. Smith" *without* being in a position to say "I am J. H. A. Smith," along the following lines:

> Concerning a man who is in fact himself, Smith intends to refer to him

so that there is no essential occurrence of a reflexive pronoun in the specification of Smith's intention *at all*. Where Smith uses an expression (standardly, of course "I") to refer to himself in the authentically first-personal way, we say something like

> Smith intends to see to it that he refers to himself

or, better, to eliminate the residual (seeming) indirect reflexive,

> Smith intends to self-refer

We now rule out the "unwitting" reading not by insisting that "himself" is a grammatically distinctive kind of reflexive pronoun but by wheeling in the Geach-style account of reflexive pronouns as not referring expressions but marks of higher-order linguistic functionals mapping, in this case, a two-place predicate to a one-place one. The "right" kind of self-reference is now conceived of not as taking an object under a distinctive, mysterious mode of presentation, much less as taking a distinctive, mysterious object, but simply as a distinctive species of referring activity.

9.4   Is the Insistence That "I" Refers Worth the Concession
That Reflexive Pronouns Do Not?

Once Rumfitt's position has been amended in this way, his dispute with Anscombe might be accounted, for now, as an honorable draw. There does not seem to be any important consideration yet adduced on either side that would decide the issue either way. One might, with Anscombe, persist in the denial that "I" can be explicated as a device of intentional self-reference, either by resisting the Rumfitt-Geach construal of reflexive pronouns (which Rumfitt certainly does not present as conclusively established), or by rejecting the "scope-ambiguity" account of the distinction between informed and unwitting readings of the *oratio obliqua* clauses in which such pronouns occur. Or one might acquiesce in the Rumfitt-Geach construal of reflexives and the scope-ambiguity account of the distinction between the two readings, and thereby preserve the explication of "I" as the device used to refer to oneself with the intention of so doing.

Yet there still seem to me to be reasons for inclining toward the Anscombe view.

What is really at stake in all this, which I have so far kept in the background of my discussion of Rumfitt, is of course the issue of whether "I" is a referring expression *at all*. It is the main point of FP to deny this, and Anscombe's argument that no noncircular account can be given of such a role for it is an important part of her case. O'Brien, Evans, Rumfitt, and pretty much everyone else who has written on the subject find Anscombe's main contention simply incredible.

Now, we have seen that Rumfitt's argument, that the self-referrer's intention can be characterized without presupposing "I," depends crucially on Geach's account of reflexive pronouns as themselves none of them referring expressions. But it seems very odd to rely on such an account in the course of defending the status of "I" *as* a referring expression. After all, it is not at all clear on the face of it why the claim that reflexive pronouns are not referring expressions should be deemed any less incredible than the same claim about "I." (Bear in mind here that most of the recorded opposition to Anscombe's view of "I" consists in little more than various versions of the "incredulous stare.") Indeed, a nonreferential account of the reflexives should perhaps be deemed if anything *more* incredible, inasmuch as "I" does seem to be, uniquely among the personal pronouns, "obviously just really weird" (as David McCarthy once remarked to me), and so more likely to require extreme measures in our semantic theorizing.

Prior's Pronoun "Self": "I" and Reflexive Pronouns Belong to a Single Semantic Kind

But more than this, a line of thought suggested by A. N. Prior raises the possibility that withholding referential status from reflexive pronouns, while insisting on it for the first-person pronoun, might be not just arbitrary or perverse but inconsistent. For Prior proposes in effect that these might all be construed as, at bottom, *the same pronoun:* "It is the same with 'I' as it is with 'now' and with 'any'—even in subordinate clauses we make it refer to the speaker of the entire sentence. In a more rational language we might have used a pronoun 'Self' in such a way that 'Self is sick,' for example, means the same as our present 'I am sick,' but 'He believes that self is sick' would mean, not the same as our present 'He believes that I am sick', but the same as our present 'He believes that he is sick'" (Prior 1967, 333).

Prior's pronoun "Self" is not some counterintuitive semantic recarving presented in a spirit of skeptical challenge, like Nelson Goodman's "grue." It is simply the first-person pronoun modified to take narrow scope, as many other expressions do: it is related to "I" rather as "currently" (which standardly takes narrow scope) is to "now" (which standardly takes wide scope). That is, while "I," like "now," normally takes its referent from the whole sentence in which it occurs, even if it occurs within a subordinate clause (so that, as the referent of "now" is the time at which the whole sentence is uttered, that of "I" is the speaker of the whole sentence), "Self," like "currently," by contrast, if it occurs in a subordinate clause, takes its referent from that clause, and not from the whole sentence. Thus, while

He said that he would be driving to Liverpool now

indicates that he expressed the anticipation of driving to Liverpool, and driving there at a time that would include the time of the utterance of the whole sentence beginning "He said . . . ,"

He said that he was currently driving to Liverpool

by contrast, indicates that, according to him, he was driving to Liverpool at the time *he* spoke; and similarly, while

He said that I was driving to Liverpool

indicates that, according to him, the person uttering the whole sentence beginning "He said . . ." was driving to that port,

He said that self was driving to Liverpool

by contrast, indicates that, according to him, the subject of the *oratio obliqua* clause, that is, *he* himself**, was driving there. The referents of "currently" and "now" converge in present-tense statements, as do those of "Self" and "I" in *oratio recta,* so that just as

I am currently driving to Liverpool

has exactly the same truth conditions as

I am now driving to Liverpool

so

I am driving to Liverpool

has exactly the same truth conditions as

Self is driving to Liverpool

said by me. In short, the reference rule for "Self" as it occurs in indirect discourse is: *"Self" refers to the speaker or thinker of the sentence or thought-report of which it is the immediate subject, not only (like "I") in direct discourse, but also (like "he*") in indirect discourse.*

This is incomplete: a full specification would require an account of the distinctive *mode* of reference of "Self." Clearly, in indirect discourse "Self" has it in common with the indirect reflexive that its meaning cannot be explained independently of "I"—or, equivalently, in this new idiom, independently of *recta* occurrences of "Self" itself, whose mode of reference (assuming there is one), in turn, is to be understood exactly *as* that of "I." The first-person dependence of Prior's pronoun in indirect discourse is therefore perspicuous, as that of the indirect reflexive is not (since it is orthographically indistinguishable from the ordinary reflexive). Thus, it takes some effort to see that "*A* believes that he ϕs," where "he" is the indirect reflexive, cannot be understood otherwise than as ascribing to *A* a belief whose content he is in a position to express using "I" (and may not be in a position to express in any other way, as in the anesthetized amnesiac case). But it is much easier to see that "*A* believes that self ϕs" cannot be understood other than as ascribing a belief to *A* whose content he can express using "Self"! Indeed, in the anesthetized amnesiac case, the relevant contents can only be expressed by "Self" in *both* the indirect *and* direct discourse cases (assuming "Self" has supplanted "I" in the language).

I take it that sentences featuring "Self" in indirect discourse, such as

(*) Smith believes that self ϕs

might be paraphrased as

(**) Smith believes *himself to* ϕ

Since Prior's "Self" functions in sentences like (*) *exactly* as the reflexive pronoun (the indirect reflexive, if there is such a thing) functions, it is hard to see how Rumfitt, if he countenances Prior's pronoun at all (as how could he not?), could deny that his and Geach's arguments for construing the reflexive as a nonreferring "higher-order functional" can be carried over to "Self" with undiminished force. Thus (*) is as suitable a case as any for the Geach-Rumfitt treatment of reflexives as "higher-order functionals" from two-place to one-place predicables, and so *not* as referring expressions of any kind.[5] (Although that treatment, if it works at all, only works for reflexives within the scope of intentional verbs if they are construed as, effectively, *indirect,* that wrinkle only makes the account run more smoothly for "Self," which has to be construed along the lines of the indirect reflexive anyway.)

The spirit of Rumfitt's elaboration of the "Geachian" proposal for reflexives clearly requires that it be subject to a certain kind of generalization. Rumfitt defines the higher-order functional Ref (ϕ), of which standard occurrences of the ordinary reflexives are "surface manifestations," as "[mapping] an arbitrary two-place predicable $h(\xi,\eta)$ to the one-place $f(\xi)$ in such a way that for every name n, $f(n) = h(n,n)$" (1994, 604). To adapt Rumfitt's own example, if $h(\xi,\eta)$ is the function that maps a pair of names n, m, to the proposition[6] got by concatenating the name n, the word "contradicts," and the name m, and $f(\xi)$ is the function that maps a name n to the proposition got by concatenating the name n, the word "contradicts," and the name n again, then

$$f(\xi) = \text{Ref}(h(\xi,\eta))$$

Thus, if our names n and m are both "Hegel," then $h(n,m) =$ "Hegel contradicts Hegel," the higher-order functional Ref maps the two-place h to the one-place f to yield the proposition $f(n)$, which is *also* "Hegel contradicts Hegel," but now the value of a one-place function best read as "ξ contradicts himself." "Himself" here is of course not a referring expression but rather the "surface trace" of our functional, Ref. The same proposition is arrived at by two fundamentally different predications. The difference is vividly illustrated by their respective universal generalizations: "Everyone contradicts Hegel" versus "Everyone contradicts himself." The case illustrates what I take to be the Fregean point that there is no such thing as *the* logical form of a sentence (Frege 1960b, 49; cf. Rumfitt 1994, 601).[7]

The unexceptionable generalization is that, *if* a reflexive pronoun that apparently occupies an argument-place of a two-place predicable should be understood as really the mark of a higher-order function Ref mapping that predicable to another, one-place one, then it would be arbitrary to resist the idea that this is a special case of a principle of interpretation that applies to predicables with any number of argument-places. Namely, a reflexive pronoun that apparently occupies an argument-place of an n-place predicable h should be understood as really the mark of a higher-order function Ref_n mapping that predicable to another, $(n-1)$-place function f. The more general principle yields the schema

$$f(\xi_1,\xi_2, \ldots ,\xi_{(n-1)}) = \text{Ref}_n(h(\xi_1,\xi_2, \ldots ,\xi_n))^{[8]}$$

Thus, for example, "Smith positioned Smith between Brown and Jones" may be parsed as a four-place predication "Positioned-between (Smith, Smith, Brown, Jones)," so that Smith is conceived of as acting on Smith in a way that he might also act on Cobbleigh ("Positioned-between (Smith, Cobbleigh, Brown, Jones)"), and Cobbleigh might act on him ("Positioned-between (Cobbleigh, Smith, Brown, Jones)"). "Smith positioned *himself* between Brown and Jones," however, should by contrast be parsed as a *three*-place predication, the reflexive pronoun serving to express a function taking the four-place predicable "Positioned-between" as its argument and yielding as its value a new three-place predicable "Positioned-himself-between," so that the proposition is parsed as "Positioned-himself-between (Smith, Brown, Jones)." On the former parsing, Cobbleigh's doing the same thing as Smith consists of his positioning Smith between Brown and Jones; on the latter, it consists of his positioning *Cobbleigh* between Brown and Jones.

We are supposing that if Prior's "Self" is a legitimate locution, then, in those contexts in which it is interchangeable with a reflexive pronoun—that is, all contexts except those in which it is interchangeable with the first-person pronoun—if the Geach-Rumfitt treatment of reflexive pronouns is the right one, it must be the right treatment of "Self" in those contexts too. But the resulting overall treatment of "Self" looks unsatisfactory. For where "Self" looks equivalent to a reflexive and takes an argument position of an n-place predicable, it is to be treated as a higher-order functional mapping that predicable to an $(n-1)$-place predicable in accordance with the procedure just described. "Self" cannot possibly be so treated, however, when its manner of occurrence makes it equivalent to a first-person pronoun with no antecedent. For its "absorption" into the predicable will leave the sentence with no component designating its author. Thus the only construal of "Self thinks," for example, that has any chance of being continuous with the Geach-Rumfitt construal of, say, "René thinks about self" leaves us with a subjectless predicate. So long as we restricted our attention to the reflexives, the condition on the mapping from an n-place to an $(n-1)$-place predicable, that n must be greater than 1, was trivial, because since every such pronoun requires an antecedent, its predicable cannot have fewer than two argument-places. When "Self" occurs with no antecedent, however, the condition is not trivial, and is violated.

If we begin, then, with a *one*-place predicable, as in

(***) Self ϕs

mechanical application of the rule takes us to a *0-place* predicable—which normally, as Prior himself reminds us, is a *sentence:* "Sentences, as [Charles

Sanders] Peirce saw, are simply those n-place predicates for which $n = 0$; an n-place predicate is a sentence with n gaps for names to go in, an 'open' sentence as it is now excellently called, and an ordinary or 'closed' sentence is one with no such gaps left. [To quantify predicate-variables but object to quantifying sentence-variables] is thus [a conception of quantifiers] which slides easily down the n's and then unexpectedly bumps to a stop at the lowest but one, leaving us gasping" (Prior 1971, 33).

But doesn't a predicate of its nature have at least one "gap" for a referring expression? Frege characterized predicates as "unsaturated": he assimilated them to function-expressions, and the concepts they name to functions from objects to truth values, so that a monadic predicate cannot name a truth value until it is "saturated" by a singular term designating an object, which the concept (that is, function) expressed by the predicate "maps" to the appropriate truth value (Frege 1960a). We need not follow Frege here in construing his talk of functions so literally that truth values must be thought of as objects in their own right, to appreciate the point that a predicate standing alone is not a well-formed formula: it is not the sort of thing that could *be* true or false.

But since our amended version of English is not a formal language, nothing prevents us from supposing that in an expression of the form "Self ϕs," although "Self" is not a referring expression, it works, as Rumfitt would put it, as "a linguistic trace of a higher-order functional"—in this case, from predicates to sentences in which they (the predicates) are brought under higher-order predicates, perhaps a kind of quantifier. (For the details of this sort of proposal, see Chapter 11.) The subject of our sentence is now the concept expressed by "ϕ" itself, but appearing in a guise that does not require it to be combined with an object of its own—in Frege's terms, our concept has now itself been transformed into an object, to be brought under a new concept in its turn.

But since "Self" on this adaptation of Rumfitt's account is always a functional and never refers, there is no expression left in a sentence like (***) to refer to anything at all as being the subject of "ϕs." So it looks after all as though the Geach-Rumfitt account of reflexive pronouns fits rather well with Anscombe's conception of "I" as not a referring expression.

Anscombe's Argument Not Yet Discredited

For all that O'Brien, Evans, and Rumfitt have said, then, Anscombe's claim that there can be no adequate noncircular account of "I" as a device of self-reference has not been falsified, and her argument for it has not been refuted. Those who would maintain that some such account is yet possible must rely on different arguments. Further, the construal of reflexive pronouns on which Rumfitt's account depends seems to lend support to the thesis of Anscombe's that he, and so many others, are most determined to reject: that "I" does not refer, and is not supposed to.

10

Can We Make Sense of a Nonreferential Account of "I"?

10.1 The Logical Profile of "I" Seems to Require Us
to Construe It as Referring

As I mentioned at the outset of Part 2, the doctrine that "I" is not a referring expression[1] has been defended, with substantial qualifications, by Wittgenstein (1958, for example, 66–67) and, with no qualifications at all, by Anscombe in FP. Accounts of (possibly unvoiced) first-person judgment with seemingly very similar implications have been argued for by Roderick Chisholm (1982) and, in a very different idiom, by David Lewis (1979). The doctrine—typically, in Anscombe's rather than Chisholm's or Lewis's presentation—has met with widespread and sometimes extreme incredulity. However, we are not in a position to reject the view until we have either shown how to solve the real problems its advocates pose for the construal of "I" as a referring expression (the *referentialist* thesis, as we may call it), thus making the radical alternative unnecessary, or worked out the most plausible version of the account that goes with the thesis in enough detail for us to be able to assess whether the thesis really is vulnerable to the various obvious-seeming objections that might be made against it in its current form. The task of working out in more detail how a nonreferentialist account might go is an urgent one for those who suspect, as I do, that the problems Wittgenstein, Anscombe, and others raise for the referentialist account may well turn out to be insoluble. (I also suspect that, as more detail is provided, at least some of the obvious-seeming objections will be seen to be inconclusive.)[2]

The most obvious objection, of course, concerns the logical profile of "I" (and its oblique cases), and the implications of this for the semantics of "I" (and its associated propositional component). This profile could hardly look more like that of a singular referring expression: it occurs in name position, it provides the basis for existential generalization, and it seems to feature in identity statements, typically alongside names and personal pronouns, which are frequently presupposed in entirely un-exceptionable inferences. Its behavior in inferences, in short, is pretty much altogether indistinguishable from that of referring expressions, so it looks hard to resist the conclusion that its semantic function is to identify an individual.[3] Accordingly, Kaplan has proposed that all there is to understand about "I" is given in the rule that, for any speaker, the content of "I," its contribution to the proposition expressed, is simply the speaker (or writer) (1989, 495, 505). On the view sketched out later, Kaplan's proposal is accepted in a modified form. "I" is a kind of "dummy name"; a "surface manifestation," as Rumfitt might put it, of a second-level concept (possibly a quantifier) predicated of the concepts the speaker self-ascribes. This second-level predication provides the hearer with a license to infer on the basis of the speaker's utterance, together with the fact that *she* uttered it (that *she* was the speaker), propositions in which reference *is* made to the speaker, in accordance with Kaplan's rule.

To take a particular case, there is the obvious problem that if I am not referring to myself when I assert "I am warm," we cannot account for the clearly valid inference drawn from my utterance by a hearer / spectator who credits it as true, that *J. D. is warm*. Doesn't the inference require that "I" and "J. D." alike refer, and to the same object, namely, J. D.?

Prior: Inferences from Utterances Can Draw on More than Their Content

This objection, I think, can be deflected by appeal to a more detailed account of the nonreferentialist position, expanded to include an extension of Prior's account of "spurious indexicals." Prior points out that if you sincerely assert "It's raining," I can validly infer that *you believe* that it's raining, even though neither you nor the attitude of belief has anything to do with the content you asserted. The inference is valid because it is based on more than that content. If the fact of who is speaking is allowed to do expressive work of its own, there is no need to look for anything in the asserted content referring to yourself, or to the attitude of belief, to ground my inference that you believe it's raining (as Wittgenstein says, there is no need for you to point to yourself [1958, 67]). My inference is based not only on the content but also on the facts that the utterance was an assertion and it was made by you:

> It is not possible to believe anything seriously without believing that this believed thing is the case, or is true; nor can one person A sincerely agree with another person B on any matter, or sincerely pronounce B's opinions to be true or right in this matter, unless B's opinions coincide with his own, or rather unless he takes B's opinions to coincide with his own. . . . Yet it seems perfectly clear that this implicit reference to the opinions of the speaker is an "inseparable accident" of the use of these phrases rather than part and parcel of their meaning. "It is the case that p" just does not mean "It is my opinion that p"; and "You are right in thinking p" just does not mean "It is not only your opinion that p, but mine also." For a man can unquestionably use the expression[s] "It is the case" and "You are right" sincerely and seriously without for a minute imagining that he himself is always right and never wrong in his opinions (as he would have to if he thought that "being right" simply meant "being believed by him"). (Prior 1967, 326–327)

Prior's opening phrase, "It is not possible . . . ," here has logical force. The inference to the speaker's beliefs (given sincerity, comprehension, and so on) is deductive: it has none of the defeasibility of other familiar inferences from circumstances of utterance, as from, for example, tone of voice.

So far, perhaps, so unexceptionable. But perhaps this strategy might be extended to cover uses of "I." The basic idea would be something like this. Anything I assert using "I" will be the basis of a valid third-party inference that, if I spoke truly, then whatever I seemingly said of *myself* (call this *the predicate*) is true of J. D. But the basis of this inference does not involve an identity between something called "I" and J. D., for there can be nothing *called* "I" since (as we are assuming) "I" is not a referring expression. Rather, the contribution of "I" is to indicate that the "predicate" (perhaps here not fundamentally functioning as a predicate—see later) is being expressed *without* a subject but in a special way—precisely the way that licenses your inference that such and such is true of J. D. on the basis of (i) what I said using "I" and (ii) the facts that it was J. D. who said it and that his saying it was a sincere assertion (or the relevant analogue of an assertion). If someone claims that "I" is not a referring expression, it is of course legitimate to ask what kind of expression it is; and the current suggestion is that it is something like an *adverb*.

I hope the parallel with Prior's observation about "I believe" is clear. But so far this is entirely programmatic. Some more detail can be added to this briefest of sketches by drawing a further parallel with what Prior has to say in that paper about other kinds of case, for he adapts his treatment of "*A* believes that" to "it is true that" and "it is now the case that." Like "*A* believes that," these are both sentence-forming operators on sentences, but both of a rather peculiar kind. The first is to be contrasted with "it is false that," and the second with "it was the case that," "it will be the case that," and so forth. But they differ from these other contrasting operators with which they are grouped because unlike those, they simply give us back the original sentence—they are, as Prior puts it, the "vacuous special case," their effect being to "multiply by one."

Primitive Uses of "I" as Marking a "Vacuous Special Case" of an Artificially Structured Utterance

My thought here is that, applied to a certain very primitive language game, this idea of a "vacuous special case" might give us an intelligible model of how certain "I" statements might be construed nonreferentially. The language game is to be understood in a "genealogical" spirit, as dramatizing hypotheses about broadly logical priorities by presenting them as relations of historical precedence.

The initial move type in the language game consists of utterances with no syntactic structure, whose point is to draw attention to some attribute of the speaker. Wittgenstein and others thought that the function of many self-ascriptions was to *express* something, where this was to be thought of as contrasted with describing something. Their typical example was the self-ascription of pain, which, they claimed, is illuminatingly thought of as some kind of expressively elaborated descendant of a groan. But the case seems to me ill chosen, in requiring this line of descent to cross the boundary dividing the involuntary from the voluntary.[4] A more plausible primitive ancestor of a self-ascription would be an utterance or sign that, while clearly expressive as opposed to descriptive, was nevertheless fully intentional, and intentional under a description *meaning such-and-such*. Take, for example, an utterance or sign intended to make others aware of a physical condition simply by being a conventionally associated concomitant: a leper ringing a bell and shouting "Unclean!" Someone who claimed that this is already an "I" statement because it is an abbreviation of something like "I have leprosy" is surely getting things the wrong way around: she imposes on the utterance structure that really belongs to the interpretation. The subject is manifesting one perceptible—aural—property, with the aim of drawing attention to another. The fact that the two properties are instantiated in the same individual, while guaranteed by the situation, cannot plausibly be thought of as "part of the meaning of the utterance."

The second move type involves the speaker drawing others' attention to a condition not of her own but of another. There are a number of ways of describing this; possibly the least mystifying would be, in the first instance, in terms of speaking *on behalf of* the other. Obviously the sign must now include, as giving a component of its meaning, some indication of *which* (other) person is being characterized. The important point is that this is the *first* point in the story at which we can recognize anything like reference, or the necessity for it. It is also the first appearance of syntactic structure in the utterance, on the assumption that these second-stage utterances will exhibit systematic phonetic variation in two dimensions, in order to pick out one of any number of subjects, and then ascribe to them any of a range of conditions.

The third stage is the most complicated. The idea is that the syntactic structure of the second move type gets reflected back, so to say, onto the first, so that the first is now thought of as sharing the second's subject-predicate structure. There are obvious reasons why this would be highly useful. This is a way for our proto-linguistic community to homogenize the form of utterances, and so facilitate many important valid inferences. It is not that there could not be canons of inference according to which someone might validly move directly from my structureless (subjectless) utterance conventionally expressing my condition C to a structured judgment "He is in C." But such canons would be cumbersomely complex. Opportunities to effect the economies of inferential principle that come with the idea of *formal* validity would be severely limited, in these cases, by the fact that the first utterance type has no syntactic form, and so a for-tiori shares no form with the second. The structured nature of the second utterance type, by contrast, fits it to figure in the formally valid inference types made possible by singular terms (or, equivalently here, verb inflec-tions). The stage is set for judgments of identity; rules for conjunction, dis-junction, and the other connectives; and the rest. The utterances of the first type would have been largely left out of this system building, had our speakers not forced them into the mold of the second type by endowing them with the same form. This requires assigning to them their own distinctive member of the set of phonetic variations (pronouns or verb inflections, for example), which, in the structured utterances of the second type, indicates the intended subject of predication, that is, effects reference.

Notice that, in this narrative, the purpose of introducing what amounts to a first-person pronoun is *not*, as it was with (whatever amounted to) the other pronouns, to pick out a subject of predication. It is, rather, to bring the unstructured utterances into the fold of formally valid reasoning. The truth and assertibility conditions of the newly structured "first-person" utterances are exactly as they were at the beginning of the story. It is not necessary, in order to understand how and why these utterances can now figure in formal patterns of inference, to suppose that their distinctive ver-sion of the phonetic feature type, which, in the *other* cases, had a referen-tial function, need have such a function in their case too. In fact, such a supposition would be idle. The tail of inferential convenience is here wag-ging the dog of syntax.

Construing "I" in Line with Prior's Accounts of "True" and "Now"

In his paper on "spurious egocentricity," Prior *contrasts* the operators "I believe that," on the one hand, and "it is true that," "it is now the case that," and, by implication, various others, on the other. As we have seen, asserting that *p* is not equivalent to asserting "I believe that *p*": although what the latter expresses may infallibly be inferred from the former (assuming sin-cerity, comprehension, and so on), the "I believe that . . ." component of it is no part of the former's content. By contrast, my saying that *p is* equiv-alent to my saying that it is true that *p*, according to Prior, *and* to my saying that it is now the case that *p*, and in that sense those operators may be regarded as part of what I said in saying that *p*—but only, Prior claims, because they add nothing to the unadorned assertion that *p*. This is because these sorts of operators come in sets, and each of these two is the "vacuous special case" of the set to which it belongs.

I have tried to give some idea of how an account of "I" as nonreferring might draw inspiration from what Prior has to say about "I believe that." Yet it seems to me that, oddly enough, such an account might *also* incorporate much of what Prior has to say about these other operators, which he is so concerned to distinguish from "I believe that."

If we treat my parable as articulating the semantic status of the first-person pronoun, we can see how, in its way, it conforms to Prior's (parable-like) account of how these operators, "it is true that" and "it is now the case that" (and, we might add, "it is actually the case that" and others), might find their way into a formal language—an account he gives in support of his deflationist or "no-truth" theory of truth, associated in his day with Frank Ramsey and A. J. Ayer:

> One might put the "no-truth" theory in a technical context thus: In certain symbolic systems a variable, say "d," is used to stand indifferently for any expression which constructs a statement out of a statement, e.g. "It is not the case that ___," "Grass is green and ___," "It is possible that ___," "Aristotle asserted that ___." Thus "d (The sky is blue)" can stand indifferently for "It is not the case that the sky is blue," "Grass is green and the sky is blue," "If the sky is blue then grass is green," and so on. In expressing logical generalisations by means of such variables it is useful to include "The sky is blue" itself, without any adornments, as being among the things that "d (The sky is blue)" can stand for. But here there is no actual expression that has been put in place of "d," and we tend to feel that this is awkward. The awkwardness, if we are really worried about it, can be relieved by simply introducing an actual expression which when put for "d" in "d (The sky is blue)" will yield a sentence meaning no more and no less than the plain "The sky is blue." If we used "It is the case that ___" or "It is true that ___" or "really" or "truly" in this way, this would be precisely its commonest use in ordinary English. (Prior 1967, 328–329)

The current suggestion is that "I" might be thought of along the lines of the "dummy" value given to "d," which gives the same content back, in Prior's explanation here. According to my story about the development of the primitive language game, at the second stage the original unstructured utterance is given a form (by being inflected, say, or conjoined with a name or pronoun) to indicate the subject of what now amounts to a predication. But our stage-one utterances, which we may now think of as the "first-person case," are formally anomalous: they have no syntactic structure, beyond being expressions of the sort that are fit for predications. They are best construed, I conjecture, as having the logical form of second-level predications, whereby the properties seemingly ascribed to the referent of "I" are brought under second-level concepts. In this way the utterances in question may be regarded as well-formed assertions and therefore truth evaluable, without positing a referent for the first-person pronoun. "I" is therefore understood, in line with Anscombe's nonreferentialist doctrine, not as a singular term but as the surface trace of a second-level concept or quantifier. This logical form is clothed in the surface grammar of a predication with "I" as subject for the sake of a massive gain in convenience in the regimentation of inference. The surface structure imposed on first-person utterances is precisely the one that characterizes the other second-stage utterances to which the former bear their most immediate inferential relations. (Note that this need not involve any phonetic innovation; the original utterance, unchanged, may now simply be treated as the "first-person" inflection of the "verb"—such a habit of thought may well be psychologically inevitable.) But this move completely disguises the semantic reality beneath a smoothly homogenous surface: the content of the first-person utterance is still identical with the subjectless utterances of stage one. It has been rendered fit for easy inferential use by being endowed with the appropriate syntactic form; but this should not mislead us into thinking that it involves *reference* to the speaker any more than, in Prior's account given previously, the "dummy" values of d make the slightest difference to the contents of the sentences with which they are combined.

The differences between my parable and Prior's are also important. In my case, the second-stage utterances, which are structured in a way that gives the self-ascribed concepts the appearance of predicate position, are not of the same syntactic type as the first, which, if we are to construe them as structured at all, bring the self-ascribed concepts under second-level concepts that indicate self-ascription without predicating the first-level concepts of anything at all.

The stage-three imposition of structure on the first-stage utterance creates the impression that it is logically and semantically "on a par" with second-stage predications—in a way, this is the point of the imposition, since it is what fits the utterances to figure in systematizable inferences. But the impression is fundamentally misleading. The third-stage utterances are not really to be understood as obtainable from second-stage ones by substituting one referring expression for another, as when "she" is switched for "he." "I" is a "dummy name" giving a syntactically misleading form to a first-stage utterance, and the first-stage utterances are logically prior to the second.

It might be helpful to think of the matter in this way. We begin (stage one) with a syntactically unstructured utterance—say, "Measles!"—which is conventionally understood as a kind of aural concomitant of measles, and so draws attention to this condition in the speaker. In the context of radical interpretation, the principle of charity might permit us to construe this utterance as a second-level predication. The second stage involves combining a component indicating the condition with a second component indicating who is in it—"She! Measles!" (accompanied by pointing), as it might be. Now the *truth conditions* of this structured utterance could be expressed thus (although this emphatically should not be thought of as "what it really means"): "She has the condition you would be entitled to ascribe to her if she herself nondeceitfully said 'Measles!'" The same analysis of the third-stage utterance "I! Measles!" gives us the truth condition (to express it in third-stage terms) "I have the condition you would be entitled to ascribe to me if I myself nondeceitfully said 'Measles!'" But this is clearly equivalent to (has exactly the same assertibility conditions as) the unadorned "Measles!" (that is, the second-level predication), which is not surprising, given the point of introducing "I" as a "dummy" pronoun. The way the story was told makes it clear that it would be perverse to insist that "Measles!" should be understood in terms of "I! Measles!" rather than the other way around.

Another possibility is that we might secure truth aptness for stage-one utterances by supposing that they express subjectless propositions. That is, we might reconstruct the stage-one utterance "In pain!" as something along the lines of "It's paining!"[5] which, like "it's raining," is, while of course grammatically of subject-predicate form, not construable as having a real ("logical") subject without a great deal of artificiality.

The Problem of Scope with "Now" and "I"

This sketch of how "I" might be understood in a primitive context of communication is of course but a tiny step toward an adequate construal of the pronoun as nonreferring. One of the most urgent complications to be addressed would be the behavior of the pronoun in indirect discourse. Here we immediately encounter difficulties having to do with scope. In the case of "now," Prior seems to underestimate these difficulties, but in a way that confirms the parallel with "I." I shall look at the two cases in turn.

Concerning "now," Prior writes, " 'He is eating his breakfast now' and 'He is eating his breakfast at present' seem to say no more and no less, apart from nuances of emphasis, than the plain 'He is eating his breakfast.' We can do without 'now,' we can do without a present-tense copula 'is,' we can do without even a special present-tense inflection of the main verb—just using the root verb-form itself, as in 'I eat' and 'They eat' in English—if we understand that this is what we have with us all the time— this is what the verb-form basically means" (1967, 331).

This is why Prior is attracted to a "multiply by one" conception of "now," which parallels the "no-truth" theory of truth—indeed, he says, it is in a way the same theory, since "It is true that . . ." is the vacuous special case *both* by contrast with "It was (will be, and so on) true that . . ." *and* by contrast with "It is false (probable, debatable, and so on) that . . ."

Now, he does acknowledge particular difficulties with "now." He earlier pointed out that if one says that something is going on *now*, this will be true if what is going on is going on contemporaneously with the utterance; but (and Kaplan makes basically the same point) this is not because, and it is not true that, "now" (or "present") *means* "contemporaneously with this utterance." We can see this from non-present-tense cases: for example, "His eating his breakfast *was* a present fact" is typically not even materially equivalent to "His eating his breakfast *was* contemporaneous with this utterance" (1967, 330). The relevance of this to Prior's overall argument is that the claim that "now" (or "present") *means* "contemporaneous with this utterance" is a rival to his generally preferred "no-present" theory. And the preferred theory seems to succeed just where the other fails: the logical equivalence of the "presentness of the occurring of X" and the simple "occurring of X" *is* preserved in nonpresent cases: just as "He is eating his breakfast" looks equivalent to "His eating his breakfast is a present fact," so "He was eating his breakfast" looks equivalent to "His eating his breakfast was a present fact."

The first difficulty Prior concedes is that sometimes "now" *does* seem synonymous with "contemporaneously with this utterance," as when one says the word in response to the instruction "Say when" when someone is pouring one a drink. "But this use of 'now' stands out so sharply from all its other uses," he writes, "that the very fact that the translation suits it is enough to show that it doesn't suit the others" (1967, 332).

The second difficulty is that it is unusual for "now" to be directly dispensable in nonpresent tenses, as it should be on Prior's account. The reason is that "now" usually "gets attached in sense to a statement as a whole, no matter how subordinate the clause in which it is immediately placed." (This is a special case of a feature Kaplan ascribes to *all* indexicals: that they *always take primary scope* [Kaplan 1989, 499].) Examples: "He said he would be in London now," "You will always be proud of what you are doing now."

The reality of the second difficulty seems to undermine Prior's solution to the first. That solution was that it is only in special cases that "now" seems equivalent to "contemporaneously with this utterance." But the fact that "now" nearly always takes primary scope itself entails that "now" is nearly always equivalent to "contemporaneously with the present utterance" just as much as it is in the response to the host saying "Say when." In his own examples, "at *this* moment" or "simultaneously with this utterance of mine" are as substitutable for "now" as in the drink-pouring case. So it is *just not true* that "this use of 'now' stands out . . . sharply from all its other uses."

Prior here neglects an enormous difference between ". . . is a present fact" and ". . . is occurring now." "He was eating his breakfast" may be equivalent to "His eating his breakfast was a present fact," but it is not equivalent to "His eating his breakfast was occurring now," which is either not intelligible at all or an idiom of vividness unusual precisely because it gives "now" narrow scope. The problem is precisely that "now" *is* usually tied to the time of utterance in a way that "present" is not.

Prior is right that "now" does not *mean* "contemporaneously with this utterance," but not for the reason he gives, which only applies (at best) to locutions involving "present." In particular, as we have seen and as Prior himself effectively concedes, the substitution in the case of "now" *does* very often preserve truth—the drink-pouring case is *not* unusual at all; it is typical. But truth preservation here is not an upshot of content preservation. It derives instead from the fact that "utterances of 'now' in any context refer to the time of that context" is a frequently sound *rule* for *fixing the reference* of "now." The rule gives not the content of "now" but its *character,* in the sense of Kaplan (1989, 505): a function from contexts of utterance to contents expressed.

These considerations show that "now" cannot be dropped in the way that Prior seems to think. If "I am tired" were equivalent to "I am now tired," then (A) "In twenty-four hours it will be the case that I am tired" would be equivalent to (B) "In twenty-four hours it will be the case that I am now tired," but it is not. The most natural reading of (A) makes it equivalent to "In twenty-four hours I will be tired"; the most natural reading of (B) makes it equivalent to "I am now tired, and in twenty-four hours it will still be true that I *was* tired right now"—a truth rooted in the necessity of (what will be) the past. "Now" normally ties the content it modifies to the time it is expressed in utterance, even when it occurs in an embedded sentence, in a way that the present tense, or phrases like "at present," do not. Consistently with all this, "I am tired" and "I am now tired" have the same truth conditions.

How does "I" behave, by comparison? Prior makes the same half acknowledgment of the primary scope of "I" as for "now," and it is here that he introduces his invented, narrow-scope pronoun "Self," which I looked at earlier in connection with Rumfitt's objections to Anscombe:

It is the same with "I" as it is with "now" and with "any"—even in subordinate clauses we make it refer to the speaker of the entire sentence. In a more rational language we might have used a pronoun "Self" in such a way that "Self is sick," for example, means the same as our present "I am sick," but "He believes that self is sick" would mean, not the same as our present "He believes that I am sick," but the same as our present

"He believes that he is sick." And then, perhaps, "He believes that self believes that grass is green" would be related to "He believes that it is true that grass is green" exactly as "It is true that grass is green" is to "I believe (ie Self believes) that grass is green." (1967, 333)

Prior's "Self" is related to "I" rather as "present" is related to "now": it is governed by a narrow-scope version of the same reference rule. As we saw in the previous chapter, the rule is, roughly: "Self" refers to the speaker or thinker of the sentence or thought-report of which it gives the immediate subject, *not only* (like "I") in direct discourse *but also* (like the indirect reflexive "he*") in indirect discourse. Prior's invented pronoun is interesting, because the most plausible and worked-out attempt I know of to argue that we can avoid Anscombe's thesis that "I" does not refer (Rumfitt 1994) depends, as we have seen, on a theory of reflexive pronouns on which *they* do not refer. Prior's "Self," in depriving "I," as it were, of its peculiar prerogative of primary scope, threatens to erase any principled distinction in the matter of referentiality between the first-person and the indirect reflexive pronoun—that is, to raise the possibility that the claims of all such pronouns to a referential function stand or fall together.

11

Strategies for Saving "I" as a Singular Term: Domesticating FP and Deflating Reference

An Attempt to Domesticate FP

How are we to understand the main thesis of FP? Unlike what I took to be the main thesis of MMP—the rejection of the vocabulary of *morality*—the main thesis of FP looks relatively straightforward. The idea that "I" is not a referring expression does not seem to present us with analogues of the many serious difficulties that beset the interpretation of the MMP thesis—difficulties that, I argued, led the vast majority of commentators far astray. Most readers of FP have understood *its* thesis in more or less the same way, and this is a plausible explanation of the more or less uniformly high level of incredulity with which it has been received.

As I mentioned in the Preface, however, the suggestion has also been made that the real import of the FP thesis, while still false, is quite different, and in particular less offensive to conventional wisdom, than has generally been supposed.

Edward Harcourt correctly identifies Anscombe's "no reference thesis" (as he calls the main claim of FP) as a thesis about the semantic category to which "I" should be assigned (Harcourt 2000, 26). He conceives of the assignment of an expression to a semantic category in terms of specifying a test such that all and only expressions that pass it are correctly assigned to the category in question.

What Harcourt calls the *normal test* for determining whether the function of an expression is to refer consists in determining whether it has the appropriate "logical syntax." He distinguishes two component conditions:

"For many, it is sufficient for an expression to belong to the semantic category of referring expressions that it have a certain logical syntax, ie, that sentences in which it occurs stand in certain inferential relations to other sentences and that it contribute to the truth-conditions of the former sentences in a certain systematic way. Let us call satisfaction of these two conditions together 'the normal test' for referring expressionhood" (Harcourt 2000, 27).

People have been amazed by Anscombe's "no reference" thesis, Harcourt conjectures, largely because they have assumed that she too subscribes to this "normal test" for whether "I" is a referring expression.[1] He questions this assumption: he suggests that she does *not* subscribe to the "normal test." He infers this from what he takes to be her concession that "I" clearly passes it:

> Curiously . . . , Anscombe herself concedes what on the view of referring expressionhood defined by the normal test appears to be quite enough to defeat her thesis. Thus for example she says that "we haven't got [the sense of 'I'] just by being told which object a man will be speaking of, whether he knows it or not, when he says 'I' " [FP, 47]. This implies that, when a man says "I," he will be *speaking of* an object, and the notion of speaking of an object does not seem very far removed from that of *referring to* it. More strikingly, she says that "I" "functions syntactically like a name" [FP, 47], that "[i]f X asserts something with 'I' as subject, his assertion will be true if and only if what he asserts is true of X" [FP, 54, 59], and thus that "I" "can be replaced *salva veritate* by a . . . name of X when it occurs in subject position in assertions made by X" [FP, 55]. (2000, 27–28)

If Anscombe rejects the normal test, her conception of a *referring expression* is nonstandard, so that her denial of that status to "I" is consistent with its counting as a referring expression on a standard conception, as is implied by her concession that it passes the normal test. It may well be, then, Harcourt concludes, that her claim that "I" is not a referring expression does not amount to a startlingly radical thesis about *I*, but merely reflects a somewhat eccentric conception of *referring expression*: "These concessions sow the suspicion that, when it is properly understood, Anscombe's thesis is not really so controversial after all, and that Anscombe advanced it not because she thought (for whatever reason) that 'I' fails the normal test but because she took a different view of the criteria for assigning expressions to semantic categories in general, or to the category of referring expression in particular" (Harcourt 2000, 28).[2]

If Harcourt's suspicion is correct, FP would be vulnerable, I think, to accusations of the kind of philosophical fraudulence I complained of in my Preface: a certain bogus sensationalism, whereby relatively unexceptionable doctrines are hidden behind a paradoxical facade falsely suggestive of exciting profundity.

Harcourt's suspicion is quite baseless, however. The many are correct in their understanding of the FP thesis as meaning what it says. What Anscombe means by her denial that "I" is a referring expression is that *"I" is not a referring expression,* and this is not significantly less revolutionary than what she meant in MMP by her denunciation of the vocabulary of morality.

Harcourt is right about the wide acceptance of something like the twofold test he cites for whether an expression is to count as having the referring function: (i) "that sentences in which it occurs stand in certain inferential relations to other sentences" and (ii) "that it contribute to the truth-conditions of the former sentences in a certain systematic way" (2000, 27). It is misleading, however, to speak of these criteria as determining that the expression in question has a certain "logical syntax" (27). For if anything counts as a *semantic* condition, condition (ii) does. A referring expression's systematic mode of contribution to the truth conditions of atomic sentences[3] in which it occurs is presumably going to amount to its identifying some object, such that the truth value of the sentence will depend on how things stand with that object. Furthermore, (i) only counts as syntactic if it is deducibility that is at issue, and not logical consequence. But the real point of inferential relations is that they express logical consequence, not deducibility. Further, even if (i) were properly syntactic, it is in effect swallowed up by (ii). For it is hard to see how an expression could make the right sort of contribution to the truth conditions of sentences in which it occurs unless it presents the syntactic profile of a singular term (Fine 2002, 58). Harcourt's "normal test" for the right "logical syntax" therefore boils down to a formulation in terms of truth conditions of the intuitive conception of a referring expression: that its function in the language be to pick out an object. If Anscombe in FP is rejecting that test, she is not just working with a nonstandard conception of *referring expression;* she is simply changing the subject: she is not really denying that "I" is a referring expression *at all.* This would be much worse than the usual kind of philosophical fraud, which proceeds by misleading associations: she would be giving a flatly false description of her own view.

However, Anscombe certainly does *not* reject condition (ii). The remark quoted by Harcourt, "we haven't got [the sense of 'I'] just by being told which object a man will be speaking of, whether he knows it or not, when he says 'I'" (FP, 47), is a red herring: these words do not imply that an "I" user is speaking of an object. Anscombe repeatedly indicates that she regards *speaking of* an object as *equivalent* to referring to it; for example, "[The following is a possible situation:] 'When John Smith spoke of John Horatio Auberon Smith (named in a will perhaps) he was speaking of himself, but he did not know this.' If so, then *'speaking of' or 'referring to'* oneself is compatible with not knowing that the object one speaks of is oneself'" (FP, 46; my emphasis).

Thus, in denying that "I" is a referring expression, she denies that it is an expression used to speak of anything. Nor does she inconsistently concede, in the passage quoted by Harcourt, that an "I" user is speaking of an object, since she is speaking ad hominem: she is simply envisaging something that might be said by someone who *does* suppose that an "I" user speaks of (that is, refers to) some object.

Her denial that "I" is a referring expression, in the ordinary sense of "referring expression," comes through on nearly every page of FP. She unmistakably argues that "I" cannot be deemed to *connect up with an object* in the manner of a referring relation: we cannot effect an assimilation to any of the familiar categories of referring expression—name, demonstrative, and so on—in a way that makes sense; and even if we could, the only thing it could possibly aspire to refer to would be something we cannot coherently suppose to be real, namely, a Cartesian ego. For example,

> Nothing but a Cartesian Ego will serve. Or rather, a stretch of one. . . .
> We discover that *if* "I" is a referring expression, then Descartes was right about what the referent was. His position has, however, the intolerable difficulty of requiring identification of the same referent in different "I"-thoughts. (FP, 57)

Getting hold of the wrong object [in using "I"] *is* excluded, and that makes us think that getting hold of the right object is guaranteed. But the reason is that *there is no getting hold of an object at all.* . . . If this is too hard to believe, if "I" *is* a "referring expression," then Descartes was right [about the referent]. *But now the troubles start.* (FP, 58; my emphases)

Harcourt's suspicion depends on overlooking, among other things, the significance of the fact that very many of our "I" judgments are *true.* The subject term of a *true* sentence cannot, it seems plausible to suppose, fail to refer.[4] Further, on the standard understanding of "I" as a referring expression, even *false* "I" judgments cannot be false on account of their subject term lacking a referent:

"I"—if it makes a reference, if, that is, its mode of meaning is that it is supposed to make a reference—is secure against reference-failure. Just thinking "I" guarantees not only the existence but also the presence of its referent. It guarantees the existence *because* it guarantees the presence, which is presence to consciousness. But N.B., here "presence to consciousness" means physical or real presence, not just that one is thinking of the thing. For if the thinking did not guarantee the presence, the existence of the referent could be doubted. For the same reason, if "I" is a name it cannot be an empty name. I's existence is existence in the thinking of the thought expressed by "I." (FP, 53–54)

If, as Anscombe argues in FP, there is no suitable object that could count as a referent for "I," then if "I" *were* a referring expression, it *would* be an empty one. This may seem inconsistent. How can Anscombe maintain both (i) that if "I" is a referring expression, it "is secure against reference-failure" and (ii) that if "I" is a referring expression, it could only aspire to refer to a Cartesian ego, which doesn't exist? The answer, I think, is that the two claims are made against the background of different presuppositions. (i) "I" would have to be secure against reference failure *if* it is a referring expression and some "I" judgments are true: that is, if it sometimes refers, it *always* refers. (ii) If we drop the assumption that some "I" judgments are true, then if "I" were a referring expression, it could *never* refer—partly for the reason that, if it did, it would have to do so infallibly!

Anscombe, presumably, rightly regards the suggestion that "I" judgments are all false as absurd. But given her reasoned conviction that "I" can have no referent, the only escape from absurdity is to deny that "I" is a referring expression at all. It is true that many regard this denial as itself absurd; but it is not, I submit, as absurd as it would be to deny that any "I" judgments are true.

Harcourt conjectures that Anscombe rejects the "normal test for referring expressionhood" in favor of nonstandard *epistemic* tests; and even if, as I maintain, she does not reject the normal test, there is a question about whether she supplements it.

He observes that she argues that it is impossible to specify an appropriate "conception" (roughly, a Fregean sense) of the sort of thing "I" would have to refer to, on the supposition that it is a referring expression, as what a competent "I" user would have to be credited with if his use were to be susceptible of a referential construal. Such arguments, he says, are "liable to raise the protest that epistemology is one thing, semantics another. Why, it may be objected," he goes on, "should the fact that a conception of the appropriate sort cannot be specified for 'I'—interesting as it may be—decide the semantic category to which 'I' belongs, while facts about the logical syntax of first person sentences do not?" (2000, 30).

But the imputation to Anscombe of some novel epistemic test is also groundless. First, if "logical syntax" means anything like logical *form* (as is strongly suggested by Harcourt's contrasting it with "surface syntax" [2000, 31]), she nowhere implies that facts about the logical syntax of first-person sentences do not decide the semantic category to which "I" belongs. Nor could she intelligibly imply this, given that an important part of the point of the idea of logical form is precisely to decide such semantic categories: to determine that an expression takes subject position in a representation of a thought that exhibits (the relevant aspects of) its logical form *is,* among other things, to conclude that it is a referring expression.[5]

Second, the other question, about why the unavailability of a "conception" is relevant to (logical syntax and therefore to) semantic classification, has a straightforward answer. Since many "I" sentences are true and known to be true, any account of the semantics of "I" as referential must be consistent not merely with "I" making the kind of contribution characteristic of a referring expression to the truth conditions of the sentences but with its often *succeeding* in making such a contribution, and in a way consistent with the truth of the sentences being *knowable*. This in turn requires, at least on Anscombe's somewhat Fregean way of seeing such things, that we make sense of the idea of a mode of presentation in connection with "I." This requirement is not *au fond* epistemic, since it follows naturally from a broadly Fregean account of the semantics of successfully referential expressions.

We saw that Harcourt was wrong to suspect Anscombe of conceding that "I" passes the second component of the "normal test for referring expressionhood," which was in effect that it contribute to the truth conditions of sentences in which it occurs by picking out an object. But what about the first component of the test, "that sentences in which [the expression] occurs stand in certain inferential relations to other sentences"? I suggested previously, following Kit Fine, that meeting the second condition is sufficient for meeting the first. But it is not necessary; so Anscombe's denial that "I" meets the second condition is consistent with her conceding that it meets the first. True, her denial that it meets the second condition essentially just *is* a denial that "I" is a referring expression, contra Harcourt's suspicions; so that ship has already sailed. But if she concedes that it meets the first condition, this would *pro tanto* vindicate Harcourt's conjecture that her conception of a referring expression is not entirely standard: it would allow her to deny that "I" is a referring expression even though the role "I" plays in inferences, whose validity she has no interest in calling into question, is the role specifically associated with referring expressions.

Here Harcourt seems to be on firmer ground. Recall the words he cites from FP as evidence of her concessions: "[Anscombe] says that 'I' 'functions syntactically like a name' [FP, 47], that '[i]f X asserts something with "I" as subject, his assertion will be true if and only if what he asserts is true of X' [FP, 54, 59], and thus that 'I' 'can be replaced *salva veritate* by a . . . name of X when it occurs in subject position in assertions made by X' [FP, 55]" (Harcourt 2000, 28).

Yet even this evidence is somewhat equivocal. The words of the second quotation occur twice in FP. At their second appearance she does say, "Of course we must accept [this] rule." But this is said on the presupposition that "I" is *not* a referring expression, as we have already established on the basis of her denial that it meets the second condition. She first

mentions the principle, apparently, in order to cast doubt on the entitlement to it, of those who suppose that "I" *is* a referring expression! This
first assertion of the principle is also not made fully in propria persona; it
is put in the mouth of "a logician, for whom the syntactical character of
'I' as a proper name is quite sufficient to guarantee it as such." Here is the
first appearance of the principle in its immediate context:

> To [the logician] it is clear that "I," in my mouth, is just another name for
> E.A. "I" may have some curious characteristics; but they don't interest
> him. The reason is that "I" is a name governed by the following rule:
> If X makes assertions with "I" as subject, then those assertions will
> be true if and only if the predicates used thus assertively are true of X.
> This will be why Kripke—and others discussing Descartes—make
> the transition from Descartes's "I" to "Descartes."
> Now first, this offers too swift a refutation of Descartes. In order to
> infer straight away that Descartes was wrong, we only need the infor-
> mation that Descartes asserted "I am not a body," together with the
> knowledge that he was a man: that is, an animal of a certain species;
> that is, a body living with a certain sort of life. (FP, 54)[6]

This goes back to the first two pages of FP. The idea is that Descartes,
following Augustine (*De Trinitate* 10.16, 2002, 56), saw more clearly than
most the implications of treating "I" as a referring expression:

> *If . . .* the non-identity of himself with his own body follows from his
> starting-points, so equally does the non-identity of himself with the man
> Descartes. "I am not Descartes" was just as sound a conclusion for him
> to draw as "I am not a body." To cast the argument in the third person,
> replacing "I" by "Descartes," is to miss this. Descartes would have ac-
> cepted the conclusion. That mundane, practical, everyday sense in which
> it would have been correct for him to say "I am Descartes" was of no
> relevance to him in these arguments. That which is named by *"I"—that,*
> in *his* book, was not *Descartes.* (FP, 45)[7]

So Anscombe does accept the principle, but her acceptance, in her own
eyes, in no way qualifies her insistence that "I" is not a referring expression. On the contrary, her view seems to be that only one who, like her,
denies that "I" is a referring expression is in a position to endorse the
principle without further ado.

Anscombe's assertion that "Certainly 'I' functions syntactically like a name" (FP, 47) is made fully in propria persona. But there is not much room left, at this point, for an interpretation of her denial that "I" is a referring expression that blunts its force. In itself this admission is of no help in that direction, since it is fully consistent with the no-reference thesis if—indeed, I suspect, only if—it is read against the background of the familiar distinction between the levels of surface grammar and logical form, so that the functioning of "I" as a name can be conceded at the former level and denied at the latter. This is presumably the distinction Harcourt invokes when he contrasts "surface syntax" with "logical syntax" (2000, 31).[8]

Yet Harcourt is surely right to seize on the admission, not because it can help revive his suspicions that the no-reference thesis is (as I should want to put it) fundamentally unserious, but because, even if the distinction between surface grammar and logical form blocks any allegation of immediate inconsistency, it is not enough to relieve a prima facie serious tension (surface tension?) between the admission, even as a matter of surface grammar, that "I" functions syntactically like a name and the no-reference thesis, which Harcourt is, by and by, happy to take at face value for the sake of argument.

The problem is that the distinction, between surface grammar and logical form, can only take us so far. Anscombe disparages surface grammar as evidence for logical form: "The essential argument [for 'I' being a referring expression] cannot be an argument back from syntax to reference, for such an argument would depend only on the form of sentence and would be absurd (e.g. no one thinks that 'it is raining' contains a referring expression, 'it')" (FP, 55). But she is overplaying her hand. As she herself effectively acknowledges elsewhere in FP, the "argument back from syntax" to the referentiality of "I" has incomparably more force than the absurd argument from the form of "It's raining." In particular, "I" frequently occurs in what for all the world look like identity statements (no one would entertain the thought that "I am E. A." is not an identity statement unless they were *already* afflicted by doubts that "I" is a referring expression). And, notwithstanding the peculiar claims Augustine and Descartes are led to make or imply, such statements, understood as identities, are frequently held to be true, and so as licensing, in extensional contexts, inferences in accordance with Leibniz's law based on substitution of coreferring terms: I am hungry, so J. D. is hungry. And further, as Harcourt points out, "I" sentences are subject to existential generalization in exactly the way characteristic of singular terms: I am hungry, so *someone* is hungry. The absurdity of treating "it" in "It's raining" as a singular term entirely turns on its *not* presenting this sort of multiply corroborated inferential profile characteristic of a singular term.

Now, it might nevertheless be thought that no credentials of an expression's surface grammar can establish conclusively that it has the referring function in the fundamental sense of being required, by the truth of any sentence in which it essentially occurs, to refer to a real object. This supposition has been challenged, however, in a way that threatens to deny even conceptual space to Anscombe's no-reference thesis.

11.2   Frege, Wright, and the "Priority of Syntax"

In his epoch-making *Frege's Conception of Numbers as Objects* (1983), Crispin Wright attributed to Frege, and argued on his own account for, the view that, if an expression has the *surface grammar* of a singular term and occurs essentially in true sentences, then it has a referent. Wright presents this doctrine as a corollary of his interpretation of Frege's famous *context principle:* "Never to ask for the meaning of a word in isolation, but only in the context of a proposition" (Frege 1953, x^e).

According to Wright,

> The substance of the claim that numbers are, if anything, Fregean objects, must . . . be simply that there are substantial analogies between the behaviour of numerical expressions and that of paradigmatic singular terms in general; the existence of numbers as Fregean objects will be guaranteed by the presence of those analogies and the fact that certain appropriate contexts involving numerical expressions are true. (1983, 12)

> The basis of Frege's Platonism is the thesis that objects are what singular terms, in the ordinary intuitive sense of "singular term," refer to. From the point of view of the correct order of explanation, the converse claim, that singular terms are those expressions which refer to objects, is true but back to front. For Frege it is the syntactic category which is

primary, the ontological one derivative. It is because Frege holds this primacy of syntactic categories that he believes that he can legitimately argue that the syntactic behaviour of numerical expressions immediately settles that numbers are if anything a kind of object. (13)

This position transcends the context of Wright's (and Frege's) immediate concern, the philosophical foundations of number theory. Wright is clearly presenting, on behalf of Frege and himself, an application to the case of numerical expressions of a completely general thesis about the priority of syntax to ontology. (I will sometimes refer to this as the *priority thesis*.) It is quite striking, it turns out, how much of Frege's work in this area, and of the abundant recent literature on it, concerns these general questions of ontology and the significance of syntax, and so are as relevant to our questions about whether "I" is a singular term and if so what it might refer to, as to Frege's questions about whether numerical expressions are singular terms, and if so what *they* might refer to.

By the phrase "the ordinary intuitive sense of 'singular term,'" Wright presumably means a sense tied to what we have been calling surface grammar. As I remarked in the previous section, the corresponding claim about "logical syntax" is more or less trivial: the question whether a singular term occurs in a logically perspicuous expression of a thought just is the question whether a certain object, the expression's referent, must exist if the thought is to be true (cf. Dummett 1991, 185).

It is not immediately clear where Wright's view leaves the idea of logical syntax as that is ordinarily understood. Of course, he is not prepared to concede a real referent to any old noun phrase that shows up in a true sentence. His version of the (surface-grammatical) "syntactic tests" for singular termhood are stringent, particularly when it becomes clear that his position requires a purely syntactic explanation of what singular terms are, "without involving the notions of object or reference" (1983, 53). There is much emphasis, as in Frege, on aptness to feature in identity statements. But beyond this, the only condition for reality of referent is that the sentences in which the terms occur be *true*. Eliminability via logically equivalent paraphrase, in particular, is neither here nor there (25–36). This inevitably makes the idea of an object rather "lighter" than the received one, even if we respect Wright's insistence that to interpret the priority thesis as merely introducing a novel use of the term "object" is to miss the point entirely (12–13). It also seems to leave the idea of logical syntax with a much diminished role. An important purpose in discerning logical syntax is to formulate thoughts in sentences whose truth would require successful reference on the part of all of its essentially occurring referring expressions. But on Wright's conception as I understand it, *all* essential occurrences of *all* referring expressions are in sentences whose truth would require ipso facto the existence of referents for those expressions in those occurrences. Thus once expressions that fail the syntactic tests have been weeded out, there is no further work for logical syntax to do by way of attuning the syntactic structure of sentences to resonate with the facts about what kinds of things there are. There are automatically as many things and kinds of things as comprise the referents of all referring expressions in all true sentences.

The relevance of Wright's general thesis to the meaning of the first-person pronoun is immediate. If he is right, Anscombe's position is not even a conceptual possibility. Wright is quite clear about this. Consider his response to a natural objection to his (and, supposedly, Frege's) priority thesis:

> But how can such considerations [that the surface syntax of an expression is referential and the sentence in which it occurs is true] be enough to settle the matter [of the existence of the integers]? For could it not, surely, simply be a *mistake* to give the syntax of our arithmetical language the kind of significance which Frege, on this interpretation, is proposing? What if there really are no such genuine objects? . . . Well, *it is evident that Frege's position requires that such doubts be vacuous; there is to be no possibility of such a mistake, no possibility that, the syntax of our arithmetical language and the truth of appropriate statements expressed in it notwithstanding, there are no such genuine objects.*
>
> Therefore, in particular, *it must not be coherent* to suggest the possibility of some sort of independent, language-unblinkered inspection of the contents of the world, of which the outcome might be to reveal that there was indeed nothing there capable of serving as the referents of what Frege takes to be numerical singular terms. Frege requires that *there is no possibility* that we might disregard the preconceptions inbuilt into the syntax of our arithmetical language, and, the scales having dropped from our eyes, as it were, find that in reality there are no natural

numbers, that in our old way of speaking we had not succeeded in referring to anything. Rather, it has to be the case that when it has been established, by the sort of syntactic criteria sketched, that a given class of terms are functioning as singular terms, and when it has been verified that certain appropriate sentences containing them are, by ordinary criteria, true, then *it follows that such terms do genuinely refer.* . . . *There is to be no further, intelligible question* whether such terms *really* have a reference, whether there really *are* such objects. (1983, 13–14; my emphases, except for "really" and "are" in the final sentence)

Let the reader not be misled by references to arithmetical language and so forth: it is clear from many other things in Wright's book that the priority thesis is intended to be absolutely general, and indeed any other construal surely makes the thesis bizarrely ad hoc.

Anscombe herself of course concedes that "I" has the surface grammar of a singular term, and it certainly meets Wright's criteria. She also clearly wants to acknowledge the truth of at least most of the "I" judgments we would ordinarily take to be true.[9] For Wright, there is then nothing more to discuss. The grammatical profile of "I" guarantees its status as a referring expression; the further circumstance, that the term occurs essentially in any number of true sentences, guarantees that it often succeeds in referring.

However, we might regard Anscombe's discussion of the semantic function of "I" as issuing a verdict on the "priority of syntax" thesis, rather than the other way around. Such a verdict would be a damning one. If Anscombe is right—and she *might* be—that we can in the end form no coherent idea of an object to which "I" might refer in all its uses, but Wright is right that we are constrained by the expression's surface grammar to regard it as having the semantic *function* of referring to an object, there is no avoiding the consequence that "I" judgments are one and all *false* (if they have a truth value at all), for want of anything for their subject term to refer to. Wright was criticized for not providing for the possibility that arithmetical discourse might be false (Field 1989, 154); but, as I have said, an error theory of *"I" judgments* looks like a form of skepticism best left notional. In this sense Wright's position leaves too many options open.

In another sense, however, it closes off options prematurely. One who accepts Anscombe's skeptical conclusions about the prospects for "I" having a referent, and is, like Anscombe, unburdened by any commitment to the priority of syntax, is free to construe the semantic function of "I" in some other way. Such a project might look quixotic, but at least we do not rule out a priori any hope of an entitlement to regard many "I" judgments as true. Wright's position here pays a heavy price for denying itself any right of appeal to logical syntax, against the verdict of surface grammar on some expression, that it is a singular term. Insistence on the supremacy of (surface) syntax leaves Wright powerless to prevent an alarming raising of the stakes, whereby a choice is forced between producing a plausible referent for "I" and denying the truth of any and all "I" judgments. What compelling interest is served by closing off philosophical options in this way? One can see the attractions, for someone who wants to defend a liberal, Wright-style conception of *object*, of denying conceptual space to a protest that a sentence might be true without its singular terms (as those are determined by surface grammar) referring to anything, but in connection with the first person such a course looks disastrous, in light of Anscombe's misgivings about the idea of a referent of "I." As I remarked at the end of Part 1 in connection with MMP's demonstration of the relevance of cultural history to our understanding of ethical concepts, *the important point does not depend on Anscombe being right in her main thesis.* Her objections to a referential construal of "I" might be answerable, but this hope already concedes that they are *cogent.* To respond with a repeated insistence that the truth of the judgments guarantees a referent for "I" as a matter of conceptual necessity starts to look rather like a kind of incantation. Worse, as we have seen, the conceptual connections insisted on by Wright, which supposedly underwrite the guarantee, can be traced back in the other direction, so that misgivings about a referent for "I," *on Wright's own account,* amount to misgivings about the truth of any "I" judgments. How can that truth be maintained at this point, without addressing, on their own terms, the objections to the idea that "I" could have a referent?

The dialectical encounter with Anscombe's position, then, leaves the idea of the "priority of syntax" looking rather like a sham, because it seems to let in again through the back door wrangles of a traditional metaphysical kind about what kinds of things are real. It is of course an important condition, in Wright's liberal conception of what it is for an object to be real, that the sentences that include an expression making apparent reference to the object be *true.* But it will often be very hard to see how to determine whether a sentence might be true without assessing the plausibility of the suggestion that objects, of a sort that some of its expressions purport to refer to, might actually exist. The case of the first person is as vivid an illustration of this as one could want.

In a way, the case of the first person provides a vindication of what I take to be one of Michael Dummett's (1991) main complaints against Wright: that his "priority of syntax" view inherits those defects of Frege's *Grundlagen* (of which Wright claims that his own view is simply a correct interpretation) stemming from the fact that it was written before Frege had formulated his distinction between sense and reference. Once that distinction is in place, the *Grundlagen* conception of "reference for free" stands revealed as semantically idle. If numbers are objects to which numerical expressions refer, and the thought expressed by an arithmetical sentence about a number is what is grasped by someone who understands it, then according to Frege's mature view, there must be a component of that thought, the *sense* of the arithmetical expression, that consists of *the way that term's referent*—the number itself—*is given* to one who understands the thought. If the reality of that object consists of nothing more than the truth of the sentence in which the relevant numerical expression occurs, any attempt to provide a nontrivial specification of such a sense will obviously be futile, and we must abandon any hope of giving an account of how the thought expressed by the arithmetical sentence is a function of the senses of its parts and their mode of combination, and of how that account in turn rests on a theory of reference in which the *referent* of the numerical expression is shown to play a distinctive role in an explanation of why the sentence is true, if it is true.

Returning to the first-person pronoun, it is no wonder that a "priority of syntax" thesis, of the sort urged by Wright, would be blind to the possibility of objections, of the sort pressed by Anscombe, to regarding "I" as a (successfully) referring expression on the model of a name or a demonstrative. For those objections have a great deal to do with the difficulties involved in accounting for how there could be an appropriate *Art des Gegebenseins* (Frege 1892, 26)—a way in which the referent of "I" is given to the "I" user. But the requirement that a separate sense for "I" should somehow be provided for is one that cannot even be formulated in the idiom of the *Grundlagen,* whose version of the "priority of syntax" thesis therefore renders such difficulties invisible.

However, *Grundlagen* also contains the materials for a more robust conception of the referents of terms that have been characterized in the broadly contextual way consonant with Wright's procedure of assigning referents to them on the basis of nothing more than their occurrence in sentences we are justified in taking to be true. This new conception involves the further step of regarding the terms in question as *defined* by fixing the truth conditions of the sentences in which they occur. More permissively still, Frege approved the introduction of new terms on the basis of a stipulation of the truth conditions of only *some* of the sentences in which they occur—namely, sentences specifying circumstances in which two of the new terms are to be deemed to refer to the same object. This is the procedure of introducing terms, and referents for them, by means of *abstraction principles*. This procedure opens up the prospect of specifying a referent for "I" in a much less gestural and dogmatic way than is provided by bare appeal to the priority of syntax. Might a referent for "I" be constructed on the basis of an abstraction principle?

11.3   Can an Abstract Object Even Be a Candidate for the Referent of "I"?

This suggestion—effectively, that "I" refers to an abstract object (*abstract*, for short)—might seem frivolous, even preposterous. How could an object characterized by an *abstraction principle*—which is to say, characterized in the way that Frege tried to characterize such items as cardinal numbers (in *Grundlagen*) and extensions (in *Grundgesetze*)—possibly provide us with the right sort of thing to serve as the referent of "I"? Indeed, it is euphemistic to describe this scenario as one in which " 'I' refers to an abstract"; for the real import of these words is surely *I am an abstract*. How could *that* be true? Apart from anything else, it doesn't seem to help much in making sense of the inference patterns, unless we are prepared to accept that *J. D. is an abstract* and, in fact, *people in general are abstracts*. How could contingent existents—on the assumption that that is what people are—enjoy the same kind of being as numbers and sets? And anyway, didn't abstraction lead Frege straight into contradiction?

Now, I have to concede that there is a whiff of desperation about the whole idea. But I consider it here in a particular dialectical context. Suppose that one is impressed by the arguments Anscombe brings to bear on the received understanding of "I." After all, it's not so much *those arguments* that people find impossible to take seriously. On the contrary, sound or not, they are of great philosophical interest. She does, I think, generate some serious mystery about "I," in pressing the circularity problem, for example, and the question of what makes the difference between "I" and the idiom of the "A" users, and the puzzle of the meaning of "I" in the thinking of the occupant of the sensory deprivation tank. The problem is more that readers find it hard to shake a conviction that *no* arguments could possibly establish that "I" is not a referring expression. However deep might be the puzzles and paradoxes generated by our understanding of "I" as a singular term, it seems to many people, I suspect, that the response of abandoning that understanding is akin to responding to Zeno's paradoxes—which, after all, also raise very deep difficulties—by conceding that *nothing moves.* There might seem to be real question, as with such a response to Zeno, about what the no-reference thesis could even mean, if it is to have any prospect of being true.

This resistance to the no-reference thesis derives much of its fierceness from everyone's thorough familiarity with the *pattern of use* of "I." Given that pattern of use and the truth of many "I" judgments (which Anscombe concedes), it is hard for many philosophers, I suspect, to imagine what more could be involved in the claim that "I" is a singular term, even if they have little enthusiasm for Wright's "priority of syntax" as a *general* thesis.

If Anscombe had, like nearly everyone else, assumed that "I" *is* a referring expression, and instead deployed the very same arguments we find in FP to argue that all "I" judgments are *false,* the analogy with Zeno's paradoxes (or, on many views of the matter, brain-in-a-vat skepticism and the like) would be even closer, and no one would regard Anscombe's claims as anything but a gadflyish incentive to hunt down the fallacy, or dissolve the paradox, and thereby deepen our understanding of how "I" judgments work—or, perhaps, to compose a therapeutic account of why the paradox could be sidestepped, or safely ignored as seeking more than could reasonably be expected, and thereby deepen our understanding of the nature of philosophical discourse and the idleness of philosophical skepticism. Everyone would suppose, that is to say, that the definite description *whatever is the correct response to Anscombe's skeptical arguments and so provides a philosophical validation for the truth of "I" judgments* was nonempty.

In a similar spirit (I conjecture), faced with FP as it was actually written, as aspiring to present a serious challenge to the virtually unanimous assumption that "I" is a singular term, rather than setting as a kind of philosophical crossword puzzle the task of refuting or undermining a position, that all "I" judgments are false, that no one could possibly believe, many philosophers are instinctively inclined to suppose that the definite description *whatever "I" has to be taken to refer to, for the true "I" judgments to come out true* is nonempty. From there it is a short step to the supposition that "I" judgments are a kind of judgment—possibly the only kind of judgment—for which something like the priority of syntax must be true.

What I have just recounted might be called a "movement of thought" that does not rise to the level of a chain of inference, or a theory. And this is where abstraction comes in. In the case of arithmetic, we might think of Hume's principle, which stipulates identity conditions for the finite cardinal numbers, as fleshing out the vague assurances of the priority of syntax by telling us enough about what our numerical expressions refer to for us to be able to account ourselves realists about the numbers. It is true that pretty much nobody thinks, when they count any collection of items, that they are referring to objects that would have to be specified in this way, any more than they think of themselves as referring to sets of equinumerous concepts, in line with Frege's considered proposal in *Grundlagen*. But (according to the Fregean account) to think of this as an objection to the characterization of the numbers is to succumb to a false conception of the reference of a term as something that might be considered independently of the sentences in which it occurs, and so to flout the context principle, which we have excellent, independent philosophical reasons to accept.

You can see where this is going. If we can formulate a suitable abstraction principle, we can "cook up" a referent for "I" whose contribution to the truth conditions of "I" judgments ensures that most of the ones we want to come out true will come out true—this is what the suitability of the abstraction principle consists in. Of course, no one outside the elect will take themselves to be talking about such an abstract object when they use the word "I" but, as with the numbers, this will just be matter of what the speaker associates with the word in isolation—in this case, presumably, some kind of confused idea of a quasi-name that, if pressed, they would not be able to distinguish from the kind of name the "A" user calls himself ("himself" here being the ordinary reflexive). This is neither here nor there, since, according to this Fregean way of seeing things, the reference of a singular term has nothing to do with such associations, but can only be understood in terms of the contribution it makes to the truth conditions of the sentences in which it occurs.

That the truth conditions should come out right will be to an important extent a matter of getting the inferential relations right. Thus the assignment of the abstract as the referent of "I" might be thought of as a kind of parallel, in the realm of semantics, to the parable recounted in section 10.3, which reconstructed the introduction of "I" as a kind of "dummy name" whose purpose was to facilitate inference; what we envision now, however, is the introduction not of a dummy name but of a kind of dummy *object* to serve as a referent, and so transform the dummy name into a real one.

This brings us back to one of the objections that immediately crowded in at the first suggestion that "I" might refer to an abstract: How can this help with making sense of the inference patterns? If "J. D. is hungry" is going to be a *logical consequence* of what I assert by saying "I am hungry," then every circumstance that makes my assertion true must be a circumstance that makes "J. D. is hungry" true. It is hard to see how this can be guaranteed unless "I" and "J. D." have the same referent; but on the current hypothesis, that in turn would require "J. D." to refer to an abstract and not, as we might have thought, say, a living human organism. And similarly for all names of persons.

But, first, if Anscombe is right, the received understanding of the meaning of "I" is in no better shape than the current hypothesis. For it accorded with that understanding (I believe she implies) that Augustine should take the referent of "I" to be his mind (*mens*), which is "certain that it alone is the only thing of which it is certain" (*De Trinitate* 10.16, 2002, 56; cf. Augustine 2015, 173), and Descartes should imply the non-identity of himself* with Descartes; and these dualistic commitments are no less troublesome than the current hypothesis when it comes to making sense of the familiar inference patterns involving "I." If we construe the referent of "I" to be a mental substance, we are, on the face of it, going to have just as much trouble modeling inferences like that from my "I feel hungry" to "J. D. feels hungry" as we are going to have on the supposition that "I" is an abstract object; for we do not ordinarily take people's names to refer to mental substances, and this is no less true on an understanding of reference that adheres scrupulously to Frege's context principle than it is on an atomistic conception of reference as determined by the speaker's association of a term with an object.

Essentially the same problem afflicts many of the many philosophers who claim to repudiate dualism but continue to speak of "the self" or "selves" as if they were speaking of a special kind of object. (See FP, 49–50: "Now all this is strictly nonsensical.") Often the *official* story is that "selves" are not a special kind of object; rather, the expression "my self" is supposed to be just a *very* special way—the *self-conscious* way—I have of referring to *myself,* that is, to J. D. Even in the official story, this way of speaking simply helps itself to an idea, as being intuitively clear, that Anscombe helps us to see is extremely obscure: that the difference between "I" judgments and the idiom of the "A" users is a difference in the mode of apprehension of the same entity, oneself. But, as so often happens, when we scrutinize the official story itself, it tends to give rise to further awkward questions. And philosophers very often make free with the idiom of "the self" in a way that seems utterly careless of the safety instructions requiring that it *not* be conceived of as a special—and, inevitably, highly mysterious—kind of object: witness the very titles of such prominent books as *Problems of the Self* and *Sources of the Self.*[10] And such a construal inevitably reproduces Descartes's problem: How do we account for the inference from my "I'm hungry" to "J. D. is hungry," if my "I" refers to a *self,* but "J. D." does not?

One might have hoped that the current (henceforth *abstractionist*) hypothesis is in *better* shape when it comes to making sense of the inferences, by virtue of furnishing us with a kind of nonstandard model of, for example, "J. D. is hungry" as a logical consequence of my "I am hungry"—nonstandard because not assigning the same object to the terms "I" and "J. D.," but a model nevertheless, since the abstract, unlike Descartes's *res cogitans,* is *designed* to underwrite the inferences.

Another such objection was (in expanded form) that, since human beings are contingent existents (pace Williamson 2002), there is something intolerable in the supposition that "I," like a numerical expression on the

Fregean account, might refer to an abstract object. But this is not a problem, because there are plenty of contingent abstract objects, starting with one of Frege's own main examples of an abstract object, the earth's equator (1953, 35). That "I" should refer to an ad hoc abstract object is no more objectionable, in this respect, than that it should refer to the center of mass of one's body.

Nevertheless, if "I" is taken to refer to an abstract object, it seems hard to avoid an error theory for a fair number of "I" judgments. For example, how can "I am a human being" be accounted true? And although "I am J. D." is reinstated as an identity statement, this is small consolation if, as it seems, it must be accounted false. But we will be in a better position to assess these issues once we have at least some inkling of how the proposal might go.

"I" as Referring to an Abstract: Sketch of a Proposal

Abstraction and abstraction principles, being fundamental to Frege's account of the foundations of number theory, have received a great deal of attention in recent decades as part of the remarkable revival of interest, triggered in large part by Wright's (1983) *Frege's Conception of Numbers as Objects,* in Frege's project and in the prospects for some kind of reconstruction of it. As a consequence, a great deal more is now known about the logic of abstraction in general—that is, even independently of its relevance to the foundations of number theory—than was known prior to the Fregean revival. Unfortunately, as Bernard Williams said of himself in a different connection, much of what is known is not known to me. The literature on this topic is now large (see also Fine [2002] and Burgess [2005] for recent discussion). So what follows is a sketch, which glosses over many complicating details, in the hope that an explicit consideration of them would not invalidate the overall approach.

The basic idea would be that the referent of "I" is an abstract defined by means of an abstraction principle of the kind familiar from *Grundlagen* and *Grundgesetze,* whereby the identity conditions of the abstract are laid down in terms of some equivalence relation on the objects or concepts with which each abstract is to be associated. Thus, to use Frege's favorite example (1953, 74–79), two lines in a Euclidean plane are said to have one and the same *direction* if and only if they are parallel to each other. The identity condition for the abstracts, then—the abstracts here being directions—is given in terms of the familiar relation of parallelism between lines—lines in this case being the objects with which the directions are associated, that is, what "have" the directions.

This is abstraction on *objects*. The kind of abstraction Frege was actually interested in, which he used this example to illuminate, was abstraction on *concepts*, and it is this latter form of abstraction that the abstractionist may be imagined as invoking in our case. The basic idea would be that the equivalences the abstraction principle "converts" into an identity on abstracts are precisely what validate the inferences that seemed to depend on the "commonsensical" construal of "I" as a referring expression.

Let us restrict our attention here to the simplest cases of self-ascription: that is, closed unquantified sentences taken as atomic, and whose surface grammar attaches first-level monadic predicates to "I" as subject and involve no other referring expressions or indexicals (unless perhaps as components of predicates, but we are not interested in their internal structure). Let's represent such self-ascriptions, for the moment respecting their surface grammar, as instances of the schema

$$\phi(\mathrm{I})^{11}; \tag{1}$$

and, supposing the speaker to be D, let's specify *the content of (1) as uttered by D* as

$$[\phi(\mathrm{I})]_D. \tag{2}$$

The abstractionist proposal is not that (1) and (2) involve straightforwardly predicating ϕ of some object. The idea is to avoid the difficulties Anscombe makes for the standard understanding of "I" by denying this. We may imagine instead that the abstractionist construes (1) and (2) in something like the following way.

If, in uttering (1), D does not predicate ϕ of some object he designates by "I," how might the content of (1) be perspicuously represented? According to the parable of 10.3, anyone who utters (1) is to be thought of as expressing the predicate ϕ in a distinctive way, without attaching it, *as a predicate*, to any singular term—again, much as Lewis (1979) thought of the objects of *all* the attitudes as properties rather than propositions.

But *however* we construe (1) and (2), they must, one way or another, and in conjunction with the fact that it is D who utters it, underwrite an inference to

$$\phi(D). \tag{3}$$

This much is agreed to on all sides. The abstractionist proposal is then that (1) is true (or perhaps assertable), and so (3) is true, if and only if

$$\phi R \iota_D, \tag{4}$$

where R is a suitable relation and ι_D is a suitable abstract. (4) is proposed as a kind of *model* for (1): the truth or assertability of (1) is not a matter of some object, denoted by "I," having the property expressed by ϕ; nevertheless (1) is logically equivalent to a proposition concerning how things stand with respect to an object (an abstract) designated by ι_D.

The idea is that the abstract ι_D is introduced in the Fregean way, by giving identity conditions in terms of some equivalence relation on a preexisting domain of (probably) concepts. Can a suitable abstraction principle be formulated, in such a way that the item ι_D thereby introduced bears some suitable relation R to the property ϕ if and only if (1) is true (or assertable) by D? I have no idea. But suppose that such a principle *is* available.

The reality of the relevant equivalence relation and of its relata are ex hypothesi already attested and so not impugned by Anscombe's arguments against "I" being a referring expression. So the identities by which ι_D is specified encode the (real) equivalences that underwrite the inferences between first- and third-person utterances.

But this cannot be dismissed merely as a vacuous gesture toward "whatever posited referents will validate the inferences." For the referents can now be specified by means of a familiar and, in certain other contexts anyway, unobjectionable type of principle, a principle of abstraction. The abstract defined by such a principle can then serve as the "referent" of "I." So "I" is still construed as, if not a referring expression, bearing a significant semantic relation to a particular object, and the validity of the familiar inference patterns involving "I" is preserved and accounted for, but without commitment to any dubious entities such as Cartesian egos. The statements about the abstracts are supposed to encode nothing more than information about equivalences whose reality is acknowledged on all sides; but an abstract is, when it comes down to it, something rather than nothing, so the truth and falsity of "I" judgments are logically correlated with how things stand with respect to something real.

11.5 Shortcomings of the Proposal

With regard to saving the appearances, the abstractionist proposal falls far short of what might have been hoped for. First, ι_D cannot really count as a *referent* for "I," except in a highly attenuated sense characteristic of certain philosophical theories. For example, we often hear that "propositions are sets of possible worlds"; but no one really means this, unless they think that a set is the kind of thing that can be true or false.[12] Rather, the idea is that propositions can be *modeled* using sets of possible worlds, in such a way that set-theoretic properties and relations can work, via the relevant logical equivalences, as surrogates for those we want to talk about in connection with propositions, like truth and necessity and validity. At best such theories give us *contextual* definitions of propositions, by showing us how to translate sentences about them into sentences about sets that don't mention them.

Similarly, ι_D is not really the referent of "I"; it is instead a distinctive abstract object whose properties and relations can be used to model "I" discourse. It cannot really be the referent for the simple reason, among many others, that the Frege-inspired abstraction principle only allows us to think of ι_D as *associated with* the properties D self-ascribes using "I." The principle gives us no warrant for saying that ι_D *falls under* the concepts D represents himself* as falling under in his "I"-involving self-ascriptions. This is what we should have expected: for Frege introduces the cardinality operator in a way that at most makes sense of the idea of the resulting abstract objects, the cardinal numbers, *belonging to* the concepts whose extensions have the relevant cardinalities, whereby a number n's belonging to a concept F is a matter of there being n Fs. The relation to concepts that constitutes the numbers as objects is emphatically not that of *falling under* them. It is true that a number, on Frege's account, can fall under a concept, and even fall under a concept to which it belongs, as, for example, the number one falls under the concept *identical with 1*, of which it is the number. And, as this example shows, a number may enter into the specification of a concept; and in Frege's definitions all numbers are required to do so. But these are so far from being the relation to concepts that makes a number the number it is that this feature of Frege's theory threatens to be a grave defect. For the possibility of numbers entering into these relations is a feature of the theory the logicians call *impredicativity*; and while some forms of impredicativity seem to be harmless, there are many cases in which it gives rise to inconsistency, one of the most famous being Frege's own later introduction by abstraction, into a higher-order language, of terms for the extensions of concepts.

In the same way, the relation ι_D bears to the concepts with which it is associated is not that of falling under them, as the referent of "I" does on what we are now taking to be a "naïve" account of the matter. The relation, in effect, is rather this: ι_D is an object associated by an abstraction principle with all and only concepts D truly self-ascribes using "I." D uses "I" to correctly self-ascribe some property η if and only if the object ι_D bears to η the distinctive relation R characterized by the abstraction principle (on the assumption, still in force, that such an R can be characterized, as part of the formulation of a suitable abstraction principle). In this way D's apparent ascriptions of properties to an object he refers to using "I" can be modeled in terms of those properties bearing a certain relation to the abstract object ι_D, but this relation is emphatically *not* that of ι_D's *having* those properties. I am *not* ι_D. The priority of syntax is not as closely connected with the idea of abstraction as one might have thought: as we have seen, the syntactic status of "I" as a singular term cannot be impugned, and so, since it features in true sentences, on Wright's principles it must refer to a real object. Wright's doctrine is inspired by Frege's context principle, which also underpins the go-to Fregean technique for specifying such a referent, abstraction principles. But so far as I can see, although abstraction on concepts might yield an object that might serve as a kind of focal point for determining the truth conditions of "I" judgments, no cogent abstraction principle can conjure an object we might think of as the *referent* of "I."

Thus the abstractionist proposal does not vindicate "I" as itself a referring expression; it makes "I" into the "surface trace," in Rumfitt's phrase, of, probably, a quantifier or second-level predicate. But it does enable us to say that the truth conditions of declarative "I" sentences can be understood in terms of how things stand with a distinctive object uniquely associated with the speaker.

But this discussion in turn brings to light another source of worry about ι_D, namely, the impredicativity of its own abstraction principle.

Abstracts have an innocuous appearance because the equivalences by which they are introduced seem to ensure that talk about them is "really nothing more than" talk about realities already acknowledged (the concepts or objects on which the abstraction is conducted).

But the equivalences by which abstracts are introduced are *not* innocuous. To assert the reality of the abstracts is always to go beyond the familiar items, because there is often a real question about whether talk about the abstracts might lead us into inconsistency, even when no such doubts arise about the old vocabulary that serves as the basis for the principle.

The fundamental problem is that, as Frege himself insisted, a definition is admissible only if (i) it succeeds in specifying a unique item (thus, for example, a "definition" of $\sqrt{x}$ as *the* number that, when multiplied by itself, yields x is inadmissible), and (ii) it does not lead to contradiction. The "abstractionist" proposal for dealing with "I" sentences, as it stands, fails on both counts.

(i) The abstraction principle leaves open any number of questions about the nature of the abstracted object. Wherever we have such a question, as to whether the abstract meets some condition c, and so far as we can tell either answer may be maintained with consistency, we have two abstracts to which "I" might refer: one that meets c and one that does not. Given a multitude of such conditions, we will thus have many candidate abstracts with no clear nonarbitrary way of choosing among them.

(ii) Nor can we be confident that the existence of our abstract—or rather, of any of the candidates—can be asserted without contradiction. A contradictory consequence of an abstraction principle might be highly unobvious, as the notorious case of Frege's Basic Law V shows, and it is provably impossible to devise in advance a general procedure for establishing the consistency of abstraction principles (Burgess 2003, 237–238).

Our evaluation of the abstractionist proposal, then, is not sanguine. It cannot deliver what the referentialist really wants, a referent for "I"; and we have as yet no sound basis for supposing that it is consistent.

Epilogue: The Anti-Cartesian Basis
of Anscombe's Skepticism

This book has been devoted to an examination and qualified defense of Anscombe's two great skeptical critiques: of the vocabulary of morality in MMP and of the understanding of "I" as a referring expression in FP.

Morality, for Anscombe, is a philosophers' fiction—but it is not *only* a philosophers' fiction. The term is everywhere in our culture, and if its currency has bad effects, its corrupting influence in philosophy is likely to be the least of our worries. Or at least, the least *pressing* of them—it may be that the most important means to the permanent eradication of bad ideas abroad in our culture is their eventual exposure as philosophical errors. Anscombe's most urgent concern with it, anyway, was practical and political. She clearly thought that the pseudo-concept of morality made consequentialism possible, that consequentialism now permeated the culture (Anscombe 1957a), and that consequentialism made possible a widely accepted "justification" of Hiroshima (Anscombe 1957b)—and countless other modern horrors.

In FP, as we have seen, Anscombe maintained that the function in the language of the first-person pronoun was not to refer to *anything*. She argued that if it *were* a referring expression, the only thing it could in the end be understood as referring to was something like a Cartesian ego. For various reasons, powerfully articulated in FP, Anscombe (2000), and other works, and partly inspired by influential arguments in Wittgenstein (1958, 2001), she was convinced that such immaterial entities do not exist, and that the very idea of them makes no sense.

It is worth pointing out that there is *a* substantive connection between the primary theses of the two papers of Anscombe's I have examined here. My book therefore has at least somewhat more unity than is secured by the mere fact that those papers were written by the same person (although the common authorship by itself is much more unifying than usual, since Anscombe is, to put it mildly, a distinctive philosophical personality). For Anscombe thought that a Cartesian conception of the mind had amplified the deleterious effects on our culture of our idolatrous devotion to *morality*. In promoting a false account of mental states and processes in general, she maintained, that conception gave rise to a false picture of intention in particular. This in turn made possible the central element of consequentialist ethical doctrines and habits of thought: the erosion of any ethically significant distinction between the results of an action that are properly intended and those that are merely foreseen:

> Against the background of certain modern traditions in philosophy—especially the Cartesian—it is hardly noticed that intention may relate to the intentionalness of the particular act that is done, as well as to the purpose for which it is done. Now there are several kinds of action which, if they are done intentionally, are evidently evil actions, no matter what they are done for. The good end only sanctifies such means as either are good considered in themselves, or would naturally fall merely under a neutral action-description. (Anscombe 1982, 20)
>
> [The principle of double effect] has been repeatedly abused from the seventeenth century up till now. The causes lie in the history of philosophy. From the seventeenth century till now what may be called Cartesian psychology has dominated the thought of philosophers and theologians. According to this psychology, an intention was an interior act of the mind which could be produced at will. Now if intention is all important—as it is—in determining the goodness or badness of an action, then, on this theory of what intention is, a marvellous way offered itself of making any action lawful. You only had to "direct your intention" in a suitable way. In practice, this means making a little speech to yourself: "What I mean to be doing is . . ."
>
> [The] doctrine is used to prevent any doubts about the obliteration bombing of a city. The devout Catholic bomber secures by a "direction of intention" that any shedding of innocent blood that occurs is "accidental." (Anscombe 1961, 58–59)[1]

In this way, she traced lines of influence from the broadly Cartesian conception of mind both to a false understanding of the first-person pronoun and, via combination with the fantasies generated by the vocabulary of *morality,* to the specifically consequentialist currents in ethics she deplored and repeatedly denounced. But the substance of her attack on Cartesian ideas about intention is contained in her masterpiece, the 1957 monograph *Intention* (Anscombe 2000), which I have not been able to discuss here.

Aquinas and Natural Law

Donagan (1977) is mistaken to suppose that the moral-rationalist position he defends is essentially that of Aquinas. On the contrary, Aquinas's views, on those of the relevant issues on which he is, historically speaking, in a position to pronounce, are Anscombe's; and the fact of his holding these views only confirms her larger historical story. Again, Donagan seems to have been distracted by the issue of the different *surface forms* ethical thought might take: a system of precepts or a theory of virtue. This distinction is not at all relevant to Anscombe's critique of morality.

It is easy to take it for granted that Aquinas has essentially our concept of morality, and the most important reason for this, as I mentioned in Chapter 1, is that there are simply no credible rivals to "morals" / "morality" and "moral" as translations, respectively, of Aquinas's terms *mores* and *moralis*. However, as I also mentioned, there are unobjectionable uses of "moral," and of words in other languages of which "moral" provides an irresistible translation. What makes them unobjectionable is their lacking the feature to which Anscombe objects: the aspiration to express an entirely sui generis ethical modality; that is, one that cannot be construed as intensionally (strictly, hyperintensionally) equivalent to a modality ultimately deriving from any other, remotely familiar categories— in particular, those of divine command, on the one hand, or *aretē* and *eudaimonia,* on the other. The concept expressed by Aquinas's predicate *moralis,* and its associated modality or brand of practical necessity, lacks this objectionable feature.

For Aquinas, "moral" precepts (*praecepta moralia*) "pertain by their nature to good *mores*" (*secundum se ad bonos mores pertinent; ST* IaIIae Q100 A1); "*mores*" here just means "customs" or "practices," and "good" means just that: *good* as this applies to customs or practices, good of *their* kind. (Compare Q1 A3: "Since, as Ambrose says, *morality (mores) is properly ascribed to human beings,* moral actions (*actus morales*) strictly speaking derive their essence from their end (*speciem sortiuntur ex fine*); for moral actions and human actions are one and the same thing"; compare also Anscombe: "The 'moral' goodness of an action is nothing but its goodness as a human action" [1982, 17].) If the idea of *mores* does not involve a special sui generis sense of "moral," the idea of good *mores* doesn't either. In the context of ethics, the species of good that belongs to *mores* is *justice,* for "the common life [of human beings] pertains to the nature of justice" (*pertinet ad rationem iustitiae; ST* Q100 A2).

One kind of force attaching to these precepts can indeed be appropriately expressed by Anscombe's "special sense" of *ought,* whereby it amounts to "'is obliged,' or 'is bound,' or 'is required to'" (MMP, 5)—not, however, because this is "the moral 'ought,'" but because the precepts are of course for Aquinas commands of God: "It is obvious that divine law fittingly sets forth precepts concerning the actions belonging to every virtue" (*ST* Q100 A2). Anscombe may well have had these very passages of the *Summa* in mind when she formulated her first definition (which she later unwittingly contravenes, as we saw in section 3.1) of a "law conception of ethics": "To have a *law* conception of ethics is to hold that what is needed for conformity with the virtues failure in which is the mark of being bad *qua* man . . . , is required by divine law" (MMP, 6).[1]

These ethical precepts, according to Aquinas, are *also* accessible to human reason as such—the basic ones discernible by everyone; the more complicated by the wise (*ST* Q93 A2). They therefore belong to the highly contested Thomistic category of *natural law;* but they do not, in this aspect, seem to be distinguished by Aquinas from those requirements of virtue (take note, not "moral virtue") that can be put in the form of precepts, for he agrees with Ambrose that every sin offends against some virtue (Q92 A1, Q94 A3). As we have seen, the virtue pertaining to human *mores* is justice, and Aquinas agrees with the Philosopher (Aristotle 1920, V.1) that "human law only sets forth precepts that concern just action" (*lex humana non proponit praecepta nisi de actibus justitiae; ST*

Q100 A2). So in this "secular" guise, the ultimate rationale for the *prae-cepta moralia* is to be found in *beatitudo,* which is one of his words for *eudaimonia.* Thus Aquinas seems to limit himself to what Anscombe implicitly claims to be the only two intelligible bases of ethics—divine command and virtue—and our notion of "morality," whose basis is supposed to be essentially distinct from both of these, is nowhere to be seen.

We can see how far Aquinas's concept of *moralis* is from our sui generis notion of *moral* from his denial that "moral" actions (*actus morales*) can be attributed to God, "except metaphorically" (Aquinas 1918–1930, 2:90, 3.34.5). It is clear that he means a *conceptual* impossibility: "It does not befit God to have passions and the like, which moral actions are concerned with" (3.34.5); that is, a precondition of the applicability of the concept is missing.[2] But in the modern way of talking, among theists and nontheists alike, it is supposed to be just obvious that God's actions would be as much subject to moral evaluation as anyone's (recall, for example, the discussion in Leftow [2013] about whether God is "morally perfect," mentioned in section 3.3).

Donagan maintains that Aquinas provides a counterexample to Anscombe's claim about the mode of obligation central to a law conception of ethics presupposing a legislator, because (as Donagan also claims) he (Aquinas) presents a coherent conception of ethical norms—*moral* norms, in fact—underwritten by nothing more than the authority of practical reason itself. Irwin (2006) argues that Aquinas *constitutes* a counterexample to Anscombe's view that the idea of a secular law conception of ethics was unheard of prior to the demise of Christian doctrine as an intellectual consensus in the West, whether his (Aquinas's) secular grounding of ethical norms in practical reason in the end makes sense or not.

It is true that Aquinas sometimes talks as though *praecepta moralia* have the status of natural law simply by virtue of being discernible by ordinary practical reason. For example, "Reason, which is the first principle of morals (*principium moralium*), has the same position in a human being with respect to those things that pertain to him, as a prince or judge has in a city" (*ST* Q104 A1 Ad 3); "Law is a certain rule and measure of actions, in accordance with which someone is led to act or refrain from acting . . . ; but a rule and measure of human actions is reason (*regula autem, et mensura humanorum actuum est ratio*), which is the first principle of human actions" (Q90 A1 Resp). But he is quite clear that law in the strict sense *does* require a legislator, and that it is essential to the relevant concept of a legislator that he have superior power, and in particular the power to punish and thereby enforce the law. Indeed, it seems very likely, again, that Anscombe's own account of these matters was partly inspired by Aquinas's position. At *ST* IaIIae Q91 A3 Resp, he says, "Human reason proceeds from precepts of natural law, as if from certain universal principles, to whatever is to be decreed in a more particular way: and these particular directives, being discerned in accordance with human reason, are called human laws, *provided certain other conditions are fulfilled,* which pertain to the nature of law, as was said above" (my emphasis).

What are these "other essential conditions"? They include that every law is of necessity ordained to the common good (*ST* Q90 A2), and also that the making of law belongs either to the whole people or to "a public personage who has care of the whole people" (Q90 A3). The second objection in this *articulus* states that any man can frame a law because, as Aristotle says, any man can lead another to virtue, and law is supposed to lead men to virtue. Aquinas's reply reads, "A private person is not able to effectively impel one to virtue; for *he can only advise.* But if his advice is not accepted, *it has no coercive force, which law must have in order to effectively impel one to virtue,* as the Philosopher says in *EN* X [Aristotle 1920]. But it is the whole people that has this coercive power, or a public person, *to whom it belongs to inflict punishment,* as will be said below [IIaIIae Q64 A3] and therefore it is *for him alone to make laws*" (*ST* Q90 A3 Ad 3; my emphases).

In the very next *articulus* he reiterates that it is in the nature of law to be promulgated: "Thus from the preceding four articles we may construct a *definition of law:* it is nothing other than some decree of reason for the common good, promulgated by someone who has care of the community" (Q 90 A4 Resp).

What, then, of the close connection between human reason and natural law? Aquinas's position seems to be that the *content* of the part of natural law that consists of *praecepta moralia* that do not concern man's relation to God (for there are some such *praecepta,* which also require a measure of faith for their apprehension) is available to human practical reason; but this availability does not by itself amount, to *any* extent, to subjection to a (promulgated, enforceable) law *as law.* In the *respondeo* of Q91 A2, "Whether there be anything of the natural law in ourselves," he writes,

Among other creatures, the *rational* creature is subject to divine providence in a more excellent way [than the rest of creation], inasmuch as he himself has a share in his own providence, and in providing for others. Wherefore he participates in the eternal law itself, through which he has a natural inclination to just and necessary (*debitum*) action and end; and in the rational creature, such participation in the eternal law is called *natural law.* This is why, when the Psalmist had said (Ps 4): *Offer up the sacrifice of justice,* he added, as if in reply to people who asked, What are the works of justice?, *The whole people say: Who shows us good things?,* to which he says in reply, *The light of your face, Lord, has made its mark upon us.* He thus implies that the light of natural reason, by which we determine what is good, and what bad, and which pertains to natural law, is nothing other than an impression in us of divine light. From this it is clear, that natural law is nothing other than the rational creature's participation in the eternal law.

Thus the eternal law, directly decreed by God, directly determines the operations of nature; except in the case of human beings, in whom the eternal law, as it were, indirectly determines its movement toward its natural end (namely, happiness), *via* natural law, which is in its first principles discernible by human reason.

The status of natural law as law is secured, in the first instance, simply by virtue of its being a determination of the eternal, divine law. It is part of that latter law that human beings should discern their end and their good by means of their own faculty of practical reason. Further, the first principles of that reason—pursuit of *felicitas* or *beatitudo,* man's natural end, for example, and avoidance of what is bad—themselves also belong to natural law since they too are in accordance with the eternal divine law. Now, the first principles of natural law are indeed discernible by human practical reason, and so are discernible even by those who do not believe in God as a lawgiver (this would include, for example, Aristotle). This does not mean, however, that they are discernible to such people *qua law.* With the notable but problematic exception of the Stoics (see Appendix B), most pagans did *not* regard divine law, as the Jews and Christians did, as determining the sovereign ethical modality. Yet the fundaments of natural law may be discernible as falling under another kind of ethical necessity, namely, *need,* or what I previously called "Aristotelian necessity"—as specifying what is required for the purpose of the attainment of *beatitudo;* and it is in this way that one such as Aristotle apprehends what Aquinas classifies as the requirements of natural law. Nevertheless, the natural law *is* law, by virtue of being a determination of divine law, which is promulgated (although not to all) by a legislator with the power to enforce obedience.

Pagans and others to whom these *praecepta moralia* have not been promulgated by such direct divine dispensation as the Hebrew Decalogue nevertheless have access that is as full as anyone else's to their falling under that different but equally necessary kind of practical necessity, *need,* or "necessity deriving from a task" (Anscombe 1978a; cf. Aristotle, *Metaphysics* 4.5, 1015a22–1015a26); the task in this case being the overarching human task of attaining happiness. The precepts are discerned under the aspect of this necessity by ordinary practical reason—which is of course another kind of divine dispensation.[3]

This account of Aquinas's view is confirmed by the response to the first objection in Q90 A3: "As was said above [Q90 A1 Ad 1], law is in something not only in the way it is in what regulates, but also by participation, in the way it is in what is regulated; and in this way every single person is a law to himself, inasmuch as he participates in the order of someone who regulates: wherefore [Paul] adds in the same place: *Who show the working of law written in their heart.*"

Thus Aristotle (for example) can be said to apprehend *natural law* by means of his practical reason, and so to understand it as expressing a kind of practical necessity, even though he does not apprehend it *as law.*

In case the question of what is essential to law might come to seem merely verbal, we should ask here a question closely analogous to one I have pressed about the putative category *moral:* What does it *add* to the practical necessity attaching to ethical precepts of a sort that would have been recognized by, say, Aristotle, and understood as they would have been understood by Aristotle, to call them part of *natural law?* The necessity attaching to the precepts by virtue of their being required for the pursuit of *eudaimonia* is all the necessity a eudaimonist with Aristotle's impersonal conception of God could want, *or even conceive of.* To say that Aristotle's virtuous man discerns the *natural law* by his practical reason can mean no more than that the *content* of the precepts he discerns coincides with that of precepts that, according to Aquinas, and *precisely because of this coincidence,* are promulgated by God to those to whom he chose to reveal his legislative will. It is very hard to see how Aquinas could maintain that people in Aristotle's position could apprehend the precepts *as* law, as he (Aquinas) understood that concept. It is equally hard to see what Aquinas could have meant by calling them precepts of natural law, if not that they expressed not only the *eudaimonia*-based practical necessity that attaches to anything Aristotle would recognize as a norm that helped constitute some virtue but also the distinct necessity that attaches to the commandments of a God with whom the Hebrews and, later, the Christians conceived of themselves as having entered into a covenant.

If this line of interpretation is correct, my objections to Donagan are fully vindicated: Aquinas himself does not propose, outside a theistic context, that practical reason can discern precepts on any other basis than is already implicit in the *Nicomachean Ethics*. The case of Aquinas only serves to confirm Anscombe's thesis that, outside of theism, there is only egoistic eudaimonism ("virtue ethics").

The attribution to Aquinas of essentially our notion of *moral precepts* as what he means by those *praecepta moralia* accessible to human reason, in addition to lacking any support from the text, is of no help in interpreting his statements about natural law, and in fact only generates perplexity: for where we had two aspects under which we might think of the *praecepta moralia*—divine law and virtue—we now have three, with the gratuitous addition of a third, purportedly sui generis, *moral* species of ethical modality, and *three* sets of interaspectual relation to explain where before we had only *one*. This is poor hermeneutical management.

So far as secular grounding is concerned, then, the testimony of Aquinas, one of Donagan's star witnesses, itself shows that Donagan is mistaken to think that the "vindication of morality" is a vindication of precepts *as opposed to* a vindication of the relevant account of the virtues. But if we think of morality as a system not merely of precepts but of *law,* whose force does not depend on their belonging to some virtue (and so does not derive directly from the end of *eudaimonia*), this conception (according to Anscombe) doesn't make sense if cut off from the idea of a divine legislator—even if (as Aquinas thought) the Law, in most of its "moral" (*moralis*) component, is constituted by the very same precepts whose observance is a condition of possessing some (nontheological) virtue.

Aquinas turns out to be an equally unconvincing witness in Irwin's case against Anscombe. Like Donagan, Irwin misinterprets both Anscombe and Aquinas. Irwin (2006, 326), like nearly all readers of MMP, supposes that Anscombe takes Aquinas, and all Christian philosophers, to subscribe to a "jural conception of morality." I have tried to show that this is not Anscombe's view. She maintains, in fact, that prior to the demise of Christianity *no one* had any conception of morality *at all*. This is confirmed by Irwin's own interpretation of Aquinas, which, apart from his ascription of our idea of morality to him, largely matches my own. "In [Aquinas's] view," he writes, "the legal aspect of morality simply consists in the fact that moral principles are action-guiding rational principles of the sort that we discover by Aristotelian deliberation. Since, therefore, Anscombe believes that Aristotle does not accept a legislative conception of moral requirements, she ought to say the same about Aquinas" (327).

Let us set aside for a moment the ascription to Aristotle and Aquinas of the contested concept *moral,* and talk only in terms of *ethics,* understanding that term neutrally with respect to the credentials of *morality.* Aquinas, as we have seen, certainly does hold that most of the principles whose legally binding force, where that obtains, constitutes his account of ethics as a law conception are identical in their *content* to the correct "action-guiding rational principles of the sort that we discover by Aristotelian deliberation." But it does not follow from this, together with the undoubted fact that "Aristotle does not accept a legislative conception of [ethical] requirements," that Aquinas does not accept such a conception either. For what marks a conception of ethical requirements as *legislative* is not only, or even primarily, the *content* of those requirements, nor whether they are discoverable by Aristotelian deliberation. What is decisive here is a conception of those requirements as *promulgated as divine law*—a conception it is as certain that Aquinas holds as it is that Aristotle does not. Given what we have seen of Aquinas's conception of law, which accords with Anscombe's, this promulgation cannot possibly consist merely in the availability of the precepts to human reason, as necessary for the pursuit of man's natural end. Nor is Aquinas's legislative conception, so understood, at all undercut by the fact that most of the precepts in question are also accessible to practical reason independently of revelation. On the contrary, this overdetermination, rightly stressed by Donagan, only reflects Aquinas's belief, essential to Christianity, in a God who is loving and just. Because he is loving, what he commands is for our sake, and so in our interest to obey even independently of any threatened posthumous divine punishment; because he is just, even those to whom this inherently beneficial law has not been promulgated *as law* nevertheless have access to it, through practical reason, under the aspect of an entirely different but equally inescapable species of practical necessity, as determined by the overarching human end of *eudaimonia*.

Irwin is wrong, then, to maintain that if Aquinas counts as accepting a legislative conception of ethical requirements, so does Aristotle; and so he is also wrong to infer, from Aquinas's acceptance of such a conception, that Aristotle accepts one too. He is right, however, to say that Anscombe says that Aristotle does not accept a legislative conception of *moral* requirements. But, again, he is wrong to say, and wrong to say that Anscombe says, that Aquinas *does* accept such a conception. That Anscombe denies this follows a fortiori from her claim that neither Aquinas nor Aristotle accepts *any* conception of moral requirements, which in turn follows a fortiori from her view that neither would have found any such conception intelligible. On Anscombe's view, this, finally, follows independently from various sets of premises; but one derivation, again a fortiori, is from her thesis that the "concept" of morality is inherently unintelligible to anyone.

Stoic Ethics: A Law Conception without Commandments?

Clearly there is *a* sense in which the Stoics taught an ethic of divine command. Yet it seems to me that Anscombe was wrong to say, in MMP, that "one might be inclined to think that a law conception of ethics could arise only among people who accepted an allegedly divine positive law; that this is not so is shown by the Stoics, who also thought that whatever was involved in conformity to human virtues was required by divine law" (5).

That is, she was wrong relative to her own account, implicit in MMP and expounded in later work, of what is involved in *law* and *command*. She is right (as she also said in MMP) that these ideas presuppose some legislator with superior power. But they presuppose quite a lot more besides, most of which seems to be missing from the Stoic picture.

The Stoics' ethical doctrines presupposed much of their physics.[1] They were *naturalists:* they believed that the natural world around us, or cosmos, was the whole of reality (surrounded by void). They were *materialists,* or something very like it: they held that everything that exists is *body,* which they defined as what is extended (Diogenes Laertius 2013 [hereafter DL], 7.135), or as "what acts and is acted upon" (Cicero, *Academica* 1.39).

They believed that *Zeus,* or *God,* or "the gods" were real and held dominion over the cosmos. Their naturalism of course then required them to *identify* God with the cosmos, or with a part of it: "God and mind and fate and Zeus are one thing, but called by many different names" (DL, 7.135; cf. Cicero, *De Natura Deorum* [hereafter *ND*] 2.21). But those Stoics who took the latter option held that God was a "part" that *permeated* the cosmos, in very various degrees of concentration (DL, 7.138); this part is *reason,* which is a kind of pervasive "fiery breath" (*pneuma*). As in Plato's *Timaeus*, the cosmos is in fact a kind of superorganism (Cicero, *ND* 2.58), either identical with God or permeated by him in the form of this divine reason. Certain concentrated fragments of divine reason are to be found in the cosmos: notably, the heavenly bodies, and the rational faculties of human beings (Cicero, *ND* 2.16).

The superorganism that constitutes the cosmos is therefore maximally *rational* and ordered. Divine reason is above all *providential* and orders everything for the best. The "large-scale structural defects" of human life (in Mark Johnston's [2009] phrase) are only apparent (Chrysippus as reported by Plutarch, *De Stoicorum Repugnantiis* 1051E).

We now turn to ethics. Like Socrates (their main ethical inspiration and, through the Cynics, their main ancestor), the Stoics held that the only unconditional goods were goods of the soul, that is, the virtues (DL 7.102, on Chrysippus; Stobaeus 5a), which are bodies of knowledge (DL 7.125–126; also implied by DL 7.111; cf. Stobaeus 5b, 5b2) that in some sense form a unity (DL 7.125–126; Stobaeus 5b7). Indeed, they were more Socratic, arguably,[2] than Socrates, denying that anything else could even be *made* genuinely good by the accompaniment of virtue. As is well known, they held that the correct way to live was "in accordance with nature" (DL 7.87; Stobaeus 6a). This might look trivial: since the fundamental nature of human beings consists in their rationality, to live in accordance with one's nature is to live in accordance with reason; but as Socrates often emphasized, the necessity of living in accordance with reason is already in a way *given* in the posing of the question, "How should I live?"

However, the Stoics meant something much more substantive: one should live in accordance not just with human nature but with *cosmic* nature (DL 7.87–88, 108). Because the cosmos is either identical with the supremely rational God or permeated by his supreme reason, it functions for us as a macrocosmic object lesson in rational order, and it cannot make sense to resist its natural operations. To study the cosmos is to acquire knowledge of God—physics *is* theology.[3]

The Stoics then worked out the details of life "in accordance with nature" in terms of the "preferred indifferents" (*adiaphora*) (for example, DL 7.102).

Epictetus reports Chrysippus as saying, "As long as the consequences are unclear to me, I always cling to what is better suited to getting what is according to nature. For God himself made me such as to select these things. But if I knew for sure that it was fated for me now to be ill, I would even seek [illness]. For my foot, if it had brains, would seek to be muddied" (*Discourses* 2.6–10).

What does this mean? Perhaps this. My foot, if it had brains (and trusted to my own reason), would happily concur in what *seemed* bad for *it* (becoming muddied), in the knowledge that it serves the purpose of the whole. But each part of nature is ordained by cosmic reason in accordance with an overarching providential plan. In this context, I might view myself as the "foot with brains" of the superorganism that is the cosmos. Thus my illness serves an overall purpose, like the muddying of my foot, and I should welcome it.

The Stoic identification of God with the cosmos was *not* simply a way of disguising a fundamental atheism (as has often been alleged in respect of a similar identification made by Spinoza). There are a number of recorded Stoic arguments for the existence of God; some of these are "arguments from design" (for example, Chrysippus as reported in Cicero, *ND* 2.16) or "cosmological" (for example, Sextus Empiricus, *Adversus Mathematicos* 9.76), others seem to prefigure the ontological argument of Anselm and the early modern rationalists (Sextus, *AM* 9.133–136), but few depend on the identification of God with the cosmos. God was not conceived as the cosmos, as it were, *by definition*. So if Stoic ethics is "not really" a divine command conception, this is not because they didn't really believe in God—they did.

The sense in which Stoic ethics *is* a divine command conception should now be somewhat clear; and this *does* seem to depend on the identification of God with the cosmos (or with cosmic reason). The supremely providential law of God determines everything that happens in nature. Indeed, the relation between divine law and nature is literally as intimate as that which would obtain between a human being and his actions were the human being perfectly rational. The Stoics were standard-issue Greek eudaimonist "virtue ethicists," as far as that went. But they also held, as other Greek schools did not, that virtuous action was ipso facto action in accordance with the law of God, and for at least two reasons: (i) virtuous action is rational action, and reason is divine; (ii) virtuous action is action in accordance with cosmic nature; that is, in accordance with what is itself determined by divine law. In this sense, Stoic ethics does fit

Anscombe's definition of a divine command conception: "To have a [*divine*] *law* conception of ethics is to hold that what is needed for conformity with the virtues failure in which is the mark of being bad *qua* man (and not merely, say, *qua* craftsman or logician)—that what is needed for *this*, is required by divine law" (MMP, 6).

Human reason on the Stoic view is not so much "supplied by" God as it is *a part of God*. We are not merely *given* reason by God as part of his providential plan; rather, the presence in us of reason makes us *irreducible agents* of providence. For cosmic providence is not imposed from without in accordance with some separately conceived divine plan: providence *just is* the presence of reason at work as a somatic principle in the cosmos. Its presence in human beings is not to be distinguished in principle from its presence anywhere else: there is no room for a deep distinction between the presiding authority of the cosmos and the various agents that put into effect the rational processes through which cosmic providence operates. Such a distinction can at most amount to one between a whole and its parts.

The main connection between Stoic ethics and physics / theology is at the level of the *nature of the practical necessity* the Stoics conceived as central to ethics: they thought of it as *both* (i) deriving from *eudaimonia,* that is, a matter of what (especially in the way of qualities of character) is *needed* for the agent's happiness, *and* (ii) deriving from a *binding obligation* to obey divine law. Something similar is found in, for example, Aquinas; *but* what's distinctive about the Stoic view—deriving from their cosmology—is that (i) and (ii) don't merely coincide—they amount to something like the same *concept* of necessity. Where a Thomist (or pretty much any Christian philosopher) says "in accordance with nature, and *therefore* ordained by God," a Stoic says (with Spinoza) "in accordance with nature, *or in other words* ordained by God." But this Stoic "ordained by" does not betoken law or command in the sense in which human beings might *abide by* a law or *heed* a command, in a way that manifests acknowledgment of the lawgiver's *authority* or *right to be obeyed.*

Thus, as it seems to me, Stoic ethics does *not* count as a divine *command* conception or, in the correlative sense, a divine *law* conception. And the reason has to do with the nature of command and law as Anscombe herself explains it, as set out in Chapter 5. The relevance of this conception is that the modern idea of *morality* is partly an attempt to express *this* form of ethical necessity, which is only intelligible on the presupposition of a divine legislator. This form of ethical necessity is sui generis and nonteleological, and it derives its character from the peculiar conventional and practice-based processes by which promising becomes a way of creating obligations, rules come to be understood as determining the course of a game, and commands come to be regarded as authoritative. It is essential to these processes that they involve *language*—or, at least, *signs*. That is, promises and commands (for example) can only be formulated in ways that involve what H. P. Grice (1957) called *nonnatural meaning*. "Natural" meaning is exemplified by inferences about natural (nonlinguistic) events: "Those clouds mean rain." Nonnatural meaning involves a speaker's intention to induce a belief in the hearer that the speaker intends the hearer to believe that the speaker . . . (and so on) intends to convey *that p*. Thus the rainbow at Mount Ararat was a natural phenomenon, but it was also a *sign—intended* by God, and known *from his testimony* to be intended, to convey a promise to Noah that the world would never again be inundated (Genesis 9:12–14).

The Stoics could not conceive of nature as excluding Grice's "nonnatural" meaning, if for no other reason than that nature includes human beings, who make such meaning in abundance. Indeed, the commitment of Chrysippus and others to seemingly irreducibly semantic elements— "sayables" (*lekta*) and "assertables" (*axiōmata*)—marks their "naturalism" as very tolerant by our standards, and indeed by some ancient standards (for example, certain versions of atomism).[4] Nor did they dissent from the almost ubiquitous Greek assumption (so prominent in the Socratic *Apologies* of both Plato and Xenophon) that the gods communicate through signs with particular mortals on particular occasions.

Furthermore, even with respect to that austerely naturalistic sense in which they took ethics to be grounded in *universal* divine law, the Stoics held that its dominion over human beings was essentially reason involving, in a way that its impersonal grip on the brutes and inanimate matter could never be. Because human beings are rational creatures, once they understand that the cosmos (or its providential reason) *is* God, they can go about trying to discern God's will for human beings in general, in the operations of nature, and perhaps speculatively treat certain natural occurrences *as* signs, and reasonably conclude that it is a good idea to act in accordance with what they take those signs to "reveal" about God's will. Thus the Stoics agree with Aquinas (*ST* IaIIae Q91 A2 Resp) that human beings participate in the divine law in a uniquely excellent way.

What the Stoics conspicuously lack, however, is belief in any *wholesale* revelatory events, whereby divine law was given to human beings as such. Some kind of preestablished system of signs is necessary for the processes by which the authority of a lawgiver, his right to be obeyed, is claimed and acknowledged; that is, there must be some kind of comprehensive divine revelation, where this is to be distinguished, on the one hand, from what might be inferred about God's will on the basis of observation of natural phenomena and, on the other, from the occasional piecemeal deliverances of dreams, portents, and oracles. Such revelation is necessary if divine law is to count as *promulgated,* as opposed to more or less speculatively discerned or surmised. Such promulgation is only possible if the law's content, and its status as law, that is, precepts thereby promulgated *with divine authority,* are sufficiently clear that anyone who apprehends it may reasonably be deemed culpable, *in the sense of disobedient,* for not abiding by it. Nothing less than this would be required for the distinctive, language-presupposing modality of authoritative command to win recognition as *the* central modality of Stoic ethics.

The logic of deontic modals is of course a rather arcane topic, and no doubt appears distant from the urgent ethical concerns of living human beings. Yet it is a marker for something ethically fundamental. The revelation on Sinai, and the whole sequence of their covenants with God, were for the Hebrews *the* momentous events of their history, events that defined them as a people, and even (as understood, for example, in parts of Isaiah, and as they were later understood by the Christians) the defining events of human history. This significance would not be diminished in the slightest by the fact, if it is one, that most of the strictly ethical components of what God commands are also accessible to human practical reason (itself, after all, an endowment from God) as necessary for the attainment of virtue and *eudaimonia.* To describe Stoic ethics as a law conception is perfectly accurate as far as it goes, but it does not go far enough to alter the fundamentally eudaimonist outlook the Stoics shared with Plato, Aristotle, Epicurus, and the rest.

Because the Stoic theodicy made no provision for law or command-ment in this overarching sense, their ethic remained within the realm of naturally intelligible "Aristotelian" necessity, of the sort that attaches to that without which certain goods cannot be obtained, or harms avoided. Since the fundamental norms of Stoic ethics lack any *logically* imperatival character, the Stoics cannot qualify as teaching an ethic of divine com-mand in that robust sense, in which divine law obliges "as rules oblige in a game."

Notes

Preface

1. There are exceptions: a few commentators interpret FP in a way that radically domesticates its main thesis, by attributing to Anscombe a highly revisionary conception of "referring expression." This would make of FP a typical case of the confidence trick I described previously, whereby "the large print giveth and the small print taketh away." I argue against such an interpretation in Part 2, Chapter 11.

1: Virtue Ethics, Eudaimonism, and the Greeks

1. In my experience the few authors who avoid more or less basic misconstruals of thesis (2) are among the few who are sympathetic to Anscombe's overall view; prominent among these are Coope (2006), Diamond (1988), Teichmann (2008), and Vogler (2006). (I did not come across Coope's paper until this book was largely written; his position on the issues I discuss, as I understand it, is essentially Anscombe's, as I understand it, and my own.) Of the many critics of MMP, the closest to getting thesis (2) right is Donagan (1977), and that is not very close (see Chapter 3 and Appendix A). According to its preface, Alan Donagan's book was conceived as a rebuttal of Anscombe's thesis (2).
2. Blackburn is presumably referring to Socrates's famous argument in Plato's *Euthyphro*, widely believed to put paid to any attempt to base ethics on divine command.
3. She once remarked to one of her daughters that "it aroused prejudice in people to tell them that a thought came from [Aquinas]," and to another that "to ascribe a thought to him made people boringly ignore the interest of it, whether they were for Aquinas or against him" ("Introduction," in Anscombe 2011, xix, quoted in Vogler 2013b, 240).
4. This is a prominent and interesting point of contact between Anscombe's thinking about ethics and that of her Cambridge colleague Bernard Williams: see especially Williams (1985) and (1993). Their outlooks were in many other respects highly dissimilar and indeed mutually repugnant.
5. The Cyrenaics may not count as eudaimonists; see Irwin (1991) and Annas (1993, ch. 11.1). For a contrary view, see Warren (2014, 201–209).

6. "In the list of thirteen virtues [Benjamin] Franklin compiled as part of his system of private moral accounting, he elucidates each virtue by citing a maxim obedience to which *is* the virtue in question" (MacIntyre 1984, 183).

7. "Egoistic" here has a "formal" sense that should not in itself be subjected to ethical evaluation. See the discussion later.

8. Take, for example, this highly representative pronouncement from Julia Annas: "All ancient theories understand a virtue to be, at least, a disposition to do the morally right thing. . . . [According to the ancients] if we do not [grasp in its own right what is the morally right thing to do], we will not have understood what makes this disposition a *virtue*, rather than some disposition which does not involve morality" (Annas 1993, 9). Such a view of ancient virtue could not be sustained even if "other-regarding," in the Greek context, could be straightforwardly identified with "moral"—which, as I argue at length later, is for many reasons very far from being the case.

9. Charles Pigden (1988, 26) reports on the basis of MMP that "Anscombe hopes to prove that it pays—in terms of our basic natural needs—to be good," a hope he disparages for its "pious impracticality." This seems to me a strange attribution. On the ancient, unmoralized conception of "good" as *good at being a human being,* this is neither pious nor impractical but rather a conceptual truth. Perhaps Pigden wants to mean "*morally* good," but on that interpretation (to anticipate arguments given later) Anscombe would denounce such a "hope" as strictly meaningless. There is something in the vicinity that is neither trivial nor meaningless whose proof she might be thought of as hoping for, namely, that being *just,* in a sense in which that excludes, for example, judicial murder, is necessary for being good at being a human being. But even this is certainly something she could not be said to hope to prove *herself.* She thinks that a great deal more work needs to be done in the philosophy of mind before *anyone* might be in a position to prove it; and she expresses no certainty that it can be proven at all:

> I am not able to do the philosophy involved—and I think that no-one in the present situation of English philosophy *can* do the philosophy involved—but it is clear that a good man is a just man. (MMP, 16)
>
> One man—a philosopher—may say that since justice is a virtue . . . and essentially the flourishing of a man *qua* man consists in his being good (e.g. in virtues); but for any X to which such terms apply, X needs what makes it flourish, so a man needs, or ought to perform, only virtuous actions. . . . That is roughly how Plato and Aristotle talk; but it can be seen that philosophically *there is a huge gap, at present unfillable as far as we are concerned,* which needs to be filled by an account of human nature, human action, the type of characteristic a virtue is, and above all of human "flourishing." And it is the last concept that appears the most doubtful. For it is a bit much to swallow that a man in pain and hunger and poor and friendless is "flourishing," as Aristotle himself admitted. (MMP, 18; my emphasis)

10. Geach gives no textual reference to Foot, but ideas of this kind can be found in Foot (1958) and Foot (1978b), although the latter was published after Geach's essay. Geach's expression "*moral* virtues" (not to be found in Foot's "Moral Beliefs") may itself seem to connote the special category of the *moral* to which Anscombe strenuously objects in MMP; but Geach seems to be following an older and unobjectionable tradition continuous with Aquinas's concept *moralis* and in which "moral virtue" translates Aristotle's phrase *aretai ēthikai*. See section 1.3 in this chapter. (Geach was writing before the idea had been dreamt of that blindness ought not to be thought of as making someone objectively worse off, but merely as a different way of being, as some philosophers have recently urged.)

11. I disregard as fantastical the suggestion that any concept might have been central to the Greek ethical outlook but unmentioned in the *Nicomachean Ethics*.

12. I mention causality partly because MMP seems to be inspired by, and even quite closely modeled on, Russell's "On the Notion of Cause" (1912), which Anscombe elsewhere described as "a destructive essay of great brilliance" (1981a, 135). It begins, like MMP, with a statement of its three theses, the first of which is summarized thus: "that the word 'cause' is so inextricably bound up with misleading associations as to make its complete extrusion from the philosophical vocabulary desirable."

13. For a good example of this peculiar dynamic, see my remarks on Bobonich (2002) in the next section.

14. I realize that here, and in many other places, I am implicitly rejecting recent efforts by interpreters of Aristotle and other ancient ethicists, and of Kant and other moral philosophers of the modern period, to show that ancient eudaimonism is not fundamentally at odds with the modern conception of morality or modern philosophers' articulations of it (see, for example, the editors' introduction to Engstrom and Whiting 1996). But it would take me far too far afield to argue the point here.

15. This fundamental eudaimonistic requirement on what it is for an action to *make sense* must be distinguished from the issue of what reasons it is the mark of a virtuous person to cite for particular actions. I shall have occasion to allude to this distinction again later, but how it should be formulated and explicated is a difficult issue I cannot go into here. On the priority of the *manifestation* of goodness (and so of *eudaimonia*) in virtuous action to the *contribution* such actions make to it, see Foot (2001): "The question is not whether we have reason to aim at being good human beings, but rather whether we have reason to aim at those things at which a good human being must aim" (53). The fifth chapter of Foot's book (66–79) is, among other things, an account of ethical reasons proper as including both what many people nowadays would call *moral* or altruistic reasons and what they would call prudential or self-interested ones. Foot argues persuasively that this distinction within ethical reasons is at best superficial.

Echoing Nietzsche and Bernard Williams, she suggests that the distinction encourages an emphasis on (a certain conception of) altruism, which seriously
distorts ethical thinking: "That we tend to speak in moral philosophy only of
volitional faults that impinge particularly on others gives the whole subject an
objectionably rigoristic, prissy, moralistic tone that we would hardly care to
take up in everyday life" (79).

16. I am grateful to Harold Langsam for impressing this point on me.

17. This idea, that the denial that any reasons are *really* altruistic is *not* supposed to
imply that all reasons are *really* egoistic, I stole from Donald Davidson. This sort
of idea is the natural expression of the outright rejection of a distinction. In the
Davidson case, "if we cannot intelligibly say that [conceptual] schemes are different, neither can we intelligibly say that they are one" (1974, 198).

18. Annas (1993) seeks support for her wholehearted identification of Greek virtue
with *moral* virtue in the undoubted fact that, for the Greeks, certain virtue-based
reasons, like some of our "moral" reasons, contribute to deliberation not via any
kind of "weighing" procedure but by "silencing" or nullifying any other reasons
that might seek to compete with them: "All ancient theories think exactly the
same way about the fact that an action is cowardly [as we do in conceiving the
refusal of cowardice as a moral requirement]: this is a consideration which is not
just weighed up against the profit and time expended, but which sweeps them
aside; and to think otherwise is to misconstrue what cowardice is" (122; cf. Mc-
Dowell 1978, 26–28; 1979, 334–335; 1980, 370). But the fact that "moral" reasons
in our culture have this "silencing" capacity gives us no reason whatever to think
that reasons that have this capacity in another culture are anything like "moral"
reasons in any respect relevant to Annas's thesis. In particular, it takes us no
distance at all toward the idea that the latter reasons constitute a unique, sui
generis category, set apart from other sorts of reason in the way that "moral"
reasons are supposed to be for us. Consider in this connection Bernard Williams's discussions of Aeschylus's rendering of the overwhelming necessity
attached to Agamemnon's reasons for sacrificing Iphigenia (Williams 1973b,
173; and especially 1993, 132–136). It is extremely implausible to conceive of
Agamemnon's reasons as having anything to do with *morality*—at least, once
we drop the surprisingly tenacious and often unwitting assumption that reasons that exercise automatically overriding authority are simply *eo ipso* "moral." It
is entirely natural, by contrast, to think of Agamemnon's reasons as ultimately
grounded, not in his *eudaimonia* exactly, since the tragedy of his predicament is
that nothing can redeem *that,* but in something that has just as much to do with
himself and what can be salvaged for himself: what *must* be done if his being as
commander of the Greeks is not to be wrecked beyond redemption. (I do not
mean to imply agreement with everything Williams says about the Agamemnon
case.) Furthermore, it is essential to prudence itself that it can underwrite "silencing" judgments. Foot points out that "foolish" and "imprudent," like "cruel"
and "unjust," "entail a final 'should' or 'should not'"; these are what she calls

"conceptually verdictive" action-descriptions, "contrasting in this respect with expressions such as 'dangerous' and 'self-regarding.'" These latter descriptions, as she says, "can be applied to an action without implying that it should not be done, whereas this is not true of words such as 'imprudent' and 'foolish'" (Foot 2001, 78).

19. The distinguished historian is Schneewind (1998, 4). I didn't exactly pick Bobonich's book at random, but there are plenty of examples of this sort of thing to choose from.

20. Quite apart from the vast discrepancies between the dominant eighteenth-century concept of morality and the ancient concept of virtue, it is pretty extraordinary that Schneewind (in 1998), with Bobonich's approval (in 2002), should describe the former as extending equal moral status to "all normal individuals." Unless, that is, "normal individuals" is to be understood as meaning something like "propertied white men"; but it would be misleading not to flag such an identification, particularly if the eighteenth-century outlook is being invoked for the explicit purpose of effecting a favorable contrast with an outlook claimed to be utterly alien to us on account of its radical exclusivity.

2: The Invention of "Morality" and the Possibility of Consequentialism

1. The fact that narrower definitions of *consequentialism* have subsequently gained some currency is no reason to deny Anscombe the prerogatives due to her as *coiner* of the term. Thus we find Bernard Williams writing in 1973, "It is perfectly consistent, and it might be a mark of sense, to believe, *while not being a consequentialist,* . . . that if an adequate . . . specification of a type of action has been given in advance, it is always possible to think of some situation in which the consequences of doing the action so specified would be so awful that it would be right to do something else" (1973a, 90). Yet such a view is clearly impossible to hold without being a consequentialist on Anscombe's definition; indeed, it is virtually a *statement* of consequentialism on that definition. Even more remarkably, Williams's implicit assent to the view he describes has been seen as a kind of *reductio* of Anscombe's "account" of consequentialism: "[Anscombe] makes it a defining feature of non-consequentialism to believe in such absolute prohibitions, and so must presumably count *Williams,* of all people, as a consequentialist" (Chappell 2015, n22). But no issues of plausibility arise in connection with the implications of a stipulative definition of a newly coined word.

2. Charles Pigden (1988, 24n4) claims that Anscombe is "simply mistaken" to identify Sidgwick as the inventor of "consequentialism or act-utilitarianism," because Francis Hutcheson was no less of a consequentialist than he. As I remarked in the previous note, we should defer to Anscombe's characterization of consequentialism, since she coins the term in MMP; and she does not seem to make it equivalent to act-utilitarianism. She denies that John Stuart Mill (for example) was a

consequentialist; and not because of the role of rules in his system but because he respects the ethical significance, subsequently destroyed by Sidgwick, of the distinction between the consequences of an action the agent intends and those he merely foresees. Pigden claims that Hutcheson "believes in precisely those aspects of consequentialism that Anscombe objects to," but does not mention the aspect Anscombe marks as decisive: "I think it plausible to suggest that *this* move on the part of Sidgwick [namely, "the denial of *any* distinction between foreseen and intended consequences, as far as responsibility is concerned"] explains the difference between old-fashioned Utilitarianism and that *consequentialism,* as I name it, which marks him and every English academic moral philosopher since him" (MMP, 12; cf. Vogler 2013b). (It seems that the fatal move was actually first made by Bentham; see Teichmann [2008, 113n30].) "Since Hutcheson was also a Christian, apparently sincere," Pigden goes on, "there must be doubts as to whether consequentialism is genuinely at odds with the Hebrew-Christian ethic." But however devout he may have been, Hutcheson's authority to determine the content of that ethic can hardly rival that of the authors of the Pentateuch, for example, or of Saint Paul (cf. Romans 3:8).

3. This is just an example. It is clear from Anscombe's emphasis elsewhere in MMP (for example, 10) on the variety of the kinds of action traditionally strictly prohibited by the Hebrew-Christian ethic, which would *all* be liable to conditional permissibility in accordance with the consequentialist latitude made conceptually possible by the vocabulary of *morality,* that she does not hold, as Roger Crisp (2004) supposes, that "the most significant characteristic of the views of these modern philosophers is that they will permit the punishment of the innocent in certain circumstances" (76). Since the reason she gives here for the ethical superiority of the vocabulary of *virtue* is that it has naturally facilitated, as talk of *moral* right and wrong does not, the framing of exceptionless prohibitions, it also seems wrong to suppose, as Onora O'Neill does (2004), that "she objects to rules and principles without divine backing" (316).

4. To be clear: the claim is that the vocabulary of morality makes consequentialism an apparent conceptual possibility. It does not in itself make consequentialism an *attractive* option: on the contrary, Kant seems to me to have done an exceptionally good job of showing how certain features many take to be essential to morality are radically inconsistent with consequentialism. (All this would ideally be expressed in a way that makes it consistent with my later claim that Anscombe holds, and it is the case, that *moral* is not really a concept at all. I believe this can be done, but it would be a rather convoluted and so distracting exercise.)

To the extent that the vocabulary does make consequentialism conceptually possible, however, it makes possible any form that countenances the idea that something very like the flavor of disapproval that traditionally went with the judgment that an action is *unjust* might, in some conceivable circumstances, properly attach to an action that would traditionally have been deemed a paradigm case of *injustice,* such as Harry S. Truman's bombing of Hiroshima. I suspect this is true of very many forms of consequentialism. (The awkward character-ization of the "flavor of disapproval" is intended to capture the fact that the consequentialist typically does not see herself as engaged in some kind of ruth-less, terrifying, Calliclean "transvaluation of values," but takes herself to be one of "the good guys.")

5. There may of course be plenty of other reasons to be skeptical about this idea, and especially about the idea that there is always a best outcome (or class of best outcomes). See Foot 1985.

6. According to Duncan Richter, Peter Winch in an unpublished paper supposed that Anscombe herself thought of virtue and the associated idea of flourishing as having primary application, in ethics, to the patient. Winch seems to have mis-judged the purpose of Anscombe's remark about the possible "influence on our actions" of facts such as that a particular plant needs a certain environment if it is to flourish: "Certainly, it all depends on whether you *want* it to flourish! as Hume would say" (MMP, 7). He takes this to indicate that she would suppose, in true Humean fashion, that any "practical necessity" attaching to the Good Samaritan's helping (meeting the needs of) the wounded man is radically con-ditional on the Samaritan's wants (Richter 1995, 75, citing Winch, n.d., 3). But Anscombe's understanding of the role of the ideas of virtue and flourishing in ethics (notwithstanding her insistence that no one's understanding of this is very advanced) is clearly and self-consciously in the tradition of the Greeks, whose eudaimonism ensures that it is the agent's flourishing that is central to a philosophical account of human ethics. This does *not* mean that his own flour-ishing need feature in the reasons the agent would give for any particular good action: if eudaimonism required a rational Samaritan to help the wounded man because this would further his (the Samaritan's) *eudaimonia rather than* because the man needs help, it would be a corrupt doctrine indeed. But the connection between the agent's *eudaimonia* as the ultimate ground for culti-vating the virtues and those virtues' requiring many reasons for particular actions to be other-directed is presumably part of what, on Anscombe's view, remains obscure in our thinking about virtue.

7. See Williams 1973a, especially 108–117.

3: The Misguided Project of Vindicating Morality

1. The mention of Stoicism makes it clear that law conceptions of ethics are not re-stricted, even de facto, to those descended from the Torah. David Conway, in a review of Anscombe (2005a), expresses a common preconception, especially among those, unlike himself, for whom MMP is a matter of hearsay, when he lists the following as the first of the "several theses" of her paper "that have be-come widely accepted . . . but which nonetheless . . . are demonstrably false": "No ethical system ever embodied a law conception of ethics that did not derive its *deontic* vocabulary from a Judeo Christian source" (Conway 2006, 678). Irwin

(1977) makes the same mistake, and unfortunately compounds it with a confusing neglect of Anscombe's distinction between ethics and morality, and a strange implication (if it is more than just infelicitous phrasing) that she ascribed a law conception to Hebrew scripture and to Protestants, but not to Catholic Christianity: "[Anscombe in MMP] mistakenly thinks [the law conception of ethics] is not a Greek, but only a Hebraic and post-Reformation view of morality" (287n6). ("Law conception of ethics" is in the text to which the note refers.) Anscombe's view is that there is no Hebraic or *pre*-Reformation view of *morality* at all, and that every version of "morality" is post-Reformation and essentially aspires to express a law conception of ethics. Irwin's counterexamples to the thesis he misattributes in this distorted form to Anscombe are not the Stoics but much earlier writers like Hesiod, Xenophanes, and Theognis (17). On Stoicism, see Appendix B.

2. Richter notes the inconsistency, but favors an interpretation that resolves it in the direction opposite to that taken here; that is, on his view, the "slip" is not her implication that there could be a secular law conception of ethics, but her earlier definition of a law conception as essentially theistic, about which he writes, "What Anscombe says here [the quoted definition from MMP (6)] is clearly not what she means" (Richter 1995, 71). His evidence is the later passage I quote from MMP (13), which *I* call a "slip," and her subsequent remarks about candidates for the role of secular "lawgivers": existing social norms, social contract theories, and "laws" inherent in the cosmos. It is not clear to me why we should take these remarks at face value, and not her earlier definition of "law conception": Why is *that* "clearly not what she means"? I do not want to press this particular point of interpretation, although it is surely unfair of Richter (1995, 72n19) to criticize Donagan for inaccuracy in his description of Anscombe as contending that "morality can intelligibly be treated as a system of law only by presupposing a divine lawgiver" (Donagan 1977, 3; cf. 1983, 804): this is precisely what Richter acknowledges she says in her definition of "law conception," even quoting her words, but maintains she does not mean. I argue later (section 6.2) that, whatever view we end up attributing to Anscombe on the matter, it makes more sense overall to think of "law conceptions" as indeed essentially theistic; that is, to think of them in line with her definition as opposed to her second thoughts. There is a closely related point of interpretation that seems to me much more important. Richter's remarks about what Anscombe says about capturing the extension of "illicit" in Aristotelian vocabulary (Richter 1995, 72; cf. MMP, 6) strongly imply that he takes Anscombe to suppose that legitimating a secular law conception of ethics is equivalent to legitimating the moral vocabulary. I argue later in this chapter that she doesn't (and shouldn't) mean this.

3. I criticize *The Theory of Morality* in sorrow because it had a huge effect on me and I still admire it very much, even though my admiration blinded me to the confusions in this account of the significance of MMP and so retarded my understanding of the paper for many years.

4. Contrast Geach's use of the expression "moral virtue," diagnosed previously as marking, perhaps infelicitously, an impeccably Aristotelian distinction.

5. On the distinctive form of practical necessity allegedly constitutive of moral norms, also see section 5.4.

6. Lear (2015) includes interesting discussions of this missed opportunity.

7. This comparison was suggested to me by Michael Thompson.

8. See Appendix B on why Stoic ethics, although technically a law conception, does not amount to an exception to this generalization.

9. See in this connection Rachel Barney's (2011) discussion of Hesiod's *Works and Days*.

10. The idea that contradictory concepts are not really concepts at all is a natural companion of the doctrine that contradictory statements are not just false but meaningless, and as such it is strongly associated with Wittgenstein and seems to be one of his few very influential late doctrines that go back to the *Tractatus*. There is a remarkable illustration of the reverence in which this doctrine was once held in Oxford in Williamson (2014).

11. In standard formal treatments of the logic of properties, a comprehension axiom will ensure that *being non-self-identical* counts as a perfectly respectable property. Frege's strategy survives in the standard definition of the empty set in Zermelo-Fraenkel set theory, as the set of all objects that are not identical with themselves.

12. This comparison was suggested to me by K. Setiya.

13. My insistence on Anscombe's denial that "moral" even expresses a concept might look like flogging a dead horse. After all, as Sergio Tenenbaum wrote to me, "it is hardly a consolation to the modern moral philosopher to learn that though incapable of being employed for any serious job in philosophical ethics, his most cherished concept could find some employment in the business of denoting zero," and conversely, "if a philosopher's most basic concepts are shown to be uninstantiable, and her theory was, for this reason, taken to be meaningless, wouldn't it be seriously pedantic to insist that, really, all that can be said against it on these grounds is that her theory is necessarily false?" But if, as I suspect, Anscombe is right about this, it makes a big difference to the dialectical situation. Many readers of MMP have supposed that it effectively issues a challenge to give an account of what the concept *moral* amounts to, which they then try to meet (Darwall is a good recent example of this). But if "moral" doesn't even express a concept, there is no such challenge, since there is no intension to vindicate. Or rather, at most, there is the anterior challenge of responding to Anscombe's argument that it is not a concept. This all bears out what I said at the start (1.1) about one measure of a piece of philosophy's profundity being how much other philosophy it puts out of business.

14. Richter concurs: "Anscombe would agree [with Baier and, he implies, with Richter] that confusion arises precisely when the moral is confused with legal notions of duty, obligation and the rest (not when *morality is coherently conceived*

on the, for example, divine law model)" (1995, 74; my emphasis). Richter also quotes Winch, in his unpublished paper, attributing to Anscombe the suggestion that "there is something unintelligible about a *moral* modality which lacks external (e.g., Christian or Aristotelian) justification" (Winch, 10, quoted in Richter 1995, 75n27; my emphasis); the clear implication is that a *moral* modality equipped with such a justification would be intelligible.

15. Admittedly such a formulation seems to imply that "morally *ought*" is "merely contradictory," so that on the broadly Fregean approach to these matters I have recommended, phrases like *what morally ought to be done* do express concepts, that is, intensions that determine extensions, even though the extension in every possible world is the null set. This is a conclusion I would of course want to resist, although at this point I am not entirely sure about the best line of resistance. One way of making out the notion as "worse than self-contradictory" might be to appeal to its essentially practical nature: the real point of "morally *ought*" is to express a distinctive kind of reason for action, but it is inherently incapable of doing this. Thus *what legally ought to be done, although not determined as such by any legislator,* might at first sight seem to have a kind of legitimate use in defining *zero,* say, like *non-self-identical* in Frege's *Grundlagen;* but because the concept is supposed to be essentially practical, this is not the kind of use that could vindicate the concept in the right way. We might contrast *what morally ought to be done,* on this way of thinking, with a practical concept like *what needs to be done to prove the completeness of arithmetic;* the set of actions falling under the latter concept is also necessarily empty, but it still has the *form* appropriate to a reason-giving concept; its practical *force* is of an intelligible *kind.*

16. More examples of the relevant attribution: Vogler (2013a): "Distinctively *moral* concepts . . . had a home in monotheistic divine law ethics, but not in atheistic moral philosophy" (304); Crisp (2004) goes so far as to attribute the view that "moral" and "commanded by God" are *intensionally equivalent:* "Her view is that the claim of a modern utilitarian, for example, that we ought, morally, to maximize utility, *may be taken to be equivalent to the claim that divine law requires us to maximize utility*" (77–78; my emphasis); Pink (2004): "Anscombe thought . . . that this was the only way to *make sense of a distinctively moral obligation. Moral obligations* would have to be imposed on us through the legislative decrees of a divine law-giver" (164; my emphasis); O'Neill (2004): "Anscombe rejects all use of the vocabulary of moral obligation that is not divinely promulgated" (316).

17. If Anscombe had conceded that it *adds* something to the idea of divine command to impart to it the "atmosphere" of a "moral requirement," how could she have ruled out the possibility that that same atmosphere might attach to norms with quite other origins—such as the norms associated with the virtues, for example? *Virtue* would then collapse into "moral" virtue after all, and we would be back with a Victorian conception.

4: The Futility of Seeking the Extension of a Word with No Intension

1. The distinction between the intension and extension of a predicate derives from Carnap (1946), where it is also applied to singular terms and whole sentences. Here I mean by the "intension" of a predicate simply that in virtue of which a predicate determines an extension, where its extension is the set of individuals to which it applies. Thus two homonymous concepts, for example, both expressed by "bank," will differ in extension in virtue of differing in intension. Beyond this, I intend no commitments with respect to such questions as whether predicates refer, what concepts are, and so on.

2. It is important not to miss a particular strangeness in the analogy: it is *phlogiston* and not *the concept of phlogiston* that stands for the concept of the moral; for it was phlogiston itself, and not its concept, that turned out to be chimerical.

3. Much less plausible but, perhaps, not inherently implausible. For a highly skeptical view with much in common with Mackie's, but explicit about using "moral" to mean pretty much whatever anyone takes as the most authoritative deontic modality, see Burgess (2007).

4. We should bear in mind that, as I argued at some length in section 3.2, Anscombe's intended analogy was not between the imagined "second life" of the word "criminal" and our word "moral," but rather between her imagined scenario in respect to the use of "criminal" *before and after* the withering away of juridical institutions, and the use of an ethically sovereign *ought* of obligation or owing *before and after* the demise of Christianity. The point is not, I think, particularly important in connection with the issue at hand; indeed, the issues may emerge more clearly if the reader *does* now think in terms of a straight comparison between "moral" and (in the imagined case) "criminal." But my returning to the analogy in this context might lead the reader to lose sight of the point altogether and, in connection with the central issues of MMP interpretation discussed in 3.2, it is *extremely* important.

5. As I pointed out at the beginning of the previous section, if *moral* were a concept, it would have to have some independently intelligible content if the questions posed by "first-order moral theory" *or* "metaethics" are to make any sense; and if the word did not aspire to express anything sui generis, then Anscombe could not possibly have any well-founded objection to it. These remarks might seem to be in some tension with the current suggestion that a consequentialist (for example) may be taken to *mean* by "moral," in part, something like "productive of the best consequences." Yet the "metaethical" enterprise does seem effectively committed to *moral* having a kind of hybrid content. On the one hand, if the inquiry is to make sense, the word cannot be thought of by the inquirer as having exactly the same intension (hyperintension) as her favored account of it, on pain of that account falling into triviality; on the other hand, the inquiry looks a lot closer to conceptual analysis than to empirical investigation, even if we suppose that different concepts might play "the morality role" in different possible worlds.

6. Another slogan associated with Wittgenstein that looks highly consonant with my referee's objection, *meaning is use,* was until quite recently very popular; but the closest thing we find to it in his writings is heavily qualified (2001, §43), and a saying attributed to him as characteristic, "Don't ask for the meaning; ask for the use!" can be read quite naturally as implying that meaning and use are distinct. (Jim Cargile once expressed to me his scorn for the idea that the meaning of a sentence could be its use by observing that one might cast a sentence in bronze and hit someone over the head with it.)

7. "In doing one's task [*Aufgabe*], one receives certain laws, of the form 'Thou shalt . . . .' This, Wittgenstein says, prompts the question: And suppose I do not do it? 'But it is clear that ethics has nothing to do with punishment or reward in the ordinary sense.' Still 'there must be something right about that question. There must be a kind of ethical reward and ethical punishment, but these must reside in the action itself. (And it is also clear that the reward must be something pleasant and the punishment something unpleasant)' (6.422)" (Anscombe 1959, 171). (I am indebted for this reference to Roger Teichmann.) See also the report of Waismann (1979, 118) on Wittgenstein's view of "ought," quoted in Pigden (1988, 32–33n10) (Pigden refers to Wittgenstein as "Anscombe's mentor").

8. We will have occasion to consider expressivist theories again in Part 2, as applied to the interpretation of statements involving the first-person pronoun.

9. In addition to Plato's Socratic dialogues and many other works, I would especially mention in this connection Jean-Jacques Rousseau's *Discourse on the Origin of Inequality* (1992), Friedrich Nietzsche's "On the Genealogy of Morals" (1989), Sigmund Freud's *Civilization and Its Discontents* (1989), Marcel Proust's *Remembrance of Things Past* (1982) and René Girard's *Violence and the Sacred* (1979). It is highly significant that Freud's profound criticisms of morality are very much directed against the version of it to which Anscombe and Bernard Williams also object; that is, the system of norms, aspiring to the status of laws, descended from the Hebrew-Christian law conception of ethics, and *not* the Greek tradition to which—as to psychoanalysis—*eudaimonia* is central. See Lear 2015, ch. 7, especially 192, 197–199.

5: What's Really Wrong with the Vocabulary of Morality?

1. That is, the conceptual innovations relative to Aquinas's Aristotelian inheritance; historically, of course, the innovations were made by the first Christian ethicists, drawing on their Jewish forebears.

2. I should emphasize that "can't make sense" here encompasses an irreducibly *practical* way of making sense, if there is such a thing (as there seems to me to be), and perhaps alludes to little else. That is, someone who knows what he needs to lead a life worth living but does not seek it need not, and typically will not, be

guilty of a failure of theoretical reason—a failure to see what follows from what. But his reason is not functioning properly, all the same.

3. To insist that the word nevertheless does have the same meaning in my mouth seems to presuppose that the relevant notion of the meaning of a term just is (or is entirely determined by) its extension (where it has one), which seems premature at this stage.

4. This clause is of course necessary to leave room for the idea of criminal or otherwise self-disqualifying orders, such as military superiors are liable to give in wartime for the murder of noncombatants or prisoners of war, for example. I take it that these possibilities indicate that the authority in question is at best *pro tanto*. On the standard understanding of divine authority in the ethical traditions in question, these possibilities are effectively excluded. This is what Kierkegaard took to be so momentous and terrifying about Christianity.

6: Assessing "Modern Moral Philosophy"

1. She clearly denies, on *ethical* grounds, that a proper practical commitment to the norms could be hostage to the philosophical work, even as she alleges that poor workmanship has distorted our understanding of what the norms are.

7: The Circularity Problem for Accounts of "I" as a Device of Self-Reference

1. Throughout this book, "self-reference" will mean a speaker's or writer's reference to him- or herself.

2. For a skeptical view, see Higginbotham (1980, 1989). James Higginbotham, however, favors a construal of the real syntactic structure of forms like "Smith intends to refer to . . . ," in which the main verb takes an infinitival complement, as involving a propositional complement with its own subject term ("PRO"). A version of Anscombe's dilemma, between an inadequate or a circular account of "I," may therefore arise when we ask about the semantics of "PRO." The propositional construal of the complement is in turn controversial; see Chierchia (1989).

3. Subsequent asterisks will have the same significance.

4. Peacocke (2008, 79–80, 83–85) does examine in some detail another exhibit in Anscombe's case against the standard account of "I," namely, her frustratingly obscure parable of the "A" users (FP, 48–49), which I discuss further later in connection with Evans. But as I understand Anscombe's paper, this parable is *secondary* to the circularity argument, since it (the parable) is intended to illustrate the possibility of a word each person uses to refer to himself that clearly does *not* function in the manner of "I." The parable may fail in its illustrative purpose without thereby impugning what I take to be the main argument.

8: Is the Fundamental Reference Rule for "I" the Key to Explaining First-Person Self-Reference?

1. "I" would in this case be on the same footing as Evans's "descriptive names," exemplified by "Julius," coined to refer to whoever invented the zip fastener (1982, 31). It is not clear that "Julius" is really a name at all. See Geach 1986, 534–535.

2. One might make out "the speaker of these very words" as a synonym for "I," but only if the latter phrase is understood in a way that presupposes "I." It is natural to take "these" as demonstrating word *tokens*. If Kaplan is right that indexicals always take "primary scope," then "these" here serves to pick out the word tokens in question in such a way that, if we imagine the circumstance as differing, so that *B* speaks the "same" words (that is, inevitably, the same word *types*, not tokens), they would not count as *these* words, as they were picked out in the original case. The case is now *like* "I": just as who *the current speaker* is can vary from one imagined situation to another but who *I* am cannot, which word tokens exemplify these word *types* can vary, while which word tokens are *these* word tokens, and which are *those* (and therefore who is *the speaker* of these, and who of those) cannot, I think, vary in the same way. Thus there is a surprisingly vast semantic difference between *the current speaker* and *the speaker of these word tokens*.

   If who counts as "the speaker of these word tokens" cannot vary from one imagined circumstance to another, is the phrase not after all equivalent to "I"? Perhaps, but the phrase still cannot do duty as a noncircular analysis of the first person. If we think about the various outlandish possible circumstances that would require me (supposing I am the speaker) to disambiguate my demonstrative expression "these word tokens" (for example, someone else is speaking at the same time, and so on), or would give us the wrong referent for the whole phrase "the speaker of this utterance" (for example, my lungs, vocal cords, and so on have somehow been commandeered by someone else as a medium of *his* expression; cf. FP, 59), we're probably not going to be able to avoid, in the limit, the necessity of parsing "the speaker of these word tokens" as "the speaker of the word tokens spoken by *me*."

3. Kaplan's account of indexicals as devices of direct reference, which expressions like "the current speaker" can never be, is partly inspired by Kripke's idea, or rather ideas, of rigid designation. But while rigid designation is a matter of a term's picking out the same individual in all possible worlds (or all worlds in which the individual exists), Kaplan defines direct reference in terms of what and how the device in question contributes to the proposition expressed by the sentence in which it occurs: it contributes simply its referent, as a propositional component, by contrast with other singular terms, which correspond to propositional components that in turn, in combination with circumstances of semantic evaluation, determine their referents. Kaplan wants his readers to think of desig-

nating the same individual in all possible worlds as a trivial consequence of his account of direct reference, not as part of that account. See Kaplan 1989, especially sec. 4, 492–497.

4. Roger Teichmann asked me how I could stop someone from using "same content" to apply to two speakers' utterances of "I am warm"; or, conversely, from using "different content" to apply to two speakers' utterances of "The speaker is warm." I can't *stop* such usage, of course, but I would object that it would be ill suited to the purpose of regimenting one tolerably clear ordinary sense of *what someone said (thought, imagined, and so on)* (one purpose of Frege's [1956] concept of a *thought,* of which most current ideas of "content" are fairly close descendants). Which sense is this? The sense in which our primary interest in what was said (asserted) pertains to whether or not it is *true* and, relatedly, what it would take to make it true. This requires us to be able to conceive, at the relevant level of detail, which sorts of circumstances would make what was said true, and which would not. Roughly speaking, if exactly the same set of conditions is associated with two utterances as fixing how the world would have to be for the utterances to count as true, they may be said to have the same content. (I'm here skating over a lot of notorious puzzles, of course—for example, the Hesperus-Phosphorus issue, the fact that all mathematical statements have the same content by this criterion as it stands, and Stephen Yablo's observation that "Here is a couch" and "Here is the front of a couch, and behind it is its back" do not have the same content [2014, 2]—but I don't think that matters for current purposes, inasmuch as I don't see how my opponent's alternative way of thinking about content helps us avoid any of those puzzles.)

If my opponent wants to say (in line with Teichmann's first suggestion; the second can be dealt with similarly) that "The speaker is warm" has different contents as said by A and B, then in his usage the connection between the idea of content and our interest in truth evaluation would in one way or another be severed. For to the extent that he wants to carry on individuating contents in terms of truth-conditions, he would also have to say the following, which I think he should be on balance unhappy about having to say: in saying "The speaker is warm," A has not said something that is true if the speaker is warm, and false otherwise. For if the obtaining of that possible situation—the speaker's being warm—were to be associated with what A said as being the condition on which, alone, it would count as true, there would surely be no nonarbitrary way of denying that the very same condition should be associated with the same statement, "The speaker is warm," as said by B. But then (the "content" of) what A is imagined as saying would be, from the perspective of the surely legitimate and lively interest we take in evaluating what people say as being true or false, exactly the same as (the "content" of) what B is imagined as saying. But this identity is just what my opponent denies. So, at the very least, I would want to hear quite a lot about what is to be gained by speaking in the manner of my opponent that would make it worth the embarrassment of having to say that if someone says "The speaker is warm," we should not, in our attempt to ascertain whether what he said was true, simply look into the matter of whether the speaker was warm—even though "the speaker" is clearly not an indexical expression. On the other hand, my opponent might be refusing to allocate any role to truth conditions in the individuation of content. My opponent's supposition, that "The speaker is warm" has a different content as expressed by A or by B, might derive from some completely different conception of content, which allowed him to also say that in saying "The speaker is warm," A *has* said something that is true if the speaker is warm, and false otherwise. But then his position would be strange in a different way. For then he'd have to say that although "The speaker is warm" has different *contents* according as it is said by A or by B (this is the core of his position), nevertheless it is made true (if it is true) by exactly the same circumstance—the speaker's being warm—regardless of who said it. So then I would still want to hear a lot more about what is to be gained from using a conception of content that cuts it off in this way from our interest in being able to determine whether what has been said is true or false.

I believe a much fuller defense of the usage I favor can be extracted from Kaplan (1989). For a sophisticated alternative to Kaplan's view of content as *the* primary sense of "what is said (thought, and so on)," see Stojanovic (2016).

5. I take it that this is what Kaplan's insistence that demonstratives and indexicals are devices of direct reference amounts to in this case.

6. An Idea is a conception of an object that enables one to distinguish it from others of the same kind. Evans also describes it as a kind of subjective counterpart to a Fregean sense (see 1982, 104, 106–107). I have amended Evans's lambda expressions for clarity. I treat these paragraphs as Evans's, although they occur in an appendix to chapter 7 of Evans (1982), and the editor adopted in the appendices the convention of referring to Evans in the third person. The editor assures us in his preface that "the substance of all the Appendices, and most of the writing, are due to Evans" (vi).

7. Geach's response to Evans's account is characteristically brusque: "Suppose the speaker has never heard of one-place concept-expressions?" (Geach 1986, 535). But presumably the idea is that this is the *sense in which* an "I" user intends to refer to herself, even though she will typically be unable to articulate it; she will also typically have some intuition that this mode of self-reference *is* distinctive. Much of Geach's own work on the logic of natural-language expressions presupposes that many distinctions of meaning, including distinctions that essentially concern the intentions of (idealized) speakers, are far beyond the ken of the typical speaker. And the real point of Anscombe's argument is to establish that there is no specification of an intention such that *anyone* uttering "I" with it *could* be said to self-refer in the distinctively first-personal way.

8. Alex Oliver (2010, 130) denies that Frege considered concept-expressions to be schemata, on the ground that "ξ" and so on are not "schematic letters" to be *substituted* by names giving arguments but rather markers of gaps into which such

names are to be *inserted*. I confess that by this point I no longer have any clear sense of what difference this difference is supposed to make; I realize it could be expressed as whether the Greek letters count as *parts* of the concept-expression or not, but that seems to me to push the problem back: What is at stake in questions about what counts as part of an expression, if a schematic letter qualifies as a part even though the whole point of its schematic status is that the letter must be *substituted* if we are to obtain a well-formed expression? Although Oliver insists on the reality of the distinction, since it is presupposed by his interpretation of Frege, he seems at least to share my skepticism about its significance: he takes these, and various other construals of predicates, to be equally legitimate, at least for the purposes for which they are designed.

9. That is, at least, for Frege from 1891.

10. My own main misgiving as to the coherence of this scenario is that "reports on one's own actions" are supposed to be made on the basis of observation and its surrogates but, as Anscombe herself emphasized in one of the central insights of Anscombe (2000), the only concept of human action we have is one according to which, essentially, the agent has *non*observational knowledge of what she is doing. The agency of Anscombe's "*A*" users cannot be dropped from the story without defeating its purpose: since speaking is an exercise of agency, if her subjects are not agents, they are not "*A*" users.

11. In quoting Evans I ceremonially suspend my objections to his splicing together of incompatible semantic idioms.

12. If Anscombe's thought experiment is not in the end intelligible, this may simply indicate an even deeper problem for the Evans account. McDowell (1998) argues plausibly that the idea of agency presupposes not only nonobservational knowledge but self-consciousness itself. Evans's account seems to face a dilemma: if Anscombe's scenario makes sense, it gives us a counterexample; if it does not make sense, that is because agency presupposes self-consciousness, in which case there is still no hope of intentional self-reference—that is, a kind of action— helping to explain the self-conscious use of "I."

9: Rumfitt's Solution to the Circularity Problem

1. The symbolism is adapted from Frege's *Grundgesetze*, §§24, 25; see Rumfitt (1994, 618n14); cf. Frege (2013, 41–42). "A_β (β refers to Smith)" effectively amounts to "the action β performs when β refers to Smith"; more generally, "$A_\beta f(\beta)$" abbreviates "the act specified by '$f(\beta)$'" (Rumfitt 1994, 618).

2. The sentences I here number (18) and (19) are each, in Rumfitt's text (where they are numbered [19] and [21]), "more explicit" (633) paraphrases of sentences (his [18] and [20]) he casts in a form determined by his adoption of a modified version of Donald Davidson's (1969) "paratactic" theory of indirect discourse, adapted for ascriptions of intention ("Smith intends to do that. Refer to Smith," and so on). See further Rumfitt (1993). My ellipses mark the omissions; I have suppressed

this part of Rumfitt's treatment because—as it seems to me—it does not bear on the issue at hand, and so would only distract from it.

3. For example, he argues that (12) cannot mean "Cato intends to kill Cato" on the ground that Cato can intend to kill himself even if he does not know his own name. More on this later.

4. The completion that follows is in fact essentially effected by Rumfitt himself in personal correspondence. A version of it was also suggested to me independently by Gideon Rosen.

5. I here assume, pace Frege, that functionals are not (incomplete) expressions taking (incomplete) objects as their *Bedeutungen*. The assumption is only for simplicity: even if Frege is right, (i) I gather that *Bedeutungen* may well not straightforwardly amount to "referents" as that is here relevantly understood, and (ii) even if *Bedeutungen are* referents, the referents of reflexive pronouns on the Geach-Rumfitt view are not the right kind of item to provide a meaningful contrast with an Anscombe-type construal of "I." If Anscombe were to concede a conception of reference equivalent to Frege's expansive conception of *Bedeutung*, she would presumably have no objection to the suggestion that "I" was a referring expression after all, so long as this status was secured by nothing more than its "referring" to a *function*.

6. In Rumfitt's idiom, a *proposition* is something like an interpreted sentence, which he takes to be a precisification of Frege's use of *Satz*; see Rumfitt (1994, 600–601, incl. n2).

7. I cannot—or, anyway, do not—do justice here to the subtlety of Frege's views on this matter. A helpful exposition is Thompson (2008, 13–19). For a contrary view, see Sullivan (2010, 95–104).

8. The notation here is potentially confusing. The subscript "n" in Ref_n does *not*, as often in such cases it would, indicate that Ref_n is an n-place function, but rather that it is a partial second-order, one-place function defined only for certain arguments consisting of n-place first-order functions.

10: Can We Make Sense of a Nonreferential Account of "I"?

1. I take *referring to* something to be a matter of *speaking of* it, and I take a *referring expression* to be an expression whose function in the language is to pick out some individual thing for the purpose of saying something about it. (I make this assumption for present purposes only, without prejudice to the possibility of plural reference.)

2. I mentioned earlier (9.4) that most rejections of Anscombe's no-reference thesis consist of various versions of the "incredulous stare." Perhaps these stares indicate a conviction that no proposition that might be deduced from her thesis could serve as a *reductio* of it, because no such proposition could be more implausible than that thesis itself. Yet surely the claim is *bizarre* rather than, what is not the

same thing, self-evidently false. So it looks as though there is *some* work to do by way of refutation. For the record, the most serious difficulty that has occurred to me is this.

If "I" is not a referring expression, then the meaning of a sentence like "I'm swimming" cannot involve any object that might count as a referent for "I." But surely it must somehow involve the concept of swimming! Perhaps on the right construal this concept is being brought under a quantifier or other higher-order concept. (Again, for details see Chapter 11.) But how would this work for a sentence like "I'm talking about myself"? For surely it is no part of Anscombe's view that a sentence like that must be deemed necessarily false! Well, the strongest line to take seems to be, first, to opt for a Rumfitt-Geach nonreferential understanding of the reflexive pronoun, so that, roughly speaking, we understand "talking about myself" as a distinctive monadic predicate we might think of as "self-talking-about," with no referent for "myself" as a separable semantic component. Then, in line with the treatment of "I'm swimming," we understand the meaning of the whole sentence as not involving a referent for "I," but still as involving the concept "self-talking-about," possibly functioning as the subject of a higher-order predication.

Fine. But whatever moves we make here, they are all in the service of having the sentence "I'm talking about myself" come out as (in the appropriate contexts) *true*. But if that's true, it's hard to see how "I'm referring to myself" could fail to be true as well. How can I talk about myself without referring to myself? Presumably we use the same moves to avoid construing this in such a way that "I" and "myself" turn out to be referring expressions. But now suppose I'm asked, "With what linguistic device are you referring to yourself?" How can we object if I reply, "I'm using 'I' to refer to myself"? But not to worry: this sentence too can be analyzed in such a way that its truth does not require first-person reference.

But this is no good. An analysis that avoids first-person reference is no help, if the point of the analysis is to have "I'm using 'I' to refer to myself" come out *true*. For by the disquotation property, *however* the sentence is analyzed, if "I'm using 'I' to refer to myself" is true, then *I'm using "I" to refer to myself*. And how can I possibly use "I" to refer to myself, if "I" is not a referring expression?

3. Anscombe said nothing about this problem, and provided no indication of how a positive nonreferentialist position might go, beyond some rather obscure hints in FP. In his own paper on the topic, Kripke remarks, "I was never able to talk to Anscombe about these matters, but I do recall a report from someone else as to what she said when queried as to why 'I' behaves as if it refers in inference patterns. Her answer as reported was 'I don't know'" (2011, 312).

4. This is a slight simplification. The line of descent is actually required to cross the buffer zone separating the voluntary from the *intentional*, which is a species of the voluntary. On the voluntary/intentional distinction, see Anscombe (2000, §17, 26).

5. This expression, and the analogy it points to, was suggested to me by Kit Fine.

11: Strategies for Saving "I" as a Singular Term

1. Since, if "I" *is* a referring expression, it surely effects singular reference, I shall here use "referring expression" and "singular term" interchangeably, ignoring plurals, general terms, predicates, and so on.
2. Harcourt's suspicions are endorsed by Candace Vogler (2006, 359n24). I should emphasize that they are only suspicions. Harcourt begins the second section of his paper by saying, "It would be strange, however, if Anscombe *did* straightforwardly intend her thesis in such a way that it could be sidestepped by relabeling. So let us assume that Anscombe accepts the normal test for referring expressionhood, and thus give the idea that the no reference thesis does have consequences for the logical form of first person sentences a fair hearing" (2000, 31). Unfortunately, he concludes that the "straight" reading of the no-reference thesis is obviously false, so he begins the paper's fourth section by resolving to revert to his first hypothesis, its strangeness notwithstanding, that "the thesis is not intended to imply any [differences between 'I' and paradigmatic referring expressions] and is based instead on a non-standard way of delimiting the class of referring expressions" (37). In other words, he is back to implicating Anscombe in fraud (although he would of course not put it that way).
3. The restriction to atomic sentences is to be understood in the rest of this discussion, and is intended merely to exclude sentences, such as certain disjunctions, in which the occurrence of a singular term might be "nonessential" and not really contribute to truth conditions.
4. Timothy Smiley argues for a theory of definite descriptions according to which they are genuine singular terms and "many simple sentences with empty subjects can be read as true" (Smiley 1981, 329). But he turns out to be talking about surface grammar. As I understand it, the "simple sentences," for example, of the form "a is F," are to be read as F(whatever is a) and formalized as $(\forall x)(x = a \rightarrow Fx)$ (329). I assume (pace Williamson 2002) that, similarly, the empty term "the cookie monster" is not going to be the logical subject of the true "The cookie monster doesn't exist."
5. I say "relevant aspects" of logical form in allusion once again to what I take to be Frege's doctrine (for example, Frege 1960b, 49) that there is no such thing as *the* logical form of a sentence, since different aspects of form will need to be isolated for different tasks of logical engineering, as we might call them; and although these aspects will of course be mutually compatible, they typically cannot all be exhibited simultaneously. See the discussion in section 9.5.
6. The reference to Kripke appears to be to the argument for dualism in Kripke (1980, 144–155).
7. It is very puzzling that Harcourt expresses a further suspicion that Anscombe's "apparently controversial claim" that "'I am EA' is . . . not an identity proposition" (FP, 59) "does not . . . concern the logical form of 'I am EA,' and is based instead on a non-standard definition of 'identity proposition,' corresponding to

a similar definition of 'referring expression'" (Harcourt 2000, 28). First, what she says about Augustine and Descartes implies that, if "I" *were, per impossibile,* a referring expression, and so referred to a Cartesian Ego, then "I am EA" *would* be an identity statement, but would *not be true,* since the Ego Anscombe would refer to by uttering "I" would not be E. A., since E. A. is not an Ego but a living human organism. Second, he seems to say that Anscombe can only deny that "I am EA" is an identity statement in the accepted sense of "identity statement" "if it had *already* been shown that 'I' is not a referring expression," but "this has not yet been shown." But she makes her denial in the following context: "*If I am right in my general thesis, there is an important consequence*—namely, that 'I am EA' is after all not an identity proposition" (FP, 59; my emphasis).

8. Harcourt seems to slide between two meanings of "logical syntax," however. When he contrasts it with "*surface* syntax," it is hard to see how he could mean anything other than logical form: roughly, the expression of a thought in a sentence, the semantic roles of whose components express, at some level of resolution, the component senses of the thought, as these roles are determined (via an underlying account at the level of reference) by the inferential relations the thought bears to other thoughts. In this sense of logical syntax, a singular term occurring in subject position in a logical-syntactic representation of a thought indicates that some object, the referent of that term, must exist if the thought is going to have a chance of being true. Thus there is no further question about whether what occurs in this way as a singular term in a logical-syntactic representation of a thought should be viewed as *really* a referring expression. In other places, however, Harcourt seems to mean by "logical syntax" something like "(surface) syntax, as that bears on inferential relations among sentences taken as they are found." With respect to *this* sense of logical syntax, questions about an expression's real semantic role can still be intelligibly raised. Thus Harcourt at one point describes himself as "in search of a feature of the logical syntax of 'I' which might yet provide a reason for denying that it is a referring expression as defined by the normal test" (2000, 34).

9. One might wonder whether sentences like "I am referring to myself" constitute exceptions. I suggested earlier (section 10.1) that these cases present Anscombe with a dilemma.

10. Williams 1973c; Taylor 1992.

11. The formal-looking notation is adopted entirely for purposes of abbreviation and disambiguation. It is not presented as a fragment of some envisaged formalized theory of the relevant discourse.

12. This way of speaking has a long history in mathematics, but in philosophy it may go back to Frege: just as a set of worlds doesn't look like the sort of thing that could be true or false, the set of all concepts with singleton extensions doesn't look like the sort of thing that could be the answer to the question, "How many moons has the earth?"

Epilogue

1. Anscombe (1961) was written for a Catholic audience; in a wider context, the relevant feature of a "devout Catholic bomber" would be a determination to avoid *intentional* killing of the innocent.

Appendix A: Aquinas and Natural Law

1. Anscombe does not often refer to Aquinas in her work, but we should not infer that she was not greatly influenced by him. It is not very plausible to suppose that when she wrote about the nature of law, Anscombe was not bearing in mind Aquinas's treatment of the topic, which is one of the most well-known and influential parts of the *Summa Theologiae*.
2. See the discussion in Grisez (1965, 183–184). Germain Grisez remarks that Aquinas denies that the ultimate end of man could consist in morally good action, citing *Summa Contra Gentiles* 3.34; but he wrongly supposes that Aquinas's reason has to do with the category of the *moral* being narrower than whatever concerns natural human ends. In other words, he supposes that by *moralis,* Aquinas means our "moral": "[Moral value] by no means exhausts human goods. The preservation of life is certainly a human good. The act which preserves life is not the life preserved; in fact, they are so distinct that it is possible for the act that preserves life to be morally bad while the life preserved remains a human good" (184). But, to repeat, Aquinas recognizes no such distinction between *bonum morale* and *bonum humanum:* "Moral acts are the same as human acts" (*idem sunt actus morales et actus humani*) (*ST* IaIIae Q1 A3 Resp). This is not a weird doctrine about what we purport to understand by *moral,* but the deployment of a different concept altogether.
3. As far as I can see, Anscombe barely mentions the issue of the accessibility of precepts of, for example, justice to unaided practical reason. But there is this, from Anscombe (2005b, 265):

> There is sometimes good excuse for . . . doing what will certainly lead to [people's] deaths, eg having a system of rail or air transport. . . . If there is no significant difference between intending and foreseeing death, it will follow that one may also plan the death of innocent people as a means to an end.
>
> Here the Judeo-Christian teaching enters its interdict, forbidding all killing of the innocent as end or as means. We might rely on religious authority for this; *but it has also generally been held that the moral law is accessible to reason.* (my emphasis)

Appendix B: Stoic Ethics: A Law Conception without Commandments?

1. With regard to attributed Stoic ethical doctrines, I focus mainly on those of the first three heads of the Athenian Stoa: Zeno (334–262 BCE), Cleanthes (scholarch 262–230 BCE), and Chrysippus (scholarch 230–206 BCE). As to sources,

I mostly use the three main surviving compendia of Stoic ethics: (i) the *Epitome of Stoic Ethics* of Stobaeus (early fifth century CE; widely believed to be a virtually verbatim report of the account of Arius Didymus [first century BCE]); (ii) book 7.84–131 of the *Lives of the Philosophers* of Diogenes Laertius (third century CE); and (iii) Cicero's *De Finibus*. The main ultimate source for all three works seems to have been some selection from the extraordinarily copious works of Chrysippus. For original texts I have relied on Arius Didymus (1999), Diogenes Laertius (2013), and Cicero (1998). For important excerpts from these and other Stoic texts on ethics, with translations, see Long and Sedley (1987a, 344–437; 1987b, 341–431); for a larger selection of texts in English, see Inwood and Gerson (2008, 113–205). For helpful exegesis and commentary, see Inwood and Donini (1999).

2. For arguments that Socrates held that virtue could make good other things, which are in turn necessary for *eudaimonia*, see Jones (2013).

3. Compare Spinoza: "Since without God nothing can exist or be conceived, it is evident that all natural phenomena involve and express the conception of God as far as their essence and perfection extend, so that the greater our knowledge of natural phenomena, the greater and more perfect is our knowledge of God: or in other words . . . the greater our knowledge of natural phenomena, the more perfect is our knowledge of the essence of God (which is the cause of all things)" (*Tractatus Theologico-Politicus* ch. 4, translation after Elwes in Spinoza [2004]).

4. On Stoic logic and semantics, see Bobzien and Mignucci (1999).

References

Algra, K., J. Barnes, J. Mansfield, and M. Schofield, eds. 1999. *The Cambridge History of Hellenistic Philosophy*. Cambridge: Cambridge University Press.

Annas, J. 1993. *The Morality of Happiness*. Oxford: Oxford University Press.

Anscombe, G. E. M. 1957a. "Does Oxford Moral Philosophy Corrupt Youth?" *Listener* 57:266–267, 271. Reprinted in Anscombe 2005a, 161–167.

———. 1957b. "Mr. Truman's Degree." Self-published pamphlet. Oxford. Reprinted in Anscombe 1981d, 62–71.

———. 1958. "Modern Moral Philosophy" [MMP]. *Philosophy* 53:1–19. Reprinted in Anscombe 1981d, 26–42, and in Anscombe 2005a, 169–194.

———. 1959. *An Introduction to Wittgenstein's Tractatus*. New York: Harper and Row.

———. 1961. "War and Murder." In *Nuclear Weapons: A Catholic Response*, edited by W. Stein, 44–62. London: Sheed and Ward. Reprinted in Anscombe 1981d, 51–61.

———. 1969. "On Promising and Its Justice, and whether It Needs to Be Respected In Foro Interno." *Crítica: Revista Hispanoamericana de Filosofía* 3 (7 / 8): 61–83. Reprinted in Anscombe 1981d, 10–21.

———. 1975. "The First Person" [FP]. In *Mind and Language*, edited by S. Guttenplan, 45–65. Oxford: Oxford University Press. Reprinted in Anscombe 1981c, 21–36.

———. 1976. "The Question of Linguistic Idealism." In "Essays on Wittgenstein in Honour of G. H. von Wright," edited by J. Hintikka, special issue, *Acta Philosophica Fennica*, 28 (1–3): 188–215. Reprinted in Anscombe 1981b, 112–133.

———. 1978a. "On the Source of the Authority of the State." *Ratio* 20:1–28. Reprinted in Anscombe 1981d, 130–155.

———. 1978b. "Rules, Rights, and Promises." *Midwest Studies in Philosophy* 3 (1): 318–323. Reprinted in Anscombe 1981d, 97–103.

———. 1981a. "Causality and Determination." In Anscombe 1981c, 133–147.

———. 1981b. *Collected Philosophical Papers*. Vol. 1, *From Parmenides to Wittgenstein*. Minneapolis: University of Minnesota Press.

———. 1981c. *Collected Philosophical Papers*. Vol. 2, *Metaphysics and the Philosophy of Mind*. Minneapolis: University of Minnesota Press.

———. 1981d. *Collected Philosophical Papers*. Vol. 3, *Ethics, Religion and Politics*. Minneapolis: University of Minnesota Press.

———. 1982. "Medallist's Address: Action, Intention and 'Double Effect.'" *Proceedings of the American Catholic Philosophical Association* 56:12–25.

———. 2000. *Intention*. 2nd ed. Cambridge, MA: Harvard University Press.

———. 2005a. *Human Life, Action and Ethics*. Edited by M. Geach and L. Gormally. Charlottesville: University of Virginia Press.

———. 2005b. "Murder and the Morality of Euthanasia." In Anscombe 2005a, 261–277.

———. 2011. *From Plato to Wittgenstein*. Edited by M. Geach and L. Gormally. Charlottesville: University of Virginia Press.

Aquinas, Thomas. 1888–1906. *Summa Theologiae [ST]*. Latin text in nine volumes with commentary by Thomas Cajetan. Rome: Typographia Polyglotta. Cited by numbers of part, question, and article (Part 1 = Ia, Part 2a = IaIIae, Part 2b = IIaIIae, Part 3 = IIIa; the numbers following "Q" and "A" give the question and article, respectively).

———. 1918–1930. *Summa Contra Gentiles*. Latin text in three volumes with commentary by Francesco Silvestri. Rome: Typographia Polyglotta.

———. 1964–1980. *Summa Theologiae*. English translation by various hands in sixty-one volumes. London: Blackfriars.

Aristotle. 1920. *Ethica Nicomachea*. Greek text edited by L. Bywater. Oxford: Oxford University Press. There are many excellent translations. An especially helpful recent one is Broadie and Rowe 2002.

Arius Didymus. 1999. *Epitome of Stoic Ethics*. Greek text edited by A. J. Pomeroy. Atlanta: Society of Biblical Literature.

Augustine of Hippo. 2002. *On the Trinity*. English translation by S. McKenna. Edited by G. B. Matthews. Cambridge: Cambridge University Press.

———. 2015. *De Trinitate*. Latin text edited by J. P. Migne. N.p: Mediatrix.

Baier, K. 1988. "Radical Virtue Ethics." *Midwest Studies in Philosophy* 13:126–135.

Barney, R. 2011. "Callicles and Thrasymachus." In *The Stanford Encyclopedia of Philosophy*, Winter 2011 edition, edited by E. N. Zalta. https://plato.stanford.edu/archives/win2011/entries/callicles-thrasymachus/.

Blackburn, S. 2005. "Simply Wrong." *Times Literary Supplement*, no. 5348, September 30, 11–12.

Bobonich, C. 2002. *Plato's Utopia Recast: His Later Ethics and Politics*. Oxford: Oxford University Press.

Bobzien, S., and M. Mignucci. 1999. "The Stoics: Logic." In Algra et al. 1999, 92–176. Cambridge: Cambridge University Press.

Broadie, S., and C. Rowe. 2002. *Aristotle: Nicomachean Ethics: Translation, Introduction and Commentary*. Oxford: Oxford University Press.

Burgess, J. 2003. Review of Fine 2002. *Notre Dame Journal of Formal Logic* 44 (4): 227–251.

———. 2005. *Fixing Frege*. Princeton, NJ: Princeton University Press.

———. 2007. "Against Ethics." *Ethical Theory and Moral Practice* 10 (5): 427–439.

Carnap, R. 1946. *Meaning and Necessity: A Study in Semantics and Modal Logic.* Chicago: University of Chicago Press.

Castañeda, H.-N. 1966. " 'He': A Study in the Logic of Self-Consciousness." *Ratio* 7 (2): 130–157.

Chappell, S. G. 2015. "Bernard Williams." In *The Stanford Encyclopedia of Philosophy*, Spring 2015 edition, edited by E. N. Zalta. http://plato.stanford.edu /archives/spr2015/entries/williams-bernard/.

Chierchia, G. 1989. "Anaphora and Attitudes De Se." In *Semantics and Contextual Expression*, edited by R. Bartsch, J. van Benthem, and P. van Emde Boas, 1–31. Dordrecht, Netherlands: De Gruyter.

Chisholm, R. 1982. *The First Person*. Minneapolis: University of Minnesota Press.

Cicero. 1998. *De Finibus Bonorum et Malorum*. Latin text edited by L. D. Reynolds. Oxford: Clarendon.

Conway, D. 2006. Review of Anscombe 2005a. *Philosophy* 81 (318): 673–682.

Coope, C. 2006. "Modern Virtue Ethics." In *Values and Virtues*, edited by T. Chappell [S. C. Chappell], 20–52. Oxford: Oxford University Press.

Cresswell, M. 1975. "Hyperintensional Logic." *Studia Logica* 34 (1): 25–38.

Crisp, R. 2004. "Does Modern Moral Philosophy Rest on a Mistake?" In O'Hear 2004, 75–93.

Dancy, J. 2004. *Ethics without Principles*. Oxford: Oxford University Press.

Darwall, S. 2006. *The Second-Person Standpoint*. Cambridge, MA: Harvard University Press.

Davidson, D. 1969. "On Saying That." In *Words and Objections: Essays on the Work of W. V. Quine*, edited by D. Davidson and J. Hintikka, 158–174. Dordrecht, Netherlands: Springer. Reprinted in Davidson 1984, 93–108.

———. 1974. "On the Very Idea of a Conceptual Scheme." *Proceedings and Addresses of the American Philosophical Association* 47:5–20. Reprinted in Davidson 1984, 183–198.

———. 1984. *Inquiries into Truth and Interpretation*. Oxford: Oxford University Press.

Diamond, C. 1988. "The Dog That Gave Himself the Moral Law." *Midwest Studies in Philosophy* 13:161–179.

Diogenes Laertius. 2013. *Lives of Eminent Philosophers*. Greek text edited with an introduction by T. Dorandi. Cambridge: Cambridge University Press.

Donagan, A. 1977. *The Theory of Morality*. Chicago: University of Chicago Press.

———. 1981. "Morality, Property and Slavery." Pamphlet, Department of Philosophy, University of Kansas. Reprinted in Donagan 1994, 107–131.

———. 1982. "Moral Rationalism and Variable Social Institutions." *Midwest Studies in Philosophy* 7:3–10.

———. 1983. Review of Anscombe 1981b, Anscombe 1981c, and Anscombe 1981d. *Ethics* 93 (4): 801–804.

———. 1994. *The Philosophical Papers of Alan Donagan*. Vol. 2, *Action, Reason and Value*. Edited by J. E. Malpas. Chicago: University of Chicago Press.

Doyle, J. 2010. "Socrates and Gorgias." *Phronesis* 55 (1): 1–25.

———. 2012. "Socratic Methods." *Oxford Studies in Ancient Philosophy* 42:39–75.

———. 2016. "'Spurious Egocentricity' and the First Person." *Synthèse* 193 (11): 3579–3589.

Dummett, M. A. E. 1973. *Frege: Philosophy of Language*. London: Duckworth.

———. 1991. *Frege: Philosophy of Mathematics*. London: Duckworth.

Engstrom, S., and Whiting, J. 1996. *Aristotle, Kant and the Stoics: Rethinking Happiness and Duty*. Cambridge: Cambridge University Press.

Evans, M. J. G. 1977. "Pronouns, Quantifiers and Relative Clauses (I)." *Canadian Journal of Philosophy* 7:467–536. Reprinted in Evans 1985, 76–152. References in the text are to the reprint ed.

———. 1982. *The Varieties of Reference*. Oxford: Oxford University Press.

———. 1985. *Collected Papers*. Oxford: Oxford University Press.

Field, H. 1989. "Platonism for Cheap? Crispin Wright on Frege's Context Principle." In *Realism, Mathematics and Modality*, 147–170. Oxford: Oxford University Press.

Fine, K. 2002. *The Limits of Abstraction*. Oxford: Oxford University Press.

Foot, P. 1958. "Moral Beliefs." *Proceedings of the Aristotelian Society* 59:83–104. Reprinted in Foot 1978a, 110–131.

———. 1972. "Morality as a System of Hypothetical Imperatives." *Philosophical Review* 81 (3): 305–316. Reprinted in Foot 1978a, 157–173.

———. 1978a. *Virtues and Vices*. Berkeley: University of California Press.

———. 1978b. "Virtues and Vices." In Foot 1978a, 1–18.

———. 1985. "Utilitarianism and the Virtues." *Mind* 94 (374): 196–209.

———. 2001. *Natural Goodness*. Oxford: Oxford University Press.

Frege, G. 1879. *Begriffsschrift*. Halle, Germany: Verlag von Louis Nebert.

———. 1892. "Über Sinn und Bedeutung." *Zeitschrift für Philosophie und philosophische Kritik* 100:25–50. Translated as Frege 1960c.

———. 1953. *Die Grundlagen der Arithmetik / The Foundations of Arithmetic*. German text with English translation by J. L. Austin. Oxford: Blackwell.

———. 1956. "The Thought: A Logical Inquiry." Translated by A. Quinton and M. Quinton. *Mind* 65 (259): 289–311.

———. 1960a. "Function and Concept." Translated by P. T. Geach. In Frege 1960d, 21–41.

———. 1960b. "On Concept and Object." Translated by P. T. Geach. In Frege 1960d, 42–55.

———. 1960c. "On Sense and Reference." Translated by P. T. Geach. In Frege 1960d, 56–78.

———. 1960d. *Translations from the Philosophical Writings of Gottlob Frege*. Edited and translated by P. T. Geach and M. Black. 2nd ed. Oxford: Blackwell.

————. 2013. *Basic Laws of Arithmetic.* Translated by P. A. Ebert and M. Rossberg. Oxford: Oxford University Press.

Freud, S. 1989. *Civilization and Its Discontents.* Translated by J. Strachey. New York: Norton.

Gauthier, D. 1987. *Morals by Agreement.* Oxford: Oxford University Press.

Geach, P. T. 1957. "Beliefs about Oneself." *Analysis* 18 (1): 23–24.

————. 1968. *Reference and Generality.* Emended ed. Ithaca, NY: Cornell University Press.

————. 1969. "The Moral Law and the Law of God." In *God and the Soul,* 117–129. London: Routledge and Kegan Paul.

————. 1972. "A Program for Syntax." In *Semantics of Natural Language,* edited by D. Davidson and G. Harman, 483–497. Dordrecht, Netherlands: Springer.

————. 1977. *The Virtues.* Cambridge: Cambridge University Press.

————. 1986. Review of Evans 1982. *Philosophy* 61 (238): 534–538.

Girard, R. 1979. *Violence and the Sacred.* Translated by P. Gregory. Baltimore: Johns Hopkins University Press.

Grice, H. P. 1957. "Meaning." *Philosophical Review* 66 (3): 377–388.

Grisez, G. 1965. "The First Principle of Practical Reason: A Commentary on the *Summa theologiae,* 1–2, Question 94, Article 2." *Natural Law Forum* 10:168–201.

Harcourt, E. 2000. "The First Person: Problems of Sense and Reference." *Royal Institute of Philosophy Supplement* 46:25–46.

Higginbotham, J. 1980. "Pronouns and Bound Variables." *Linguistic Inquiry* 11 (4): 679–708.

————. 1989. "Reference and Control." *Rivista di Linguistica* 1 (2): 301–324.

Hursthouse, R. 1999. *On Virtue Ethics.* Oxford: Oxford University Press.

Inwood, B., and P. Donini. 1999. "Stoic Ethics." In Algra et al. 1999, 675–738.

Inwood, B., and L. P. Gerson, ed. and trans. 2008. *The Stoics Reader.* Indianapolis: Hackett.

Irwin, T. 1977. *Plato's Moral Theory: The Early and Middle Dialogues.* Oxford: Oxford University Press.

————. 1986. "Aristotle's Conception of Morality." In *Proceedings of the Boston Area Colloquium in Ancient Philosophy* 1, edited by J. J. Cleary, 115–143.

————. 1991. "Aristippus against Happiness." *Monist* 74 (1): 55–82.

————. 2006. "Aquinas, Natural Law, and Aristotelian Eudaimonism." In *The Blackwell Guide to Aristotle's "Nicomachean Ethics,"* edited by R. Kraut, 323–341. Oxford: Blackwell.

Jespersen, B. 2001. "The Quest for Hyperintensionality." *Pro-Fil* 2 (1). http://profil.muni.cz/01_2001/jespersen_hyperintenzionalita.html.

Johnston, M. 2009. *Saving God.* Princeton, NJ: Princeton University Press.

Jones, R. 2013. "Wisdom and Happiness in *Euthydemus* 278–282." *Philosophers' Imprint* 13 (14): 1–21.

Kaplan, D. 1989. "Demonstratives: An Essay on the Semantics, Logic, Metaphysics, and Epistemology of Demonstratives and Other Indexicals." In *Themes from Kaplan,* edited by J. Almog, J. Perry, and H. Wettstein, 481–563. Oxford: Oxford University Press.

Korsgaard, C. 1996a. *Creating the Kingdom of Ends.* Cambridge: Cambridge University Press.

———. 1996b. *The Sources of Normativity.* Cambridge: Cambridge University Press.

Kripke, S. 1980. *Naming and Necessity.* Cambridge, MA: Harvard University Press.

———. 2011. "The First Person." In *Philosophical Troubles,* 292–321. Oxford: Oxford University Press.

Lear, J. 2015. *Freud.* 2nd ed. London: Routledge.

Leftow, B. 2013. "God's Deontic Perfection." *Res Philosophica* 90 (1): 69–95.

Lewis, D. K. 1979. "Attitudes De Dicto and De Se." *Philosophical Review* 88 (4): 513–543.

Long, A. A., and D. N. Sedley, ed. and trans. 1987a. *The Hellenistic Philosophers.* Vol. 1, *Translations of the Principal Sources with Philosophical Commentary.* Cambridge: Cambridge University Press.

———, ed. 1987b. *The Hellenistic Philosophers.* Vol. 2, *Greek and Latin Texts with Notes and Bibliography.* Cambridge: Cambridge University Press.

Louden, R. 1984. "On Some Vices of Virtue Ethics." *American Philosophical Quarterly* 21 (3): 227–236.

MacIntyre, A. 1984. *After Virtue.* 2nd ed. Notre Dame, IN: University of Notre Dame Press.

Mackie, J. L. 1977. *Ethics: Inventing Right and Wrong.* London: Penguin.

McDowell, J. H. 1978. "Are Moral Requirements Hypothetical Imperatives?" In supplement, *Proceedings of the Aristotelian Society* 52:13–29.

———. 1979. "Virtue and Reason." *Monist* 62 (3): 331–350.

———. 1980. "The Role of Eudaimonia in Aristotle's Ethics." In *Essays on Aristotle's Ethics,* edited by A. O. Rorty, 359–376. Berkeley: University of California Press.

———. 1998. "Referring to Oneself." In *The Philosophy of P. F. Strawson,* edited by L. E. Hahn, 129–145. Chicago: Open Court.

Nagel, T. 1970. *The Possibility of Altruism.* Princeton, NJ: Princeton University Press.

Nietzsche, F. 1989. "On the Genealogy of Morals." In *On the Genealogy of Morals and Ecce Homo,* translated by W. Kaufman, 15–163. New York: Vintage.

O'Brien, L. 1994. "Anscombe and the Self-Reference Rule." *Analysis* 54 (4): 277–281.

O'Hear, A., ed. 2004. *Modern Moral Philosophy.* Cambridge: Cambridge University Press.

Oliver, A. 2010. "What Is a Predicate?" In Potter and Ricketts 2010, 118–148.

O'Neill, O. 2004. "Modern Moral Philosophy and the Problem of Relevant Descriptions." In O'Hear 2004, 301–316.

Peacocke, C. 2008. *Truly Understood*. Oxford: Oxford University Press.

Pigden, C. 1988. "Anscombe on 'Ought.'" *Philosophical Quarterly* 38 (150): 20–41.

Pink, T. 2004. "Moral Obligation." In O'Hear 2004, 159–185.

Plato. 1959. *Gorgias*. Greek text edited with commentary by E. R. Dodds. Oxford: Clarendon.

———. 1997. *Plato: Complete Works*. Edited by J. Cooper. Translated into English by various hands. Indianapolis: Hackett.

Potter, M., and T. Ricketts, eds. 2010. *The Cambridge Companion to Frege*. Cambridge: Cambridge University Press.

Prior, A. N. 1967. "On Spurious Egocentricity." *Philosophy* 42 (162): 326–335.

———. 1971. *Objects of Thought*. Edited by P. T. Geach and A. J. P. Kenny. Oxford: Oxford University Press.

———. 1976. "The Cogito of Descartes and the Concept of Self-Confirmation." In *Papers in Logic and Ethics*, 165–175. London: Duckworth.

Proust, M. 1982. *Remembrance of Things Past*. 3 vols. Translated by T. Kilmartin. New York: Vintage.

Rawls, J. 1971. *A Theory of Justice*. Oxford: Oxford University Press.

Richter, D. 1995. "The Incoherence of the Moral 'Ought.'" *Philosophy* 70 (271): 69–85.

Rousseau, J.-J. 1992. *Discourse on the Origin of Inequality*. Translated by D. Cress. Indianapolis: Hackett.

Rumfitt, I. 1993. "Content and Context: The Paratactic Theory Revisited and Revised." *Mind* 102:429–54.

———. 1994. "Frege's Theory of Predication: An Elaboration and Defense, with Some New Applications." *Philosophical Review* 103 (4): 599–637.

Russell, B. 1912. "On the Notion of Cause." *Proceedings of the Aristotelian Society* 13:1–26.

Scanlon, T. 1990. "Promises and Practices." *Philosophy and Public Affairs* 19 (3): 199–226.

———. 2000. *What We Owe to Each Other*. Cambridge, MA: Harvard University Press.

Schneewind, J. B. 1998. *The Invention of Autonomy*. Cambridge: Cambridge University Press.

Smiley, T. J. 1981. "The Theory of Descriptions." *Proceedings of the British Academy* 67:321–337.

Spinoza, B. de. 2004. *A Theologico-Political Treatise; and, A Political Treatise*. Translated by R. H. M. Elwes. Mineola, NY: Dover.

Stern, R. 2014. "On Darwall on Anscombe on 'Modern Moral Philosophy.'" *Mind* 123 (492): 1095–1122.

Stojanovic, I. 2016. "Speaking about Oneself." In *About Oneself: De Se Thought and Communication*, edited by M. Garcia-Carpintero and S. Torre, 200–219. Oxford: Oxford University Press.

Sullivan, P. 2010. "Dummett's Frege." In Potter and Ricketts 2010, 86–117.

Taylor, C. 1992. *Sources of the Self.* Cambridge, MA: Harvard University Press.

Teichmann, R. 2008. *The Philosophy of Elizabeth Anscombe.* Oxford: Oxford University Press.

Tenenbaum, S. 2000. "Ethical Internalism and Glaucon's Question." *Nous* 34 (1): 108–130.

Thompson, M. 2008. *Life and Action: Elementary Structures of Practice and Practical Thought.* Cambridge, MA: Harvard University Press.

Vogler, C. 2006. "Modern Moral Philosophy Again: Isolating the Promulgation Problem." *Proceedings of the Aristotelian Society* 106:347–364.

———. 2013a. "Anscombe, G. E. M." In *The International Encyclopedia of Ethics,* edited by H. LaFollette, 303–309. Oxford: Wiley-Blackwell.

———. 2013b. "Aristotle, Aquinas, Anscombe and the New Virtue Ethics." In *Aquinas and the "Nicomachean Ethics,"* edited by M. Pakaluk, 239–257. Cambridge: Cambridge University Press.

Waismann, F. 1979. *Ludwig Wittgenstein and the Vienna Circle.* English translation by J. Schulte and B. McGuinness. Oxford: Rowman and Littlefield.

Warren, J. 2014. *The Pleasures of Reason in Plato, Aristotle and the Hellenistic Hedonists.* Cambridge: Cambridge University Press.

Williams, B. A. O. 1973a. "A Critique of Utilitarianism." In B. A. O. Williams and J. J. C. Smart, *Utilitarianism: For and Against,* 77–150. Cambridge: Cambridge University Press.

———. 1973b. "Ethical Consistency." In Williams 1973c, 166–186.

———. 1973c. *Problems of the Self.* Cambridge: Cambridge University Press.

———. 1981. "Persons, Character and Morality." In *Moral Luck,* 1–19. Cambridge: Cambridge University Press.

———. 1985. *Ethics and the Limits of Philosophy.* London: Fontana.

———. 1993. *Shame and Necessity.* Berkeley: University of California Press.

Williamson, T. 2002. "Necessary Existents." In *Logic, Thought and Language,* edited by A. O'Hear, 233–251. Cambridge: Cambridge University Press.

———. 2014. "How Did We Get Here from There? The Transformation of Analytic Philosophy." *Belgrade Philosophical Annual* 27:7–37.

Winch, P. n.d. "Professor Anscombe's Moral Philosophy." Unpublished manuscript.

Wittgenstein, L. 1958. *The Blue and Brown Books.* New York: Harper.

———. 1980. *Culture and Value.* Translated by Peter Winch. Oxford: Blackwell.

———. 2001. *Philosophical Investigations.* Translated by G. E. M. Anscombe. Oxford: Blackwell.

Wright, C. 1983. *Frege's Conception of Numbers as Objects.* Aberdeen, UK: Aberdeen University Press.

Yablo, S. 2014. *Aboutness.* Princeton, NJ: Princeton University Press.

Acknowledgments

I am very grateful to Danielle Allen, Mark Johnston, and Laurie Schafer for very helpful conversations about these matters, and especially for encouragement when things became difficult. I would also like to thank Melissa Lane and Philip Pettit for steering me in the direction of a book of this kind, and Laurie for giving me the idea of this book in particular.

I would like to thank the Institute for Advanced Study, Princeton, and in particular Peter Goddard and Donne Petito, for financial and administrative support, and for provision of a uniquely tranquil scholarly environment for a period of more than five years, during which a good portion of this book was written.

I am grateful to my friends Sergio Tenenbaum and Kieran Setiya, and to an anonymous reader for Harvard University Press, who read the whole book in manuscript; it has benefited a great deal from their comments. I owe particular thanks to Ian Rumfitt, whose willingness to give the highest priority to sending detailed comments, usually within a few hours, on the latest error-strewn draft chapter, sent to him out of the blue by someone he barely knew, defies explanation, unless by uncommon kindness and consideration.

In addition, I would like to thank Adam Beresford, Sarah Broadie, Daniel Callcut, Jonathan Dancy, Cora Diamond, Andy Egan, Anthony Everett, Kit Fine, Jennifer Frey, Warren Goldfarb, Rusty Jones, James Ladyman, Melissa Lane, Harold Langsam, Dave Lee, Steven Lukes, David McCarthy, Dick Moran, Lucy O'Brien, Alex Oliver, Philip Pettit, Gideon Rosen, Daniel Rubio, Jorge Secada, Ravi Sharma, Michael Smith, Roger Teichmann, Michael Thompson, Dean Zimmerman, the wonderful Rutgers philosophy of religion reading group 2013–2015, and audiences at the Institute for Advanced Study, Princeton, at Michael Smith's ethics seminar at Princeton University, at the Arthur Prior Centenary Conference at Balliol College, Oxford, in August 2014, at Rusty Jones's ancient philosophy workshop in Tahoe, California, in May 2016, and at the Philosophy Departments at the University of Bristol and at the University of Virginia for fruitful conversations and helpful comments on earlier versions of this work. Chapter 10 was initially published as "'Spurious Egocentricity' and the First

Person," *Synthese,* Volume 193, Issue 11 (October 2015): 3579–3589. © Springer Science+Business Media Dordrecht, 2015.

Finally, I would like to thank my first and best teacher of philosophy, Bill Makin, who made everything possible.

Index